D0407789

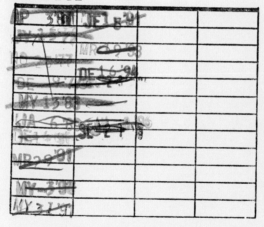

PRISONERS OF WAR

A. J. Barker

PRISONERS
OF
WAR

UNIVERSE BOOKS
New York

Published in the United States of America in 1975
by Universe Books
381 Park Avenue South, New York, N.Y. 10016

© A. J. Barker 1974, 1975

Second printing: June 1975

Issued in Great Britain as *Behind Barbed Wire*

Library of Congress Catalog Card Number: 74-27244

ISBN 0-87663-214-2

Printed in the United States of America

CONTENTS

ILLUSTRATIONS

Preface

The prisoners of the Vietnamese War were repatriated in 1973. Like human fall-out from some past explosion, these men left one kind of limbo for what may well have proved to be another. Years of captivity left them socially by-passed and their return presented the home countries with a problem. Few of the Communists who were released got a proper welcome; judging by their glum expressions as captured by the cameras, some of them knew how politically inconvenient they were to Hanoi. The United States, with more human feeling, laid out the red carpet. But Operation Homecoming, as the American preparations were called, was a long and painful and continuing business. Some of the ex-prisoners, one fears, will never be fully assimilated back into society.

With the arrival of the first of the captives back in the United States, tales began to circulate of maltreatment and torture in Hanoi's prison camps. And, despite the trim and healthy appearance of the majority of those who spoke of their experiences, it was soon clear that the long ordeal was far from over, and that, for years to come, many will be suffering from the physical and emotional after-effects of their internment. It is still too early to judge exactly how they will eventually remember their imprisonment. It seems safe to forecast, however, that legends will grow from the horrors of both their imprisonment and that of the Viet Cong. Reminiscences are part of the heritage of war, and many of the prisoners in Southeast Asia were in captivity longer than their counterparts in the two World Wars.

By and large the American prisoners who returned appeared to be in better shape than the American Government expected. In some of Hanoi's camps the mortality rate reached about 45 per cent—higher than the death rate at the infamous Camp O'Donnell in the Philippines during World War II. Consequently, with few exceptions only those among the fittest of the prisoners who possessed a high morale fibre and who were prepared to adopt a code of rigid self-discipline survived the ordeal. In effect the seemingly vigorous appearance of the repatriated prisoners was generally deceptive—a mask for physical and psychological scars. Like the captives in other wars, most of the former prisoners quickly recovered from physical wounds but many are still suffering mental anguish as a result of their experiences. Some were back to normal within a few weeks of stepping off the aircraft bringing them back from Southeast Asia; some will take a few years to get properly back to sane living, some will never recover.

Like the Japanese in World War II, the Vietnamese do not hold the same view about human life as Europeans and Americans. They are conditioned to the belief that life on earth is only a short interlude; not only is there nothing to fear in death, but death opens doors to greater things. And this colours their view of prisoners of war. Reports of bestiality in Hanoi's camps have, perhaps, been over-emphasized, and much of the ill-treatment in the camps amounted to neglect. The captors did not have medical supplies and could not be bothered to produce them. Conditions in the camps in South Vietnam, where most of the captives suffered from chronic malaria, dysentery, and various forms of skin disease, were probably the worst. Shaking with fever, weakened by constant diarrhea, bodies covered in sores, and their feet and ankles swollen from lack of protein, these men had to work to survive. And to do so the Viet Cong prison diet of three cups of rancid rice a day had to be supplemented by protein from rats and snakes caught by the prisoners themselves. After six months the average prisoner of the Viet Cong had lost 40 to 50 per cent of his weight, and it is hardly surprising that in such conditions men cracked under the strain. Some, despairing of life, lost the will to live; many of those who did survive the dysentry, beri-beri, malaria and severe loss of weight and returned home are still suffering painful after-effects—anaemia, heart murmurs, blood circulatory problems, and brain damage caused by lack of protein. Occasional lapses of concentration are apparent even in those with no apparent after-effects.

Conditions in North Vietnam were reputedly better than those in the south. Prisoners confined in Hanoi's 'Hilton' had clothing and shelter denied to their fellow prisoners in the south. But solitary confinement and torture were regularly used to induce answers at interrogation sessions. The North Vietnamese wanted to extract military information and to generate propaganda material, and coercion would be used. When prisoners failed to respond to questioning ill-treatment did not follow a set pattern, but if a man refused to talk violence generally followed. Some of the Americans found ways of avoiding being beaten up—usually by feigning stupidity; a few preferred to show docility and even to collaborate with their captors. (These individuals have had to answer for their conduct since their repatriation. Wisely, the American Government has played down the role of active collaborators, and little publicity has been given to the outcome of charges of treason brought against them by fellow prisoners.) Apart from the active collaborators there were other passive prisoners who cooperated with their captors to a greater or lesser extent. Few became sincere converts of Communism—indeed, many of those who accepted the easy way out knew little of the aims and machinations of Communism and did not understand what the war in Southeast Asia was all about. As in Korea twenty years before, these particular prisoners of war knew too little about the United States, its ideals and traditions; mentally and spiritually they were ill-prepared for a war in which every soldier runs the risk of capture by an enemy steeped in totalitarian ideologies.

Some of the instruments and methods of torture used on American prisoners in Vietnam were displayed at March Air Force Base in California during April 1973. Colonel Lewis Shattuck demonstrated the so-called 'rope-trick'—a method of trussing a man up into a ball, with his toes in his mouth, which stopped the circulation of his blood; and Major Charles Tyler showed off the pair of flesh-biting manacles that he had managed to smuggle out of Hanoi. Other prisoners displayed more personal, painful and permanent souvenirs. Air crews captured when their aircraft were shot down over North Vietnam showed pathetic evidence of their experiences. Broken bones incurred in the course of their escape from crippled planes had received little or no medical attention and the men were left with foreshortened arms and legs and with elbows and knees which could no longer be bent.

Other evidence of neglect, which has been forthcoming since repatriation, has included several cases of arthritis, due to prolonged inactivity; kidney troubles, from periods of dehydration; heart disease, a side-effect of beri-beri; and an array of stomach troubles and dental problems. Most of these can probably be corrected, but many of the ex-prisoners subject to Hanoi's 'vitamin-free' diet suffer from eye ailments that are likely to impair their vision permanently. At best, even those not directly afflicted may expect some after-effects. World War II actuarial figures and Korean War statistics indicate that in general, ex-prisoners of war have a shorter life expectancy than other men, and a greater proclivity for broken marriages, accidents, and psychiatric problems—including insomnia, depression, and alcoholism. Joy at the first moments of freedom has to last returning prisoners of war for a long time. The Americans repatriated from Vietnam went back to a different kind of America, without the sort of instinctive bearings which make any native feel at home. And the changes were swiftly apparent at almost every level. Several of the prisoners faced immediate marital problems: for instance, the first Air Force pilot to be captured in Vietnam returned to find his wife had divorced him more than two years previously. But even when tragedies of this kind—familiar enough in war-time—are overcome, assimilation is still hard. The returning Americans found the United States poisoned by the debate over the war in Indochina and by racial hostilities in addition to erosion of the framework of social life by the natural passage of time. As one small example, several generations of automobiles had come and gone since that first pilot was captured nine years before. A society like that of America, which changes rapidly all the time in any case, makes the home-comer's dilemma particularly acute. Having been removed from the mechanism which made America tick during the years of their incarceration, the prisoners of war were bound to have difficulty settling down into a new niche.

In their absence also, the cultural change was as great as the difference between Doris Day and Jane Fonda; between the last days of home-porch America and the spread both of urban ghettos and of suburbia; between Coke and cannabis. Above all, this was a period when the United States went through one of those seminal periods of heart-searching and bitter argument which puts any country on a different course. Caught up in the front-line of Vietnam, the released prisoners probably did not understand the domestic trauma which the war brought home to the streets of Washington and of every other American community. Saddled with attitudes and emotions which were political light-years from the public mood of the world to which they returned, they probably still have to look at reference books in order to learn what most Americans know by instinct about their country.

The euphoria of homecoming and the adulation of a grateful nation are now past and the accolades have faded. Yet many of the prisoners of war freed in April 1973 have yet to find their way back from the years they spent in the desolate lunar landscape of the mind that their incarceration created. Some will never return. Time may heal, but—as with the prisoners of other wars—the emotional scars will remain.

1
From the Beginning
of Time

Prisoners of war have always had a miserable time. Primitive man and his barbarian descendants annihilated all his captured foes. Occasionally a captured headman or leader was held as a hostage. But the vanquished of the ancient world usually faced extermination. According to Scripture (Samuel 15:3): '. . . thus saith the Lord of Hosts . . . go and smite Amalek and utterly destroy all they have, and spare them not.' Because he took a few Amalekite prisoners, Saul was considered disobedient. Six centuries later Hemocritus of Syracuse was exiled for refusing to slaughter all Athenian captives. In an era when it was hard enough for a man to keep himself at subsistence-level, captors were apt to think of captives merely as extra mouths to be fed—and therefore better dead than alive. Only when the captor turned from hunter to husbandman and his food supply became more secure did new considerations begin to modify this entirely primitive view.

Sun Tzu thought it was better to capture troops than to destroy them, and Tamerlane is said to have instructed his commanders to avoid needless cruelty, ordering that prisoners be spared because 'a living dog is of more use than a dead lion'. Mankind's conscience was sometimes responsible for this attitude; but the fundamental motive usually stemmed from the realization that prisoners could be employed on tiresome or dirty work which the captor disliked doing himself or making his own people do. The Greeks, who acknowledged the highest human dignity only in their own race, executed those prisoners who were of no use to them or whose death would serve as a warning to other belligerents, and sold the rest into slavery. The Romans used their captives for target practice or as gladiators, and tortured others for public amusement. Captured warriors rowed Caesar's galleys to North Africa and Britain and were killed when they could no longer pull an oar. Gradually, however, the practice of using POWS as slave labour took precedence over extermination, and the economic self-interest of the captors led to an improvement in the position of the wretched captives. In the later years of the Roman Empire the killing of Roman slaves was made illegal, and the spread of the Christian doctrines of equality and brotherhood also brought better conditions for the prisoners of war.

During the Middle Ages the captured mediaeval soldier continued to face death or enslavement, and many of them preferred to fight on and risk death rather than surrender. For the knights, however, the evolution of a code of chivalry enhanced the chance of survival. The true knight refused to slay for slaughter's sake; conquering, he could be merciful to a gallant opponent. But the code of chivalry was often honoured more in breach than in observance, and it was beset by intolerant ideologies and the fanaticism which fosters atrocities. During the cruel pogroms and religious wars which raged in Europe, the Christianity of the Middle Ages was interpreted to condone greater severity in warfare against infidels. On the other side, the followers of Islam rarely showed mercy to their prisoners unless there had been extenuating circumstances, such as a conspicuous display of gallantry by the loser. On both sides the element of gentility obtruded in favour of the knight who usually obtained substantially preferential treatment at the time he was captured, and subsequently in captivity.

War itself was still a savage business, but the idea that a soldier disarmed is a defenceless human being with a claim to protection against ill-treatment steadily gained acceptance. POWS were still being sold as slaves in the seventeenth century, but the proponents of the humane treatment of captives then found voice in Hugo Grotius—a Dutch lawyer, humanist, and one of the world's great democratic thinkers. Grotius, who had been a prisoner of war himself, attempted to devise a set of rules which combatant nations could follow to mutual advantage. His efforts did not meet with immediate success, but they did publicize the problem of prisoners of war.

In effect the concurrent rise of nationalism had aggravated the problem. As national armies expanded the complexities of war and soldiering grew. A conquering army usually had few facilities for confining a mass of captives; castle dungeons were few and far between, and great camps had to be built to house prisoners. (The original prison on Dartmoor was built to hold French troops captured during the Napoleonic Wars.) Prison hulks—old warships with cannon removed and masts truncated—were used when cells overflowed, and because guards were shorthanded, prisoners were frequently chained in droves. In Europe during the eighteenth century, however, this situation gave way to a more civilized approach. The idea of ameliorating captivity by allowing those prisoners who could afford to buy their release was employed by the Greeks and Romans, but it did not really come into fashion until the Crusades.* Up to then the question of who was to be ransomed and the amount of money or goods to be paid was an individual business, often subject to the sort of haggling associated with a Middle Eastern bazaar. The next step was the establishment of a fixed tariff, based on a prisoner's rank. In 1648 the Treaty of Westphalia, ending the Thirty Years War in Europe, stipulated that prisoners of war on both sides should be repatriated without ransom. After this the practice of holding POWs for ransom when a war ended became less frequent. There followed international agreements for a fixed scale of ransom payment during a war. In 1675, for instance, a French general was worth 50,000 livres and a private soldier about 7 livres.

On the fixed price basis the ransoming of prisoners during a war continued for about another hundred years. But the ransom institution could not continue in the changing economic and social climate. As soon as the knight ceased to be a feudal vassal of his overlord, the King, and became a professional servant paid by the Crown, the principle of ransoming privileged individuals gradually turned into one of 'exchange'. The feudal knight was now a commissioned officer paid by the Crown, and so the responsibility for paying his ransom became that of the Crown he served. By mutual agreement rival governments could, and did, offset ransom-claims against each other. For the officer this was sometimes a mixed blessing; although he no longer had to reach down into his own pocket, the process of effecting his release invariably took longer. For the 'other rank', however, the blessing was unmixed. Where, before, he was seldom freed at all, he might now hope to be—even though the delay for him would be longer than for his officer. All in all it was a considerable advance in the history of prisoners of war.

Economic and social considerations aside, the principle of exchange did have a fundamental humane basis. This derived from the recognition by nations of the civilized world that war was the result of a quarrel between two respective governments—neither of whom had any wish to penalize or incommode the men doing the fighting any more than necessary. Men taken prisoner were lost to the enemy's war effort in the same way as men who were killed. As this dilemma was the same for both belligerents, the position would clearly not be altered if captives were exchanged. In the Seven Years

---

* Because this necessitated prisoner identification, a rule evolved in regard to prisoner interrogation. A captive knight was permitted to divulge his name and rank, and under the Geneva Convention the same rule holds today: 'Every prisoner of war, when questioned on the subject, is bound to give only his rank, date of birth and army regimental, personal or serial number.'

War between Britain and France this principle was put into effect, and a series of pro-rata 'cartels' were effected—general being swapped for general, captain for captain, private for private; always in equal numbers. The result was that many who would otherwise have languished in captivity for a long period quickly regained their freedom; and those who were less fortunate retained that first necessity of all prisoners—hope: hope that their names would figure on the next cartel. Equally as important to both the British and French was the practical consideration that problems of accommodation, guards, and the clothing and feeding of large numbers of unprofitable bodies were kept to manageable proportions.

In the eyes of those who favoured this arrangement and made it work, there was probably no reason why it should not continue to do so. Unfortunately, however, both sides had to stick to the rules or it broke down. If, for instance, an exchange of say 1000 men of similar grade was agreed and one side sent only 950, or the other included only 50 sergeants among his 1000 when he had promised 100 the whole scheme was bound to go by default. This in fact is what eventually happened when Napoleon Bonaparte flouted the code.

Exchange covered all prisoners; in practice, however, the officers benefited from it more surely and more quickly than the other ranks. Almost always the latter had to wait for cartels, and batches—often of many hundreds—then had to be assembled and shipped home. If an officer was lucky his term of captivity might be remarkably short, because it could end as soon as a similar-ranking exchange could be arranged. In 1797, for instance, Lieutenant Thomas Masterman Hardy, captured in January, was back in England a free man in February. Four years later Lord Cochrane did even better. Taken in the *Speedy* on 3 July, he had been exchanged by the 14th and was again his own master. These are extreme examples to illustrate the working of the exchange which at the beginning of the nineteenth century had displaced the old institution of ransom.

Not that the ransoming of prisoners had ceased completely. Faint though unmistakable traces of the practice survived well into the Napoleonic wars, and a number of attempts to revive a version of what could be termed ransom en masse have been made in modern times. In 1916 General Townshend suggested that a gold ransom might be paid by the British Government to secure exceptional terms for the surrender of the garrison in Kut. More recently it was rumoured that the US Government would be prepared to pay a ransom to secure the release of American prisoners held by the North Vietnamese. By the time Napoleon entered the lists, however, exchange was regarded as the norm, and instances of ransoming as

obsolete recrudescences.* But exchange as a means of liberating
prisoners during hostilities was already past its heyday. When
France's First Consul flouted the code in attempts to gain advantage
from the Franco-British cartels, the institution of exchange was
bound to fall into disrepute.

Parole, a concurrent amelioration of captivity—also of major importance to officers—had come into favour with the development of
POW exchange. Like exchange it stemmed from the concept that the
soldier in any national army was a servant of his government, and as
such he could not be held responsible for the actions of his political
masters. So, he was not subject to punishment for going to war.
Thus, it was reasoned, that if a person was prepared to promise not
to serve against his captors until his government could arrange to
exchange him, there was no reason why he should be put to any
unnecessary discomfort. The idea was not new. The Greeks and
Romans sometimes freed prisoners on parole to negotiate a treaty, a
ransom, or an exchange of other captives. Hamilcar released the
Numidian captives on condition that none of them would bear arms
against Carthage. By the middle of the eighteenth century, however,
parole had come to be interpreted as a promise not to take up arms
until a specified time, or until the end of the war. Unfortunately the
scope of the system was distinctly limited by class privilege because
only gentlemen were regarded as trustworthy enough to keep their
promises, and only officers were gentlemen; the institution of parole
clearly worked in favour of those who held a commission. That it did
convey definite privileges may be judged from the comments of
Emeric de Vattel, a Swiss-German neutral†:

> By a custom which reveals at once the honour and humanity of
> Europeans, an officer, when taken prisoner, is released on his
> parole, and enjoys the comfort of spending the time of his cap-
> tivity in his own country, surrounded by his own family; and the
> side which has released him remains as perfectly sure of him as
> if it held him confined in chains.

Permission for a prisoner to return to live on parole in his own
country was exceptional; the general rule was for such individuals to
set up home in the captor's country and for the prisoner's family
to join him there. In England during the Napoleonic wars French
prisoners were permitted to live on parole almost anywhere they
wished, although the tendency was for them to congregate and form

* As late as 1807 when Lord Yarmouth was released on orders from Paris, it was
generally believed that his father, the Marquess of Hertford, had retrieved his son by
the secret payment of a ransom.
† Emeric de Vattel, *Les Droits des Gens* (Paris 1758), III, p. 3.

enclaves in towns like London, Edinburgh, Bath and Tunbridge
Wells, where they enjoyed the company of the English gentry.
French officers 'of cultivated minds and polished manners' who lived
near Bristol were, according to William Roberts in his *Life of
Hannah More*, frequent guests of Hannah More, who acted as their
interpreter and learned the French language from them.* In France
the story was much the same as in Britain. English officer prisoners
enjoyed the same three basic freedoms that their French counterparts
enjoyed in Britain. Many lived at Verdun, where a flourishing English
colony enjoyed the high life. In America during the Revolutionary
War, Congress respected the principle of parole, but prisoners were
permitted freedom only in specified areas of the colonies. In Britain
American officers were allowed more freedom, and Britain was more
liberal in allowing paroled officers to return to their homes.

Being a question of honour, most officers kept their paroles. Those
who did break them invariably ran into serious trouble from their
own governments as well as that of their captors. If he was recaptured, an officer who broke parole was stripped of his commission
and either packed off to prison or sent back to his captors. The
British, who had stricter views about the general sacrosanctity of
paroles than most other governments, were the most ruthless in
dealing with offenders. In 1806 a young midshipman named Temple,
left Verdun without cancelling his parole, leaving debts amounting
to some £4000 behind him. He reached Russia, where he obtained a
passage home in the brig HM *Childers*. Meanwhile, however, an
account of his doings had reached home by way of the Senior Naval
Officer at Verdun, and a shock was in store for midshipman Temple.
His friends cut him dead; he was evicted from his club; and there
was talk of him being sent back to France. His family managed to
prevent this but he was discharged from the Royal Navy with infamy.
Another similar case was that of Roger Sheehy, an ensign of the
89th Foot, who broke his parole at Verdun under circumstances
nearly as bad as Temple's. When he got back to England he reported
for duty, and was promptly sent back to France under arrest. As it
was now March 1814 he was quickly released, but he was never
permitted to rejoin his regiment.

Up to this point consideration of any 'rights' enjoyed by prisoners
of war has been focused on those captives taken in wars between
independent sovereign states. As revolutionaries and freedom
fighters are not considered to have prisoner of war status, they were
—and still are more often than not—classed as common criminals.
This was the case during the American Revolution, when George III

* Herbert C. Fooks, *Prisoners of War* (J. W. Stowell Printing Co., Federalsburg,
Maryland 1924), p. 298.

decreed that all Americans who rebelled against the Crown authority would be dealt with according to the law of England. If captured on land they could be hanged for treason; if taken at sea, they could expect to be treated as pirates. Thus every American colonist who took up arms against Britain did so under the shadow of the gallows. In the event an outcry by English liberals brought a relaxation in the law, and conditions in the field made its application impractical. Nevertheless if the Revolution had been suppressed, some of the Americans who were captured in the course of the war would undoubtedly have stood trial. Some exchanges of prisoners were effected but the arrangements for these were concluded by the opposing commanders, virtually as private transactions in which the question of one side recognizing the sovereignty of the other was specifically excluded.

During the Revolution the Americans apparently tried to live up to the rules of international law as it was then constituted. The British, on the other hand, appear to have vacillated between the rules observed in a European war, and the methods used to quell domestic disturbances. In general, Americans in British hands were treated less favourably than French prisoners taken in the Napoleonic wars, and Dr Franklin told Lord Stormont in Paris early in the war: 'The United States are not unacquainted with the barbarous treatment their people receive when they have the misfortune of being your prisoners in Europe.' Stormont's blunt reply was: 'The King's Ambassador receives no applications from rebels unless they come to implore His Majesty's mercy.'

One view of British POW prisons in America comes from the pen of Ethan Allen, himself a captive:

> The prisoners who were brought to New York were crowded into churches by the slavish Hessian guards. . . . I have seen sundry of the prisoners in the agonies of death, in consequence of very hunger; and others speechless and near death, biting pieces of chips; others pleading for God's sake for something to eat, and at the same time shivering with cold. . . . The filth was almost beyond description. . . . I have seen in one of the churches seven dead at the same time, lying among the excrement of their bodies. . . . I saw some sucking bones after they were speechless. . . . I was persuaded that it was a premeditated and systematized plan of the British Council to destroy the youth of our land.

From Burne's *Romance of the Revolution* comes an equally harrowing account:

> Of all the atrocities committed, those in the prison ships are the most execrable . . . there is nothing in history to excel the

barbarities there inflicted. Twelve thousand (American POWs) suffered death ... on board the filthy and malignant ships. The scenes enacted in these ships almost exceed belief. Of these prison ships the hulk of the *Jersey* anchored in Wallabout Bay, Brooklyn, was probably the most infamous; skeletons of dead prisoners thrown overboard from this particular ship are said to have silted the bay.

Propaganda warfare had not yet come into vogue, but what was written about POW life in America at this time suggests that there were those who were prepared to exaggerate and exploit the conditions for political ends. The Revolutionary war was an emotional issue, so this was to be expected. On their side the British accused the Americans of tarring and feathering loyalist colonials and of compelling British troops to work in appalling conditions down American mines.

Irrespective of the general treatment of American POWs in British hands, one feature which was singled out for special condemnation was the pressure put on prisoners to induce them to desert. The Americans had little compunction with those who did so; to them any Revolutionary soldier who changed sides was guilty of treason—irrespective of the fact that he was already guilty of the same offence in the eyes of the British. Laws were passed establishing the death penalty for any who, after capture, took up arms in the service of the enemy. And in 1781 a precedent was recorded when an ex-prisoner faced trial for serving the British after capture. The accused, claimed that he was forced to do so under duress. But the court decided that the duress was insufficient—that only the threat of imminent death would constitute adequate excuse—and the man was executed. Clearer cases of treason were made against Americans who deserted their posts and went over to the British. Amnesty was granted to deserters but not to those who deserted to the enemy.

During the American Civil War POWs were exchanged, and belligerents' rights were accorded by the Union to the Confederate troops. As in the Revolutionary War, however, the rights of sovereignty were not conceded, and bitter controversies arose over the exchanges that did take place—both sides charging the other with violating cartels. Even more controversy arose over the question of the conduct of prisoners after capture. Over 3000 Union prisoners and nearly 5500 Confederates changed sides in the course of the Civil War. One famous company of 'reconstructed Rebs' was sent to a Western frontier station to release the regular Union garrison for active service against the South. Both sides were naturally concerned about the attitude of their troops towards captivity, and in the middle of the war the Union Government issued an order to curb wholesale surrenders by men eager to obtain parole and so evade further military service.* Among other things this order made it clear that it was the duty of a prisoner of war to escape. It also stated that only 'extreme suffering and privation' which endangered the prisoner's life *might* justify his turning his coat and joining the enemy. It was his duty to rejoin his own side as soon as the opportunity presented itself; if he did anything to support the enemy—unless he was coerced into doing so—he could expect to be punished.

Much has been written about the harsh conditions prevailing in the American POW camps during the Civil War. In the Confederate camps, particularly those at Andersonville and Florence, the inmates were half-starved and deprived of medical comforts. On the Union side the prison on Johnson's Island in Lake Erie has been described as a 'bleak Alcatraz', and the camps on the Potomac as 'hell holes'. Appeals for an improvement in all the camps and for more lenient treatment of POWs followed disclosures of what was happening, and public concern compelled President Lincoln to take action. In 1863 he asked the eminent German-born professor of constitutional history and public law at Columbia college in New York, Francis Lieber, to draft a code of war governing the Union Army's conduct in the field. Lieber had soldiered with General von Blücher at Liegnitz, Waterloo and Namur and had been wounded in the course of his service, and his *Instructions for the Government of Armies of the United States* turned out to be the first comprehensive codification of international law issued by any government. Based on moral precepts which recognized an enemy as a fellow human being with lawful rights, Lieber's 'Instructions' embodied the first code appertaining to prisoners of war. In it were the following injunctions:

No belligerent has the right to declare he will treat every captured man in arms . . . as a brigand or a bandit.

A prisoner of war is subject to no punishment for being a public enemy, nor is any revenge wreaked upon him by the intentional infliction of any suffering, or disgrace, by cruel imprisonment, want of food, by mutilation, death or any other barbarity.

A prisoner of war remains amenable for his crimes committed before the captor's army or people, (for crimes) committed before he was captured, and for which he has not been punished by his own authorities.

* US War Department General Order No 207 of 3 July 1863.

A prisoner of war . . . is the prisoner of the government and not of the captor.

Prisoners of war are subject to confinement or imprisonment such as may be deemed necessary on account of safety, but they are to be subjected to no other intentional suffering or indignity.

A prisoner of war who escapes may be shot, or otherwise killed in flight; but neither death nor any other punishment shall be inflicted on him for his attempt to escape, which the law of order does not consider a crime. Stricter means of security shall be used after an unsuccessful attempt at escape.

Every captured wounded man shall be medically treated according to the ability of the medical staff.

Although it has been criticized on the grounds that some of its provisions reflected the fratricidal nature of the Civil War, Lieber's Code was to exercise influence on the subsequent developments of international law regarding POWs. Unfortunately its commandments proved easier to publish than to put into effect. As an example: the Code stipulated that a prisoner should receive rations similar to those issued to his captors. In practice the military and economic situation often made it impossible for the captors to follow this rule. The Confederate Government agreed to recognize and apply Lieber's code but the South was slowly starving under the pressure of the Union's blockade, and at times prisoners in Southern hands were even granted rations superior to those given Confederate soldiers in the field. The Confederacy was not accused of violating Lieber's rule, but strict observance of it did not always provide sufficient rations.

One problem facing a prisoner of war on capture recognized by Lieber was that relating to the giving of information. An officer or man who gave his captors military information was clearly as dangerous as a deliberate traitor. Yet information might be wrung out of him under pressure or by inducement. So Lieber set down the rule:

Honourable men, when captured, will abstain from giving to the enemy information concerning their own army, and the modern law of war permits no longer the use of any violence against prisoners, in order to extort the desired information, or to punish them for having given false information.

Like the rule about rations, this commandment was easier to recite than to observe. On the one hand there was the interrogation out to acquire vital information—intelligence which might win a battle, and save many lives. On the other hand there was the prisoner, sworn to withhold information which might cost a battle and the lives of his countrymen. Lieber's attempt to outlaw violence by the captor during an interrogation was a significant contribution towards the theory of regulation of warfare by ethics then being formulated at Geneva.

The Civil War in America had followed on the heels of the Crimean War in Europe, and in both wars the troops engaged suffered terrible privations. But it was a smaller war which initiated the series of events leading to a further amelioration of the conditions of prisoners of war. In 1859 a young Swiss writer, Henri Dunant, witnessed the carnage at Solferino, where the French Emperor Napoleon III fought a battle in his campaign to free the Italians from Austrian rule. Deeply moved by what he had seen, he wrote an account of the ghastly plight of the victims of the battle, sparing his readers none of the harrowing details. It was this book, *Un Souvenir de Solferino*, published in 1862, which set the stage for a conference at Geneva in 1864—and subsequently for the founding of the International Red Cross.* The first conference produced the Geneva Convention providing for the relief of wounded combatants, regardless of the flag they served, and subsequent conferences in 1868 and 1906 extended and reviewed the rules drawn up in 1864. In 1907 a Hague Convention extended them further to cover maritime warfare.

Prisoners of war were first considered in 1874 by a conference in Brussels, called at the instigation of the Russian Government. Delegates of all the major European nations attended, and a code based on that which Lieber had drawn up for the American Army was considered. Many of Lieber's original stipulations were embodied in it. Prisoners of war were to be considered as lawful and disarmed enemies, who were captives of the hostile government—and *not* in the power of individual captors or jailors. Humane treatment was obligatory; unruly prisoners could be punished for insubordination. In the event this 'Brussels Code' was not ratified, but it strongly influenced the first Hague Conference which met at the turn of the century.

Sponsored by Czar Nicholas II, the delegates of the 26 nations attending this Conference considered disarmament proposals and the possibility of establishing a world court were discussed as well as the prisoner of war 'Brussels Code'. Racial prejudice, nationalism, distrust and ancient grudges hampered the proceedings but at the close of the Conference 24 nations ratified the Convention which emerged. Eight years later, in 1907, a second Hague Conference was

---

* The work of Florence Nightingale during the Crimean War probably did much to ensure the excellent reception of Dunant's work.

called, during which the delegates of the nations which had signed
the 1899 Convention re-affirmed their adherence to its principles.
Not everybody believed that the attitude being cultivated at Geneva
and the Hague was necessarily the right one. There were those who
believed that the new rules spelt out a form of mollycoddling which
would undermine a serviceman's discipline: 'Today, the prisoner of
war is a spoilt darling', wrote a prominent writer on the law of war
in 1911*;

> he is treated with a solicitude for his wants and feelings which
> borders on sentimentalism. He is better treated than the modern
> criminal, who is infinitely better off under the modern prison
> system than a soldier on a campaign. Under present-day condi-
> tions, captivity—such captivity as that of the Boers in Ceylon and
> Bermuda, and of the Russians in Japan—is no sad sojourn by the
> water of Babylon; it is usually a halcyon time, a pleasant experi-
> ence to be nursed fondly in the memory, a kind of inexpensive
> rest-cure after the wearisome toil of fighting. The wonder is that
> any soldiers fight at all; that they do so, instead of giving them-
> selves up as prisoners is a high tribute to the spirit and discipline
> of modern armies. . . .

Few ex-POWs—especially those who survived the horrors of
Turkish prison camps in World War I or suffered under the Japanese
during World War II—would be inclined to agree with the author of
this statement.

In 1914 another Hague Conference was in the making; fifteen
years were to elapse before it took place. Meantime as some of the
belligerents of World War I had not ratified the 1907 Hague Convention, their participation in the war made the Convention legally
inoperative amongst those who had done so. In practice, however,
almost everybody accepted that the Hague rules represented nothing
more and nothing less than a declaration of international law on the
subject. On this basis, therefore, they were generally observed.

In the course of World War I a number of bilateral agreements
relating to the treatment of prisoners of war were concluded. Not all
of them were ratified, during—or even subsequent to—the war.
Nevertheless these agreements had a considerable effect on subsequent efforts to develop the rules of war concerning POWs. (The
treaty between Germany and the United States which was signed on
11 November 1918, for instance, bears a striking resemblance to the
Geneva Convention of 1929.)

The next advance came in 1929 when the delegates of 38 nations—

* James M. Spaight, *War Rights on Land* (1911), p. 265.

which did not include Soviet Russia—assembled at Geneva to frame a treaty which could supersede the Hague Conventions. The aim was to make International Law, and not just to draft a summary of rules based on existing international law. In due course a Convention was drawn up and signed. Its importance lay in the fact that it was binding between individual states—unlike the Hague Rules which were effective only if ratified by all the belligerents in a war.

No further steps towards the perfection of a prisoner of war charter took place until 1949. And in the intervening twenty years there had been many disquieting developments in the treatment of prisoners of war; not least of these was the terrible death-toll of prisoners in World War II. The aim of the 1949 Conference was virtually the same as that of the delegates who had met in 1929: to formulate and define higher standards of treatment for POWs. In the event the articles of the earlier Geneva Convention were clarified and strengthened, and 57 nations signed the new Treaty. (The Soviet Union and eight other nations in the Communist bloc were among the signatories. But the USSR and its satellites had some reservations about certain clauses of the agreement.)

This then is the historical background to the continuing saga of prisoners of war. In the wake of the war in Vietnam and conflict in the Middle East, the Geneva Convention of 1949 may already seem to be out of date.

2

Who is a Prisoner of War?

To the average reader the question, 'Who, and under what circumstances, is a man entitled to be considered a prisoner of war?', may seem redundant or even nonsensical. Yet the answer is of paramount importance, because it will govern his mode of life in captivity. The Geneva Convention and international law provides certain safeguards for the man who has the 'status' of POW, guarantees various privileges during captivity and generally assures his well-being. If he is not recognized as a legitimate prisoner of war, he may be treated as a terrorist or a bandit. What can happen then is best illustrated by the example of Patrick F. Morris, an American infantryman who was captured by the Germans near Malmedy in December 1944 while on a reconnaissance mission. Having been taken for a guerilla or saboteur of sorts, Morris was denied 'official recognition' for about a month. During the interim period he was compelled to work with a Russian-Polish slave labour gang loading and unloading munitions. When he protested, he was told that he was 'only' a civilian and that he could be shot for disobedience.

Fifty years before the event Morris would probably have automatically become a POW as soon as he was captured. Today he might count himself lucky at not being shot out of hand. Hostilities nowadays—with operations by saboteurs and commandos, devastating air attacks, and 'special missions'—are committed in a manner never vizualized before. Ideological differences have complicated matters further. Even the traditional meaning of 'traitor' has been extended from 'disloyalty to the State' to 'disloyalty to the State's ideology'. Thus a man who has disowned an ideology may well not be recognized as a legitimate prisoner of war if he is captured while fighting against it—even if he has emigrated and all the other circumstances attached to his soldiering are perfectly legal.

When the revised Geneva Convention was framed in 1949, its

prescriptions for the treatment of prisoners of war were written against the background of two World Wars. War was seen in traditional terms as an open conflict between two or more sovereign nations. There was simply 'war' and 'peace' and the problems that are now associated with 'cold war' and coercion were not apparent. Thus there was no provision for Gary Powers to claim POW status when his U-2 was shot down over Russia, although he was on a military mission. Nor were the Indian troops kidnapped by the Red Chinese forces in Ladakh in April 1960 regarded as prisoners of war.

If only because the exploits of 'freedom fighters' have become an increasingly important factor of ideological warfare, they deserve mention. Pressure is often exerted to persuade a country which is being ravaged by civil disorders to accord prisoner of war status on those who are apprehended while creating the disturbances. But the Geneva Convention makes no provision for 'freedom fighters'. Such individuals are usually regarded by the state from whom they are trying to secure their freedom as rebels. And if they are caught the question of their being granted POW status does not usually come into the picture. For their acts of violence they usually are punished as traitors or criminals, unless they can persuade the existing government by threat of reprisals, to grant preferential treatment. Foreign states supporting the rebels may also try to force international recognition of a partisan movement. (In the Malayan Emergency in the 1950s Communist terrorists were known by themselves, and Red China, as the Malayan Peoples Liberation Army.) Where concessions have been made to freedom fighters, as happened in Algeria, the effect of doing so has been to weaken the government and confer a degree of legality on the rebels. It is not difficult to understand why freedom fighters should be excluded from recognition; since all countries are reluctant to acknowledge the application of 'international' prescriptions in their domestic affairs. In spite of this, however, history does not lack instances of internal conflicts when prisoner of war status has been granted to rebel captives who would otherwise be regarded as traitors.*

While the problem of how to treat insurgents exists now, and promises to become more acute in future, public opinion does not usually think of captured rebels as prisoners of war. POWs are regarded as being the victims of the old-fashioned type of war when two or more states fought over differences in political, religious principles or for economic gain. At the turn of the century the question of who was and who was not a POW was relatively easy to

---

* During the American Civil War, and in the French Indo-China War (see the *New York Times*, 14 April 1954).

decide. Ever since then, 'total' war and new ideologies have brought progressive complications.

In a straightforward sort of war the status of a prisoner is usually determined by his activities before capture. A soldier, serving in the army of a country which is recognized as being at war with his captors' nation, who is taken prisoner in the course of a military operation is a clear case of a person entitled to POW status. Even if the soldier concerned is a foreign mercenary, there can be no dispute about his right to be treated as a POW provided he is a member of a properly constituted military organization and wears a uniform. Most soldiers are only too conscious of their 'membership of a military organization'. Probably only a few appreciate that in time of war international law views such membership as a prerequisite to recognition of the legality of their actions on the battlefield. Without it they may well be classed as war criminals and shot as such when they are captured. In any recognized army there is a chain of command, and soldiers are organized and trained to observe the rules of war. The massacres at Lidice and My Lai give lie to the suggestion that illegal acts can never be perpetrated by troops of a properly constituted army. But the training, organization and discipline of such a force make them less likely. The fact that violations of the accepted rules of warfare usually bring a tirade of adverse and prejudicial comment from the outside world is another factor.

Irregular combatants, fighting on their own initiative, are outside the shelter of the Geneva Convention's umbrella. And if they are caught they are likely to be dubbed war criminals and shot. In the Franco-Prussian War of 1870 such individuals were called *Franc-tireurs*. When they were captured the Germans asked if they carried a permit or an authorization from the French Government, and as no such document existed they were shot. Similarly, during the South African War the British refused to treat Boer snipers as proper combatants, as many of them did not belong to any organized unit. Their subsequent treatment was not so harsh as that which the German meted out to the wretched *Franc-tireurs*. Nevertheless those who were caught had their farmhouses burnt down, and many were deported. In World War II many resistance groups in the territories occupied by the Axis powers were treated as bandits. For these individuals capture could only mean one thing—death, and the question of whether they deserved to be accorded the rights of a prisoner of war never arose. The resultant fear of capture further inflamed their patriotic passions and prompted less concern for their behaviour than might otherwise have been the case. This in turn brought an escalating round of retributive action to discourage their activities. In Yugoslavia—where the situation deteriorated to a point where neither the occupying troops nor the indigenous populace would take prisoners—the Germans learned the truth of that well-worn cliché, 'Violence breeds violence'.

To forewarn his adversaries and to ensure that he is not mistaken for an unauthorized combatant, a soldier is expected to wear a uniform. There is nothing new in this. Savages ornamented themselves with paint and tattoos; the Gauls, Germans and Franks made helmets from the heads of wild animals to distinguish themselves in battle; the Greeks wore scarlet clothes. (Because scarlet was the same colour as the blood from their wounds.) The Crusaders sewed a silken cross to their vests; when standing armies first came into being regiments carried the Colours of their colonel, and the colourful uniforms of the eighteenth and nineteenth century followed. These went out around the turn of the century and the accent now is on utility. On occasions a single, relatively inconspicuous item, such as a brassard on the arm, can constitute a legal uniform. Similarly, although an airman may not wear his uniform while he is fighting a combat mission, the insignia on his aircraft exposes his hostile character. If he is forced down in hostile territory where there is a chance of his being mistaken as a spy this is essential for his protection.

In the old days there was never any question of a man captured in battle wearing a uniform being treated as anything but a soldier. Now it is not so simple. In World War II, political commissars went into battle with the Soviet Army and the control they exercised over the troops was often more effective than that of the Russian regimental officers. On the grounds that the commissars were not soldiers but political indoctrinators and that their actions were cruel, inhumane and dictated by hatred, Hitler ordered them to be shot on capture. And some of them were shot in accordance with his order. After the war, when both the actions of those who carried out the executions and Hitler's order authorizing them were condemned by the Nuremberg Court, this particular issue seemed to be resolved. Not all countries are satisfied that the decision was the right one, however. If the status of a commissar is compared with that of a chaplain, there can be no argument. And if communist political indoctrinators have the same rights as soldiers in a future war, presumably psychologists and counter-indoctrinators in other armies will be entitled to those rights also.

The status of commandos and similar individuals captured on 'special' missions was also the subject of some dispute in World War II. In total war hostilities are no longer restricted to military targets; they are extended to industrial and strategic installations deep inside enemy territory. Selected individuals and groups have also organized underground resistance movements in occupied territory, where their sabotage and terrorist activities have inflicted considerable damage. To curtail such activities in the autumn 1942 Hitler issued his infamous 'Commando' order:

> From now on all enemies on so-called Commando missions in Europe or Africa challenged by German troops, even if they are to all appearances soldiers in uniform, or demolition troops, whether armed or unarmed, in battle or in flight, are to be slaughtered to the last man. It makes no difference whether they are landed from ships or aircraft or whether they are dropped by parachute.

When news of this order reached the Allied Powers there was an immediate outcry. At the Nuremberg trials it was described as criminally barbaric and a violation of the Geneva Convention, and Nazi commanders responsible for publication and execution of the order were subsequently arraigned as war criminals. In their defence the Germans argued that Hitler's order was a realistic attempt to curb the 'illegal acts' of Allied commandos.* British commandos, they alleged, were outside the aegis of the Geneva Convention. Many of them had been recruited from convicts; they had shackled their prisoners and worn German uniforms or civilian clothes when it suited their purpose; and they had generally behaved in a perfidious manner totally unbefitting the honourable profession of arms. So they were not entitled to be treated as soldiers.

The commandos may well have done many of the things of which they were accused: to be successful, commandos often had to resort to the sort of tactics associated with gangsters. Some of them may even have been ex-convicts. No attempt was made to rebut the German allegations, because the real point was that the threat that captured commandos would not be treated as prisoners of war was the age-old threat of reprisal dressed up as military necessity. In 1942 commando raids were doing a lot of damage—especially in occupied Europe where their operations encouraged the latent resistance organizations.

Whether the wearing of enemy uniform is considered illegal depends on the enemy in question. The Hague Convention of 1907, which dodges the issue by saying there should be no 'improper' use of the enemy's uniform, has not been rephrased in more precise terms. And different countries take different views about 'improper' use of another's uniform. Some allow that enemy uniform can be worn for tactical purposes. Others like the French have adopted conflicting

---

* Trial of War Criminals before the Nuremberg Military Tribunals—UN Official Records (Prosecution and Trials of the Major War Criminals), pp. 73–74.

attitudes. For example, although France prescribes the use of enemy uniform can be a legitimate ruse, the wearing of French uniforms by enemy troops is illegal. At least that was the attitude in World War II, when German parachutists wearing French uniforms who landed in France were ordered to be shot on the spot. The Americans are among those subscribing to the view that enemy uniform can be worn as a deception measure. But this did not inhibit them from trying to punish German soldiers who donned US Army uniforms for Otto Skorzeny's daredevil operation in the Ardennes in December 1944.*

Uniform and 'membership' of a recognized military unit of the other side, and capture in what might almost be determined conventional circumstances, still does not constitute an automatic ticket to POW status. Trouble looms for anyone labelled a 'traitor' or a deserter, or who has violated parole. As ideological conflicts are likely to cause these labels to be used with increasing frequency, they warrant a brief mention.

No definition of a traitor seems necessary. From time immemorial any person who is a national of one state and has gone over to the enemy (or potential enemy), has been given this appellation. In the twentieth century, however, the definition has been extended to other categories, and the word 'traitor' can now also connote an ideological defection. In the French Indo-China war, for instance, the Viet-Minh captured men of the French Foreign Legion who were nationals of Iron Curtain countries.† In Communist eyes such men were traitors to the communist cause, and they were sent back to their original homelands to be punished as traitors. Democratic countries may regard the Communist ideology with distaste but men who believe in it are not automatically classed as traitors, and during hostilities they would normally be treated as ordinary prisoners of war.

Deserters who have joined the enemy's camp may not seem to be such an awkward category. In the eyes of most nations they have behaved as traitors. As such they are not considered to be legitimate prisoners of war and are treated as criminals who have violated their own country's laws and they are usually sentenced to death.

Parole has been discussed in Chapter 1. A man who violates his parole ceases to be entitled to prisoner of war status. This may mean a great deal of hardship, but he is not usually shot. At the most he may be classed as a war criminal, when he is entitled

---

* Skorzeny's so-called Panzer Brigade 150 broke through the US First Army front and part of it penetrated as far as the River Meuse. Skorzeny's men were wearing American uniforms and driving captured American vehicles. Many who were caught were summarily shot. Skorzeny himself was tried by an American tribunal at Dachau in 1947 but acquitted.

† *New York Times*, 19 December 1954.

to the benefits of Article 85 of the 1949 Geneva Convention (see Appendix A).

Like parole violators, deserters and traitors, airmen who evade capture are special cases. A man who bails out of his aircraft and lands in enemy territory tries to avoid capture and to get back to his side. If he changes into civilian clothes there is always the danger of his being mistaken for a spy, and being condemned as such. What he has to do in such circumstances is to prove his bona-fides. Tired, and faced with an impatient captor, this may not be easy. Spies get short shrift in Communist hands, and the stand taken by Red China in regard to 11 American aviators who were captured during the Korean War serves as a salutary warning of what can happen to evadees.*

Medical and religious personnel, merchant seamen, neutrals and some government officials are usually accorded special treatment as POWs. In another era such people often used to be released on parole; in modern times they are incarcerated with the rest. In general the attitude towards the medics and the chaplains has not changed, as their role is the same as it has always been. But changes in the traditional role of merchant seamen have been followed by changes in attitude towards them. In 1907 the Hague Convention laid down that enemy merchantmen should not be held as prisoners of war so long as they undertook to take no part in hostilities. In World War I, however, submarine warfare resulted in officers of the merchant marine being commissioned as naval reserve officers. Merchant ships armed for self-defence could easily be converted to warships. And the issue was further confused with an extension of the rule of self-defence by which an armed merchantman could act in anticipation of an attack on her by an enemy submarine. So men of a belligerent country's merchant navy have come to be regarded as members of their country's armed forces. Foreigners who happen to be serving in such ships are also seen in the same light, and if they are captured they also go into the bag. Neutrality is no excuse in such circumstances.

The fate of government officials is unlikely to be of general interest. But it is worth recording that the Japanese, whose reputation for the treatment of those who fell into their hands is universally condemned, appear to have followed the terms of the Geneva Convention with surprising exactitude when they occupied the International Settlement at Shanghai in December 1941. Commander C. S. Sheppard RN was the British naval attaché with the British Embassy when Japan declared war. With the rest of the Embassy and British

* *New York Times*, 26 November 1954. These men were accused of being spies and denied the rights of POWs.

Consulate-General staff, he was interned in a POW camp. But in August 1942 he and 11 other British officials were released. With the exception of two Americans this is the only known instance of the Japanese allowing any of their prisoners to go free during the war.*

For the majority of prisoners of war, the question of 'status' never arises. To suggest that they had any status at all would be calculated at best to raise a ribald laugh. Nevertheless the Geneva Convention and international law does confer some protection, which in World War II was sometimes denied to the armies of occupied territories. Germany, for instance, often demobilized the armed forces of the countries she overran, released them on parole, but subsequently interned them on the grounds of security, thus depriving them of POW status on the pretext that they were no longer members of the armed forces. The Allies did the same after the German surrender.†
If internment then means the imposition of conditions which cannot legally be applied to POWs—as happened with the Germans—international law has clearly been flouted. If it makes no difference because conditions as a POW are against the spirit of the Geneva Convention—as was the case in the Japanese camps—the individuals concerned are unlikely to care.

The act of becoming a prisoner of war implies surrender. But if units continue to fight on after their government or their commander has surrendered and they are subsequently captured POW status is arguable. The position becomes more complicated when the defeated government professes to function in exile, and purports to control the activities of its nationals. This happened between 1939 and 1945 when the governments of some of the occupied countries of Europe established themselves in London or Africa and were recognized as such by their undefeated allies. Most of their armed forces had been demobilized, interned or released on parole, but some scattered forces continued to fight. The question was whether they should be considered to be regarded as the legitimate forces of the country concerned, or as partisans. International law does not prohibit partisan warfare, and many people in the world today uphold such activity. Because the clandestine operations of partisans and guerillas present an unusual danger the victors are only too anxious to terminate their activities, even if it means outlawing them. In 1941 the Germans ruthlessly suppressed guerilla activity in the wake of their victorious armies during Operation Barbarossa; any Russian who harassed their troops was executed without any reference to his rights as a prisoner of war. It appears that the Allies were prepared

---

* Letter from Commander Sheppard to the author.
† J. R. Wilhelm, *Can the Status of Prisoners of War be Altered?* Article in the *Révue Internationale de la Croix Rouge*, July/Sept. 1953.

to act in a similar fashion in 1945. 'Hostilities will end officially at one minute after midnight tonight, Tuesday 8 May', Churchill announced. 'The Germans are still in places resisting Russian troops, but should they continue to do so after midnight they will, of course, deprive themselves of the protection of the laws of war, and will be attacked from all sides by the allied troops.'*

This warning made it clear that the Allies had no intention of treating German soldiers, sailors and airmen who battled on after the surrender as lawful belligerents. Confirmation of this was forthcoming when the Allies prosecuted some Germans who had continued to be hostile after the official surrender. For example, a German naval officer was punished for scuttling a submarine, and German intelligence officers were awarded heavy sentences for continuing to collect and collate intelligence news.

Finally something must be said about the position of the members of the armed forces of states which have not been recognized. All that has been said about prisoners of war 'status' implies the recognition of one belligerent by the other. The Arab States have never recognized Israel as a sovereign state since its creation by the United Nations in 1947. Yet they are in daily contact with Israel and they have attacked her three times. Badoglio's troops, De Gaulle's Free French and the Free Poles and Free Czech armies whose allegiance was not recognized by the Axis Powers and who were treated not as prisoners of war but as criminals, can be cited as another example of this anomaly. In 1949 the Geneva Conference attempted to resolve it by ruling that the captor nation should treat any captured troops of the opposing side as POWS irrespective of whether the captors recognized the authority of the captives' government or not. In theory this should go a long way to alleviate the hardships experienced by troops of the armies of unrecognized governments.

* *New York Times*, 9 May 1945.

3
Capture

To say that a fighting man becomes a prisoner of war as soon as he is captured may well seem to be a blinding revelation of the obvious. But the conditions affecting POW status outlined in the previous chapter indicate the problems that encompass captivity in war. 'When' is likely to be hedged with as many difficulties as 'who'.

In the simple case, a man becomes a prisoner because he cannot continue to fight, and cannot get away. He may have been over-powered, or run out of ammunition; alternatively he or his commander has voluntarily opted to give in. Whatever the cause he is helpless and hors de combat, and when his opponents realize it they take control. This is the customary sequence of events. But it does not always apply. Fundamentally this is because the last 70 years have seen a steady decline in Montesquieu's theory that 'states should do the greatest good towards each other during peace and minimum harm during war'. Changes in attitude towards war have led to an erosion of the rules of warfare which were invented to salvage what is left of humanitarian values during hostilities.

Granting quarter*—excepting a surrendering enemy from death—is one of these rules that has been flouted all too often. After a long and bloody fight, it is possible to visualize circumstances when men will kill rather than take pity on an enemy who decides to surrender when it suits him to do so. In the heat of battle there is not much opportunity for sentiments of pity, and the sight of the dead and dying may weaken a soldier's sense of fairness. Refusal to grant quarter in such circumstances is understandable, even if it is not justifiable. When surrendering troops are killed on the orders of

* In this sense the expression was probably derived from the sixteenth-century convention at which the Spanish and Dutch agreed to spare the lives of prisoners of war on payment of a ransom equal to one quarter of their annual salary, and that captives who were not ransomed would be put to death.

decision-makers far from the scene of the action, however, those who carry out the orders are committing murder. Such was the decision of the War Crimes Tribunal after World War II. And if the same Court had sat in 1918 it is more than likely that the Kaiser would have been found guilty, for in 1914 he issued a typical 'no quarter; no man to be spared' order.*

In this instance the Kaiser's order had two purposes: to deter Germany's enemies, and to instil in the German troops the fear of surrendering themselves in case they should meet the same fate. How far the order was effective is difficult to assess. But the same technique was used in World War II, and some of those who put it into practice were tried as war criminals.

During the closing stages of a battle the men who are intimately engaged in the fighting are not usually concerned about anything other than their immediate task. Few men brought up in Western society are imbued with the idea that it is better to die than be captured. Nor, until the moment of truth actually arrives, do they give much thought to the idea of becoming a prisoner of war. Death or disablement is a possibility—albeit one that is more likely to come to others. But capture and incarceration in an enemy POW camp does not usually enter the fighting man's mind. Perhaps this explains why an order to hold a position 'at any cost'—to hold position or die in the effort—seems to be more acceptable than an order to hold on 'for as long as possible'. The clear-cut finality about the do-or-die appeals to latent heroism, while the 'hang-on-and-then-spend-the-rest-of-the-war-languishing-behind-barbed-wire' order promises only monotony and misery. During World War II Japanese troops rarely surrendered. 'We talk a lot about holding a position to the last man and the last round', wrote Field Marshal Lord Slim. 'The Japanese actually do it.' Japanese fighting men had been trained to accept death and die courageously. Under the impact of ideological persuasion Japanese airmen were prepared to fly suicide missions in an effort to turn the tide of war in Japan's favour. On Saipan a Japanese officer cut off the heads of his kneeling men with a Samurai sword, and others blew themselves up with grenades rather than become prisoners of war.

When the situation deteriorates to the point where the choice is

---

* At Bremerhaven in July 1914 he inspected a contingent of German troops, before they embarked for China. His farewell speech, reported in the local newspaper, contained the following instructions: 'As soon as you come to blows with the enemy he will be beaten. No mercy will be shown! No prisoners will be taken! As the Huns under King Attila made a name for themselves, which is still mighty in traditions and legends today, may the name of Germans be so fixed in China by your deeds that no Chinese should ever again dare to look at a German askance . . . open the way for *Kultur* once and for all.'

capitulation or death, most westerners choose to surrender. Suicides in the Japanese mode are said to have occurred in panics in Flanders and at Caporetto during World War I, and the ancient historian Plutarch has described the self-slaughter which followed the Romans' defeat of the Cimbres near Vercella. Nowadays it is only on rare occasions that a guilt complex, resulting from shortcomings in battle, provokes self-chosen death. Faced with the prospect of losing his freedom, a man may be desperate. But the primitive will to survive stops him from taking the ultimate step into the unknown.

Right up to the transition from combatant to prisoner of war, the fighting man's task usually keeps him fairly occupied. In battle his job is to kill or be killed and when the fighting stops it is a traumatic moment. Everything then seems to happen very quickly, and for the next 48 hours at least he is almost certain to undergo considerable physical as well as mental hardships. Sometimes, however, there is a twilight period while the decision to surrender or to fight on is taken. In war, as elsewhere, circumstances often arise when it is difficult to know what to do. With troops locked in battle such a decision must be made under very trying conditions. The age-old idea that it is better to die fighting than to be captured is part of the soldier's code, but it represents an idealistic view of a soldier's standard of bravery. What happened to some French troops who did not measure up to this standard will serve as an illustration: in June 1916, an infantry company commanded by Lieutenant Herduin was defending a position near Verdun. The Germans attacked, broke through, and Herduin's company suffered severe casualties. From Verdun itself it looked as if Herduin's position had been overrun. So the French artillery was ordered to shell it. Under heavy fire, and with another German assault in the offing, Herduin was faced with three choices: annihilation, surrender or evacuation of the position. In the event Herduin opted for the third course, and with some difficulty managed to get the sorry remnants of his company back to Verdun. Two days later he and the only other surviving officer were ordered to report to their regimental headquarters. There they were told that the brigade commander had ordered their execution, on the grounds that they had abandoned their position to the enemy. Nineteen men's lives had been saved but Herduin's part in this was not seen as initiative. So both officers were executed by a firing squad.

When the surrender of a large force is being negotiated the 'twilight' interval preceding captivity may be prolonged. And men who are not involved in the actual fighting may be bewildered by the sudden turn of events which precipitates their captivity. In February 1942 General Sir Archibald Wavell issued a typical 'last man, last round' order to the garrison of Singapore. 'I look to you and your men to fight on to the end . . .', he wrote to General Percival. So the blackened, sweaty troops fought on. Within five days, however, Singapore was rapidly becoming a shambles. Every hour brought more depressing rumours and frightening facts. Explosion after explosion, which meant more places were being demolished made the troops realize the battle was nearly over. Nevertheless the whispers that General Percival was negotiating a surrender still came as a shock:*

> . . . as from 8.30 pm we were to cease firing and lay down our arms in good order . . . Because they wore rubber boots we did not hear the approach of seven Japanese soldiers. Surprised and a little fearful we watched the approach of these strange individuals. Although thick-set, they seemed abnormally small. The Japanese NCO proceeded to chalk strange characters on the petrol pumps and various articles of machinery in the garage. When this was completed he called his men together and gravely bowed to us, to which we responded with an inclination of the head, before departing.
>
> Left once more to ourselves, we were capable of one comment only: 'To think those little bastards beat us!'

Staff officers, clerks, orderlies, cooks and others who happen to be with various headquarters in the field are generally closer to the battle, although they may not be involved in it. Being not too far and not too close to the scene of action can be a privileged position from which to predict the outcome. And sometimes to get away. In June 1940 Lieutenant-Colonel Cyril Whitcombe was a staff officer with the Headquarters of the 51st (Highland) Division. Part of the division was retiring towards Le Havre when the Germans cut the road south of St Valery, where the Royal Navy had hoped to evacuate troops back to England. With the Germans astride the road and the French on the verge of throwing in the sponge, all hopes of getting the main force away were dashed. Under cover of darkness the navy managed to send some boats in to the beach in front of the German road block and the divisional commander, General Sir Victor Fortune gave permission for anyone who wished to get away to do so. Some men did so, but Whitcombe was not one of them.

> At 4 am on the 12th [he recalls†] I note that I was somewhat depressed at the prospect of waiting for the Germans to come, and suggested to my CRA we might take advantage of General

---

* Ronald Hastain, *White Coolie* (Hodder & Stoughton, London 1947), pp. 65–67.
† In a letter to the author.

Fortune's suggestion. He said he wouldn't as he must stay with the General, but if I liked to go I could. In fact I hung on a bit longer but about 5.30 or 6 am I could hang about no longer and went down to the beach to see what was going on there. It was full of troops and owing to a wet and misty morning the West-Cliff where the Germans were was obscured and they were unable to see what was going on. There were boats near Veule-les-Roses and many people were getting into them. I moved along the beach but before I had got very far the mist lifted and the Germans opened up, and I had to scuttle to the nearest cover which was practically nil. I was also very tired and could not move very fast. Our French Liaison Officer, Jacques Bingen, who had been slightly wounded the night before passed me at great speed and did in fact get on a boat and got home. (He later joined the Resistance, was parachuted into France and eventually picked up by the Germans in Paris and committed suicide rather than give his pals away.) Being so slow I did not get away but I did get on a boat, which I only discovered later was aground—this boat was hammered by German guns having fired its own guns to the end. Anyhow by the time I saw any Germans the whole sad story was over and I was well separated from most of the rest of the divisional staff. My feelings? Mainly I think philosophical—we've had it! A bit numbed and downcast naturally and I think inwardly very angry. You see, even if what happened was necessary—and even now I do not think it was—we all thought we had been badly let down by those responsible at home, and a lot of the blame was likely to be put on us. I was indeed tired and hungry—no sleep for 48 hours and nothing to eat for 24. Even before that things were erratic and spasmodic.

When headquarters are overrun senior officers are usually accorded special treatment. In the western world vestiges of the mediaeval code of knighthood linger, and professional etiquette is bolstered by hopes of gaining valuable information. Both Field Marshal Montgomery and Marshal Rommel were criticized for their attitude towards enemy generals and the hospitality they proffered. It is doubtful whether information of real value was ever divulged by German and Italian generals to Montgomery, and still less by British senior officers to Rommel. Conversely, the other side's respect for rank has produced dividends in the way of concessions to the newly-taken captives. The Second South African Division was captured at Tobruk, and Brigadier F. W. Cooper who commanded the 6th South African Brigade, relates:*

* In a letter to the author.

Rommel had the General and Brigadiers in front of him and
was very cross because we had destroyed the water distillation
plant and all the storage tanks, saying it would be our fault
if the prisoners suffered from thirst. General Klopper replied
to Rommel: 'You are a soldier and so am I. It was my task to
hamper you in every way I could and I did so. It is your task to
see prisoners get food and water and I hope you'll do it.' After
that Rommel cooled down and gave instructions for the General
and Brigadiers to be accommodated in a house in town, not in the
main POW camp. The Germans treated us well and gave us
cigarettes and tobacco—from captured stocks, of course. . . .

The late Brigadier James Hargest, a New Zealander who succeeded
in making a spectacular escape from the British Generals' POW Camp
near Florence, was captured by the Germans at Sidi Aziz, Libya, in
November 1941. In *Farewell Campo 12** he recalled the moment of
capture:

And the end did come at last. . . . There, not a hundred yards
away, through the smoke of the burning tanks, I saw a line of
enemy tanks coming in smartly. . . . They were not firing; but
from the tanks on the left flank I could see an almost continuous
stream of hand grenades being tossed out and bursting behind—a
method of terror tactics.

One huge machine came straight for me as I stood. A burnt-out
truck was in the way and the tank pushed up to it, paused a
moment, climbed, crashed down over it, and came straight on. I
did not raise my hands but stood watching the wicked-looking gun
pointing straight at my middle. Just as it seemed about to run me
down, it suddenly slewed off and passed right over two of my men
in a slit trench beside me, leaving them unharmed. As it went I
heard the crackle of machine gun fire and, turning, saw a young
RAF officer, McIntyre, with an old-fashioned Lewis gun to his
shoulder giving the tank the whole drum. It did not deign to
reply. Other waves of tanks came in, and, meeting detachments
of our men, ran round shepherding them into groups until the
German infantry in caterpillar trucks dashed up and secured them.

So it ended. I remember looking at my watch—it was nine-
fifteen am. The battle had lasted for two and a quarter hours.

After a while a tank drew up beside me and a bespectacled German officer spoke to me from the turret top where he was standing.

'Are you the Commander?'

'Yes.'

* Brigadier J. Hargest, *Farewell Campo 12* (Michael Joseph, London 1945), pp.
17–20.

'I am General Kramer and I speak English. Will you please come beside me?'

I told him that I had received a blow on the hip from a shell, and I could not manage to climb. Someone assisted me and I got up somehow. He was courteous and most anxious to please.

'Your men fight well', he said, 'and fight like gentlemen. So do we; but I have been in Russia where that is not so.'

From the top of the tank I could see that my men had been herded into a group near the dressing station not far away, and we drove over to them. I asked Kramer if, in view of his opinion that we were gentlemen, he would allow me to send my men to their respective slit trenches to get their coats, blankets and food, as they had not breakfasted. He consented at once. When one of his officers pointed out that I still carried my revolver he refused to disarm me; but the moment his back was turned I was rapidly deprived of it and of my field glasses.

There was a little stir among the Germans and another officer appeared. It was Rommel. He sent for me. I bowed to him. He stood looking at me coldly. Through an interpreter he expressed his displeasure that I had not saluted him. I replied that I intended no discourtesy, but was in the habit of saluting only my seniors in our own or Allied armies. I was in the wrong, of course, but had to stick to my point. It did not prevent him from congratulating me on the fighting quality of my men.

'They fight well', he said.

'Yes, they fight well,' I replied, 'but your tanks were too powerful for us.'

'But you also have tanks.'

'Yes, but not here, as you can see.'

'Perhaps my men are superior to yours.'

'You know that is not correct.'

It was a perfunctory conversation. He asked me if he could do anything for me and I said that I would be glad to have access to my kit for some clothes. He agreed and appeared to give the necessary orders; but nothing transpired, and I never saw a particle of my kit again. He walked away, and a few minutes later, acting on what seemed to be merely spoken orders, the whole motor column set off westwards at a great pace. Apart from his momentary annoyance at the beginning of our talk, he showed me every courtesy. He was quiet in manner and in dress, and did not wear a monocle, the badge of most of his kind. Although he had been fighting for over a week and was travelling in a tank, he was neat and clean, and I noticed that he had shaved before entering the battle that morning.

We were left in the hands of a company of infantry whom I had seen following the tanks into the camp—undoubtedly the 'moppers-up'. For the most part they moved about quietly and methodically, collecting the men and searching them for weapons, papers, snapshots, etc., and as far as I could see not attempting any bullying nor stealing articles of personal value. The Commander, however, was a typical bully. As soon as his superiors had withdrawn he began to assert his authority. I was standing aside from the group of officers when he approached and, pushing his pistol into my back, began to prod me to make me move. I stood it for a moment and then turned on him, caught the arm holding the pistol and drove it up in the air, where I told him to keep it. He looked a little abashed and walked away, and after that left me alone. I wanted to go to the dressing station near by to see our wounded, so approaching a German sentry I asked him to come with me and I set off, the sentry following faithfully behind and never leaving me. I kept him until I was sent to Bardia.

Inmates of dressing stations and field hospitals are expected to be well treated. The tide of battle generally flows over and past them, and it is some time before the implications of what has happened become apparent. For the wounded, therefore, the moment of capture may seem to be of little consequence compared with the physical pain they are experiencing. As always everything depends on the captors. Two hundred British wounded were murdered by the Japanese Imperial Guards on the banks of the Muar river in Malaya in 1941. A few weeks later other Japanese troops got out of hand at the fall of Singapore. General Percival described the scene like this:

The Japanese troops entered the great military hospital at Alexandra Park and there a tragedy took place. They claimed Indian troops had fired from the hospital. Whether they did so or not, I cannot say.

As a reprisal they bayoneted some members of the staff and patients including one poor fellow as he lay on the operating table. Next day they murdered 150 of the staff and patients. There were many horrors in the last war but for cold-blooded barbarity this deed will surely rank very high.

The Japanese lost the war, so retribution was inevitable. Because the Germans also lost the war, the Russians did not have to answer for their behaviour at Stalingrad. According to one German officer who lived through that particular holocaust about 105,000 officers and men remained in the ruins when Stalingrad fell.* Many were already dead and the problem of tens of thousands of wounded was resolved by tossing explosive charges into the hospital shelters. On 3 February 1943 the Russians dynamited the entrances of the enormous Timoshenkobunker, burying the thousands of German wounded who were lying inside.

Waving a white flag (or something which has been improvised to look like a white flag), throwing away one's weapons, and raising open hands above the head are the usual ways of indicating a willingness to surrender. These gestures are recognized as the traditional message of an enemy who wishes to give up the fight, throw himself on the mercy of his captors and accept captivity. If they are used as a deceptive device and the deception fails the individuals concerned can expect no quarter. In all non-hostile communications good faith is absolutely essential, and instances of men holding up their hands as a token of surrender and then committing some hostile act have usually ended in slaughter. In both world wars there have been countless cases of men purporting to surrender, changing their minds when a favourable opportunity was presented, producing a gun and taking pot shots at their captors. More often than not this has resulted in the captors seeing red and butchering all prisoners in sight. It only needs one man to behave in this fashion and the rest of his group pay the penalty whether they were party to his treachery or not. Men who pose as casualties and suddenly come alive to resume the battle are in a similar category. During the battle of the Somme in 1914 German troops allowed the British to advance over them and then fired on them from behind. The Germans concerned halted the British attack, but the infuriated survivors turned back to shoot the lot. No prisoners were taken that day, and it was a long time before German cries of 'Kamerad' were accepted with any confidence by the British troops involved in the action. At General Yamashita's trial the Defence Council pleaded that the massacre in Singapore's Alexandra Hospital had been provoked by shots from troops supposed to have capitulated.

Open hostility at the time of surrender is an obvious breach of the tenuous understanding established when men surrender. Lesser infringements can also be rated as treachery. Preparations for some future hostile act are just as likely to rouse the ire of the captors if they are disclosed. An illustration of preparations that fortunately were not detected will make the point. At the fall of Singapore John

* According to Erich Kern, *Dance of Death* (Collins, London 1951), 235,000 Germans took part in the defence of Stalingrad. Of these 40,000 had been flown out wounded; 90,000 fell into Russian hands as prisoners; and 105,000 have never been properly accounted for.

Milford was a gunner subaltern whose battery was defending Government House. Milford recalls the 'correct' behaviour of the Japanese when a fellow subaltern of Milford's unit committed suicide because he was unable to face captivity. (This was an attitude which they thoroughly appreciated.) When one of Milford's sergeants was seen burying the body of another fallen comrade in the grounds of Government house, other Japanese soldiers bowed, saluted respectfully, asked no questions and did not interfere. Had they known that the 'body' was in fact a Bren gun and ammunition wrapped in oiled silk the sons of the Son of Heaven would have acted very differently.

Opportunities to strike a blow at the enemy may occur after capture. Those who seize these opportunities may indeed be continuing to act as a soldier—which is what a fighting man is supposed to do—but they may also be hazarding the lives of others who are with them. Mr H. O. Whiting was a Bombardier with a field artillery regiment of the 78th Division when the British 1st Army invaded North Africa. When his unit was surrounded and out of ammunition the guns were destroyed and those who had survived the action were forced to surrender.

> I remember that the Germans were affable . . . but the atmosphere deteriorated . . . we were given some cognac and told to sit by the side of the road along which ran a German telephone cable. This was cut fairly quickly—undoubtedly by one of our signallers. A feldwebel promptly asked for an interpreter and a Jewish soldier stepped forward. Even without translation it was evident from the bearing of the feldwebel and the gestures he made with his Schmeisser that any further incident of this nature would result in our being shot. As a punishment we were made to sit in the sun. That day we were marched to the hills, carrying an officer corpse sewn in a blanket and as we lay down by some tanks (the crews of which in their conversation referred to the British trait of trying to do too much with too little—a sentiment with which the prisoners who could understand inwardly agreed) the corpse marked the end of the line—any movement beyond that would earn a shooting. . . .

At the end of a battle most men are too tired, too hungry, too sickened by what has happened and too apprehensive of the future to consider doing anything that might cause trouble. Geoffrey Stavert was a gunner officer in Tunisia in February 1943:

> At the instant of surrender itself I didn't feel too bad. Tired after the day-long battle, dazed with the noise of bomb and shell, dis-

gusted and still half-incredulous that our first action had to end in this way, but not hopelessly craven. At least we had given them a run for their money (some POWs didn't even have a fight to look back on, having for example come up as reinforcements and walked straight into the arms of Jerry). Besides, when you have seen your 25-pounder AP tracer bouncing off the front of a Tiger, a certain disgruntlement sets in—its easy to blame the equipment. With the guns all bent and the ammunition on fire, and the Battery Commander himself mustering us, it seemed only the reasonable thing to do. I remember quite clearly thinking, 'Oh well, perhaps I'll get to a prison camp and become somebody by making a famous escape.'

Our BSM didn't feel the same. He was a regular soldier, keen on his career in the Army. He never got over it.

A man's immediate reactions to the sudden realization he is to become a POW obviously depend largely on the circumstances of his capture. If he was captured after an operation in which comrades have been killed his first feelings were usually of relief that he had managed to stay alive. This feeling may endure for some time. Pilot Officer W. Towler, one of the crew of a British bomber shot down over north Germany in September 1941, has described his feeling as one of resignation. Twenty-one-years-old, barely through his basic training, imbued with the dare-devil spirit and glamour which the RAF encouraged to bolster the morale of air crews, Towler found himself lying in a field near the coast at 1 am in the morning. He was alone, he had a bad cold, and his ears were tingling, from the crash-landing of his plane; otherwise he was uninjured. But he had no weapons—and would not have known how to use them if he had—and no escape kit. He was also worried about the rest of his crew, who had parachuted into the sea before the aircraft crashed. As he saw the situation, the odds were against his finding a boat and rowing to neutral Sweden. So he decided to stay where he was and surrender to those who were bound to be on their way to investigate his crash. At dawn the Luftwaffe arrived to pick him up.

Frustration is a common feeling among soldiers who feel that they have been let down by their commanders. Many British troops in the Far East experienced this feeling when Hong Kong, Singapore and Burma fell in quick succession. So did the Germans. Just before von Paulus surrendered the German Sixth Army at Stalingrad, Goering broadcast from Berlin. The 'holy saga' of the Stalingrad warriors was drawing to an end, he said cheerfully—implying success was in sight. Some of the so-called Stalingrad warriors heard these words in a dug-out in the battered city. 'That fat swine has sold us',

one man of Lieutenant Erwin Hermann's men blurted out. He and
the rest of the Germans besieged in the Russian city knew exactly
what was going to happen. Russian loud-speakers had for days been
blaring out details of the arrangements the German High Command
should follow when it was ready to surrender, and no sooner had
Goering finished than a cipher message was received from Lias'
divisional headquarters. The divisional commander had apparently
decided to surrender on his own responsibility and his message had
not been properly deciphered

> . . . before some Russian soldiers came over to our lines shouting
> that we were their prisoners. They had no white flag, but merci-
> fully no one fired at them . . . immediately afterwards the Russians
> turned their searchlights on and very soon we were being hustled
> by our captors past their outposts . . . our feelings were indescrib-
> able as we stumbled into and out of potholes, over the carcasses
> of many dead men buried, or rather hidden, just under the surface
> of the snow. We all had a great contempt for Russian military
> skill, though not for the bravery of the Russian soldier, and we
> found it impossible to believe we had really been defeated. I my-
> self felt sure I must be dreaming. When I compared notes after-
> wards with my comrades, I found they thought the same. . . .*

Frustration such as that described by Lias is of a generalized
nature—anger with the system, the High Command, the weapons
that proved inadequate, the reinforcements that never arrived.
Goering's broadcast provided a momentary focus, but most of the
Germans at Stalingrad realized that the root of the Wehrmacht's
defeat lay much deeper than the snow of Stalingrad and the mis-
calculations and mistakes committed by von Paulus. But feelings of
frustration can also be more personalized. If a soldier becomes a
prisoner through the incompetence of his immediate superior then a
mixture of bitterness, anger, helplessness and hopelessness will be
directed towards the man who is seen to have caused the disaster.
In 1941 Jim Witte was serving with the Essex Yeomanry, a gunner
regiment of the Royal Horse Artillery in the famous 7th Armoured
Division. As the driver of the regimental water truck he was considered, next to the Colonel and the Regimental Sergeant Major, the
most important man in his unit. In the course of Rommel's unsuccessful drive to Cairo, the Essex Yeomanry were caught up in the
Eighth Army's retreat. Witte's vehicle was moving with the regimental
'B echelon', commanded by a recently-joined subaltern, and in the

---

* Godfrey Lias, *I Survived* (Evans Bros., London 1954), p. 19.

general helter-skelter back towards Egypt B echelon had lost track of the main body. Witte describes what happened then: *

Sergeant Johnson was all for going on to Tobruk, the most sensible course to take because that was where all the vehicles were heading. But not he [the subaltern]; he was going to take us southwards into the desert towards Fort Mekili where he believed we would find the Regiment.

Sergeant Johnson pleaded with him and pointed out the flood of trucks coming *back* along the track which led to Mekili.

'Now don't argue, Sergeant,' he said. 'We are going to join *the* Regiment. We leave at 0700 hours tomorrow morning.'

Sergeant Johnson shrugged his shoulders and walked away. We watched uneasily. If I hadn't been so tired I would have crept away during the night and thumbed a lift on a Tobruk-bound vehicle. But, as it was, I got my bed-roll out and within seconds I was fast asleep. I woke next morning thoroughly refreshed but still filled with gloomy thoughts. All that the party had in the way of trucks were six three-tonners. We clambered aboard next morning and set off on the desert track to Mekili. By this time the traffic heading towards Tobruk had thinned out. An occasional vehicle passed us going hell for leather the other way, its driver making frantic signals to us that we were headed in the wrong direction. But our commander took no notice and pressed on intent on winning himself a gong.

The afternoon wore on as we approached Mekili. It looked rather like P. C. Wren's Foreign Legion Fort Zinderneuf, it was just as deserted. Our gallant commander looked nonplussed. Sergeant Johnson exploited his confusion and asked whether or not we should withdraw. But his pride was hurt and he didn't like to admit that he had made a mistake.

'We'll bivouac for the night and wait until the morning. I am certain that the regiment will be here by then.'

I don't know how Sergeant Johnson controlled himself. He walked over to us dejectedly and sat down. We brewed him some tea and anxiously discussed the situation. It wasn't very bright, but there was very little we could do about it. Next morning it was quiet, too quiet for comfort. Suddenly there was a burst of shell-fire a few miles to the rear of the fort. Soon afterwards a fifteen-hundredweight truck with an anti-tank gun mounted on the back dashed into our bivouac. It belonged to the 3rd RHA who were apparently fighting a desperate rear-guard action against Rommel's tanks. The sergeant yelled to us to get out of it quickly.

* Personal narrative to the author.

'What the hell are you fucking idiots doing here? Get going before it's too late.'

The chief 'fucking idiot' appeared and started to question the sergeant. But he didn't stop to argue; his driver put his foot down and disappeared in a cloud of dust. It then dawned on our commander that we had better do as the RHA sergeant said. We withdrew hurriedly from Mekili and went back the way we came. But instead of fanning out in desert formation Snurdge kept us in column of route, a dangerous practice when the Germans were so near.

By mid-afternoon we began to believe that we would escape the tightening Panzer ring. But suddenly a fusillade of shots ripped through the canvas of our three-tonner. We stopped abruptly behind the vehicle in front and dived beneath our own. For a few minutes nothing happened. We crept out and there a few yards away was a solitary German half-track. Its occupants had captured the entire column without us making a single move to escape. A German soldier marched briskly down the line of vehicles shouting *raus* (out), a word which we were to hear a lot of in the months to come. We were lined up and counted and put back into one of our own vehicles but this time driven by a member of the Afrika Corps. Meanwhile the cause of our capture had disappeared, to where we didn't know. All we knew was that the Germans always quickly separated officers from the men.

The sequel to Witte's tale is also best described in his own words. It took place in the Italian POW compound at Derna a few days after capture:

I was strolling around one day, watching people brewing up and cooking all sorts of weird and wonderful concoctions on little fires made against the walls of the huts when in walked Snurdge (the subaltern) accompanied by an Italian officer. He made a bee-line for me and one or two others from the mob. We all sat down on the deck deliberately, knowing full well that you had to stand when addressed by an officer.

Our subaltern looked a bit annoyed, but he got more annoyed when someone said, 'If it hadn't been for you, you cunt, we wouldn't be here now.'

Our subaltern departed hurriedly with an amazed Italian officer who couldn't believe his eyes at the sight of common soldiers who laid around when they were addressed by a superior. Later on we learned that Snurdge managed to get himself repatriated as he only had one eye. . . .

Frustration can also stem from what appears to be unfair action resulting in capture. On 2 August 1914 Percy Shaw was the chief engineer on the SS *Nicoya*, a cargo vessel which had docked in Hamburg with a cargo of bananas. The bananas had not been unloaded but the British Consul came down to the ship and advised the captain to get the *Nicoya* out of German waters without delay. War was near, he said. The captain was ready to comply. Knowing the Germans had already mined the mouth of the Elbe, however, he reckoned it would be the height of folly to attempt to sail without a pilot who could guide them through the minefield. The dock superintendent was asked to supply a pilot, but none appeared, and when war was declared on 4 August, the whole crew of the *Nicoya* was marched off into captivity at Ruhleben. Bitter and resentful, Shaw and other members of the crew brought a case against the German Government when the war ended. In defence of their action the Germans pleaded that the *Nicoya* might have been carrying explosives. In the event Shaw won his case and was awarded £3000 compensation.*

Hopelessness is akin to frustration, and like frustration it can be provoked by a variety of circumstances. In 1940 French morale was low, and many French soldiers were overwhelmed with despair. Jean Hélion could not comprehend what was going on:†

They arrived in armoured cars, roaring so that the trees shook. It was five o'clock, 19 June 1940.

In the first car, a German officer stood up, his arms raised well above his head, and he shouted in French: '*La guerre est finie, vous serez chez vous dans trois jours.*'

Moving slowly behind their shields, the machine guns were covering the woods. Two observation planes circled above, very low.

They didn't need to be afraid. Nobody was going to shoot. The sad show was over, incomprehensible as far as I was concerned, right to the last moment. They lifting up their hands, and sending us home!

Out of the woods came my comrades. One by one they went towards the cars. Some of them had their arms lifted, just like the German officer. They meant, perhaps, that they agreed?

Followed by three sergeants the German officer jumped onto the road, and shouted again:

'The war is ended. You will be home in three days.' He laughed broadly, engagingly.

---

* Story related to the author by the late Percy Shaw's brother, Mr R. Merryweather Shaw.

† Jean Hélion, *Ils ne m'auront pas* (E. P. Dutton, New York 1943).

A few men cheered. Ernest and I came out of hiding, to see who had thus disgraced themselves. There, clad in French uniforms, five or six men had raised only one arm and were giving the Nazi salute. I heard this distinctly:

'. . . *wir haben nie geschossen.* (We are Alsatians, we have never fired a shot.)' They smiled.

It is true that three or four others, who could not have been Alsatians, also smiled, or tried to.

From all the cars, German soldiers jumped down and lined up. They carried hand grenades ready to throw. So they had two kinds of arguments. This one was less humiliating.

In 1944 British morale was riding high in Normandy. And men who became prisoners at this time were less concerned about the overall situation. They knew then that Germany would be defeated, and when they were captured it was because resistance in their particular situation had no future; it was hopeless to fight on. Mr N. Webb was a twenty-year-old infantryman when he was captured.*

On 24 August 1944 the British Army reached the Seine at Vernon, to find that the Germans had destroyed the only bridge. On the far bank were high bluffs, in which enemy snipers were harassing the Sappers who were erecting a Bailey bridge. Our company (or what was left of it) were detailed to cross the river and keep these 'few snipers' away from the approaches to the bridge. We crossed in the late afternoon, and soon discovered that the 'few snipers' were in fact a company of SS armed with automatic weapons. Despite appeals to Bn HQ on our W/T no reinforcements were sent, and in the early hours of the morning, with our ammunition expended and only four of us un-wounded, we had the choice of being wiped out or surrendering. No doubt we should have died gloriously in our ruined cottage, but in the event we decided to surrender—a difficult task as none of us spoke any German. Personally, I found it almost insuperably difficult to step out of the illusory safety of the ruins, and quite expected to be met by a burst of Schmeisser fire.

When men have a responsibility for others, hopelessness can be allied with shame: In April 1951 the 1st Battalion the Gloucestershire Regiment defended a vital crossing over the Imjin River in Korea—an action which has passed into British military history as an epic. After suffering casualties the battalion withdrew to Hill 235 'Gloucester Hill', where it continued to fight until almost completely surrounded. Realizing the position was hopeless Colonel Carne, the

* Narrative to the author.

Battalion Commander, ordered the remnants of his battered unit to
attempt a break-out. In small groups the survivors tried to get away.
One of the groups was commanded by Captain (now Major-General)
Tony Farrar-Hockley:*

> All the way up the valley I had heard machine-gun fire sounding
> and resounding among the hills; but none had been directed at us.
> Only now, as we drew near to the saddle, as the walls of the valley
> seemed to close right in upon us in this dark and cheerless spot—
> now almost a ravine—did we feel the breath of the enemy's fire.
> From the hills on either side, from the hills to our rear, light and
> heavy machine-guns fired towards us. Yet they did not hit us.
> There can be no doubt that, had they wished to, they could have
> mown us down like grass before a scythe. Exposed entirely to
> their weapons, we moved along the path under the very muzzles.
> The message that they conveyed was quite plain: we are up here;
> you are down there; you are exposed; we are concealed and you
> are in our sights. As we moved on, the fire from three machine-
> guns came down again, this time a good deal lower—unmistakably
> lower. I knew there was but one course open to me if the men
> with me were to remain alive for more than five minutes. Feeling
> as if I was betraying everything that I loved and believed in, I
> raised my voice and called:
>   'Stop!'
> They stopped and looked towards me, their faces expectant. I
> shall never know what order they anticipated. Then I said:
>   'Put down your arms!'
>   A few seconds later, just at the foot of the saddle, I heard Sam
> say the same thing to those with whom he had moved. The words
> rang in my ears like an echo, a shameful echo. After all that we
> had done, after all the effort we had exerted in fulfilling our task,
> this was the end: surrender to the enemy!

Anger, disappointment, frustration, helplessness, hopelessness,
shame, resignation or relief—whatever a man's feelings happen to be
in the first few moments of becoming a POW, they are not likely to
last long. Wonder about what lies ahead is likely to engender feelings
of fear, especially if he is roughly treated on capture. Prisoners of war
may know about the Geneva Conventions, but they can never be sure
that the men who hustle them towards the enemy rear know about it
also—or if they do, that their captors are quite so appreciative of
POW privileges as they, the captives, had suddenly become.

* A. T. Farrar-Hockley, *The Edge of the Sword* (Frederick Muller, London 1954),
p. 67.

4

The First Ordeal

After capture the majority of prisoners are destined to spend the rest of the war in detention. Many will hope to escape, some will try, and a few will succeed; some of the rest may also be freed—the lucky ones being liberated unharmed in the course of the war, the less lucky being repatriated because they are judged to be of no further use to the country's war effort. But the vast majority, 95 per cent or more, will be concentrated and herded together in camps. There they will wait impatiently for an end to the war or for some dramatic change in the course of hostilities which will enable them to go home.

In the first few hours of captivity the newly-taken prisoner may think of the POW camp as the end of the line. Tired, hungry, thirsty, depressed, he may even look forward to reaching the sanctuary of a place where he can expect to relax and recover after his recent shattering experiences. Between capture and camp, however, there usually lies an ordeal which may well be the worst he has to suffer during the whole course of his captivity.

Prisoners of war have tramped through the pages of history on countless 'death marches'. In May 1915 a long ragged column of about 12,000 British and Indian prisoners set out from Kut in Mesopotamia on a 500-mile march to Turkey. Genghis Khan and Tamerlane could not have organized a more vicious journey. Every step was agony for the weak, emaciated men whose physical condition had deteriorated in Kut. But the column was kept moving throughout days of intense and suffocating heat. Parched with thirst, blinded by the sun, choked with dust as they stumbled and staggered forward, those who lagged were beaten with whips and sticks, or clubbed with the rifle butts of the Arab guards. Complaints to the Turkish officers were sternly rejected, the British prisoners were now subject to Turkish discipline their spokesmen were told.

When the column reached Baghdad it was paraded through the

streets as tangible evidence of a Turkish victory. Then, after a three-day halt in a stinking, fly-ridden compound where there was no protection from the sun and no sanitation, the sad and sorry remnants of the column were sent off in batches to continue their journey to Anatolia. Considering their physical condition and how ill-equipped they were to withstand the climatic conditions, it was amazing that any of the prisoners reached their final destinations. During the second stage of their journey some of the younger British soldiers were compelled to submit to the homosexual appetites of their captors; most were too weak to object, those who did resist were simply beaten into submission. Boots quickly wore out on the rough and stony ground and as the old puttees and strips of blanket which took their place are poor protection against sharp stones the feet of those who had no boots were soon cut to ribbons. For food the captives were given a daily issue of a handful of wheat, a handful of flour and a spoonful of ghee (cooking oil); there was no firewood, and few of the British prisoners had any idea how to prepare such rations. To avoid starvation men were forced to sell the clothes they stood up in to wayside Arabs for scraps of food. Across the desert the track taken by the plodding column became a Via Dolorosa, along which the sights hardly bear telling. The dead lay unburied and stripped of their last clothing; parties of starving men in their last throes lay in mud hovels by the way to await their end, subsisting solely on the few scraps thrown to them by passing Arabs. Thus it is that there is no record and nothing is known of the ultimate fate of 3000 of those who surrendered at Kut and who died between the time Khalil Pasha announced, 'Your troubles are over, my dears; you will be treated as honoured guests of the Sultan,' and their arrival in the primitive camps which had been prepared for them. Had it not been for the efforts of the American Consul at Mersina, and the American ladies and doctors at Adana and Tarsus, many more of the sick and exhausted men who survived the journey would also have died.

Like other journeys into captivity which preceded and followed this particular death march, the suffering of the prisoners reflected the peculiarities of the captors' character. Some of these—at any rate to the distant spectator—were sufficiently picturesque; others could be attributed to the dead weight of Asiatic indifference and inertia; others again were actively and resolutely barbarous. In World War II the veneer of civilization was seen to be as thin on the Japanese Emperor's soldiers as it had been on those of the Sultan. Americans captured by General Homma's forces in the Bataan Peninsula and at Corregidor were lucky if they reached a prison camp alive. In tropical heat they were forced to march 135 miles, and it took them 11 days to do so. For five days they were given no food at all, and then only a handful of rice on the days that followed. During their short rest period they were made to sit on the road under the full glare of the tropical sun and were not allowed to seek shade. When they marched through occupied villages, Japanese troops would line the route and beat the prisoners with sticks as they marched by.

In Europe and North Africa the Germans and Italians usually behaved more humanely towards new prisoners than their Japanese allies. Much depended on the prisoner's nationality, where he was captured, and what stage in the war. British and American soldiers captured in the fighting in the West could be sure of a better reception than Russians taken on the eastern front. In 1940 the British and French fighting men, who were captured before the fall of France, saw flashes of Teutonic arrogance displayed by their young captors. Two years later British troops captured in North Africa noticed a guarded respect; the Germans had come to appreciate the fighting qualities of their opponents. By 1944 there were times when they expressed whole-hearted admiration at the way their prisoners had stood up to them before capture.

Major Whitcombe, captured on 12 June 1940, thought that he and those captured with him were treated in a 'lousy' fashion.*

We were marched away later in the afternoon and it was about 10 pm before we were planted in a large field and given a small tin of British 'Maconchie' between three of us. I see that at this time it was 36 hours since I had eaten and 60 since I had slept. Throughout the march we were badly fed and often slept in fields. Normally nothing before we left on a march of 15 or maybe 20 miles and a meal in the evening of thin soup and a piece of bread. We were saved by the French people, who came out and fed us as we passed through the villages, in the mining area round Bethune where we had been earlier in the year. They were particularly generous. At first the guards tried to stop it, but later they gave up; there were too many of us and too few of them. Any food we did get at night was provided by the French on German orders. We eventually reached Holland after a march of about 250 miles done in 17 marching days, with three rest days. In Holland we were crowded into river steamers or barges and sailed down the Maas and Rhine to Wesel. The state of these boats had to be seen to be believed. I was in the *Konigin Emma* and was lucky—there was a saloon which was occupied by the Germans and they too used the only toilets. We were all officers on this boat and we were packed on the decks like sardines, if we managed to sit down we could not

* Narrated to the author.

stretch our legs out; after we left a piece of wood was slung over the side for use as a latrine in full view of anyone on the banks of the canal or river, most of us had some form of diarrhoea due to lack of food and we had to battle our way over bodies to reach the spot and then probably queue to be able to expose ourselves over the side. The unfortunates in the barges were worse off as they were battened down to make sure none of them escaped. For the trip we had one loaf of bread, stale brown. We left at 6 pm on 29 June and reached Emmerich at 9 pm on the 30th where we stayed on board a second night, reaching Wesel about 11 am on 1 July. The Dutch like the French did their best—at Dortrecht they gave us bread and sausage and a little butter and honey, but for the two days on this boat this was all we had. When we were landed at Wesel we were given some bread and a piece of cheese and some coffee. At 3 pm we were warned to get ready to entrain with a quarter loaf of bread and a bit of cheese for the journey. After a lot of hanging about we were marched to the station and put in carriages with hard wooden seats, in our case only six to the compartment. At 2 am we were turned out at what we found was Hemer, not far from Dusseldorf. We were put into new unfinished barracks here and were I suppose comparatively comfortable, overcrowded of course with a straw bed. They also gave us a little to eat, but not much. Here we stayed till 6 July when we entrained at 4 pm with one-fifth loaf of bread (always stale brown) and a bit of cheese—this seemed to be the travelling ration irrespective of how far one was going or how long the journey would take. This time we were nine in a hard seated compartment. At midday next day we were told we would get a meal at Nuremberg in three hours' time. We did go through Nuremberg but got no food. We reached Laufen at 1 am on 8 July and marched to what was to be our home for the next 15 months. Here we were given a half-loaf of same bread and told it was to last two days—nothing else—this after 24 hours without food.

The Germans did everything they could to humiliate us. They thought they had the war won and that was that, we did not matter and no one could call them to account for anything they did. Their guards did nothing but shout at us and did not seem to realize—or didn't care—that most of us did not understand a word they said. They had given us less than minimal food and even water was hard to come by. When we reached Laufen we were stripped and medically examined, de-loused and had all our hair cut off, and then photographed holding our number on a slate in front of us just as though we were convicts. The Germans were greatly surprised and, I think, disappointed, that in such a decadent people as they had been led to believe we were, not one case of VD was discovered. . . .

Mr A. Greenshields was captured a few miles north of the beach where Whitcombe had tried to get away. Greenshields, a Lance-Corporal of the 2nd Battalion The Buffs, had been wounded and was on his way to Dunkirk when a Stuka dive-bomber forced the ambulance in which he was travelling off the road. Teaming up with a gunner who was in a similar plight, Greenshields set off walking towards the coast. The two men did not get far because they were picked up by a German armoured column. Greenshields' immediate reaction was one of relief, coupled with apprehension about what would happen to him when he did eventually get back to the Buffs. Both feelings rapidly disappeared when he joined thousands of others on the long trek into Germany.

I recall that my captors appeared to me to be giants of men and looked very professional. Their Unteroffizier was a keen football fan and favoured a particular English team and asked if I supported it. I know I agreed with him that it was a very capable team for fear of upsetting him but I know that football was far from my mind. A decision made quite early that appeasement might be the wisest course to take and it certainly was for the earlier years in captivity.*

Regimental Quartermaster Sergeant G. E. Lyons of the Royal West Kents was also impressed by the professionalism of his captors. Following a brisk, unorthodox, and unprofessional little action by the storemen, cooks, drivers and batmen of battalion headquarters 'B echelon' Lyons tried to spirit his little group away from the scene. His efforts ceased when a feldwebel's pistol was pushed into his ribs while other Germans surrounded his men.

. . . we were disarmed and marched into a large farmyard. That night we slept on the ground and were joined by some French Moroccan troops, who reeked of garlic and other smells. . . . In the morning we were formed into small parties to bury the dead, civilians and troops. In the afternoon we started a march across Northern France, Belgium and Luxembourg which lasted 20 days. Up to this point we had had no food and we soon realized that we had to keep our eyes open for anything edible. . . . As we passed through villages we broke away from the ranks and dashed into empty houses seeking food. . . . On one of these raids I rushed into one room and another man made a beeline for the other.

* Letter to the author.

Then I heard a shout 'Heraus', followed by a shot ... the other man had been shot through the chest by a German guard standing at the door ... my feelings can well be imagined. So this is German discipline. ... On the march we walked from sunrise to sundown. Fresh guards took over about every five miles ... some were friendly, talked, and turned a blind eye to our foraging for food. Others were trigger happy and fired at the slightest excuse. ... We eventually arrived at Trier on the Moselle where we were put on a train 40 men to a closed goods wagon. I helped to count the men into the wagons and when we got to the last one there were 60 men left. I suggested spreading the surplus along the train. But no! We were hustled in at the point of bayonets. We were issued with some soup before getting into the train, but the only receptacles we had were those we had picked up on the march. Some men put the soup in their water bottles and as there was some to spare, they filled up again for the train journey; the soup was very salty and they soon realized that they had forfeited water for soup. The journey started at 6 pm on a Friday and finished at 8 pm on the Sunday. The train stopped only once, when we were given a drink of ersatz coffee (less sugar or milk). No sanitary arrangements at all, so one can soon visualize the state of the wagons and the spirits of the men. Three men in my wagon died and this was only discovered when we arrived at Shubin in Poland. I feel this journey was the worst period of our captivity.*

Before he started on his march into captivity Jean Hélion was also impressed with German equipment and discipline. Their uniforms looked neater and 'better conceived' than the French, he noted; discipline was noticeably stricter, with NCOs pushing round and shouting orders at private soldiers responding with lots of heel-clicking and 'Ja-wohls'. Respect was quickly dulled, and after six days of weary plodding Hélion came to believe that their miseries were all part of a preconceived plan to subdue the French.

It would have taken many regiments of guards to escort the thousands and thousands of prisoners bagged every day. In the enormous confusion created by the speed of the invasion, they might have escaped easily. Here is a six-day solution of this problem:

1st day: Give them nothing to eat, and march them 15 miles.
2nd day: 25 miles and nothing to eat.
3rd day: 30 miles and no food.
4th day: 35 miles and ditto.

* Narrated to the author.

5th day: a tiny platter of soup, and 42 especially well-selected miles.

6th day: a mere 15 miles, and a little French tobacco wrapped in a thin, brown paper.

It solves the question of transportation too.

Of course, after the third day, you have to count on a certain amount of butt-end pounding of the ribs to keep these people from falling down. You may, on the other hand, improve their resistance considerably, by building up their morale with the reiterated affirmation that the war is over, and they will be sent home soon. Wretches will fall for the sweetest lure any time and swim into the net.*

Driver Jim Witte, resentful and angry after his capture near Mekili in the Western Desert on April Fools Day 1941, was hustled into a circle of stones where 2000 other Allied prisoners had been collected. Witte had an idea that a rough journey lay ahead, and he spotted an opportunity to make some provision for it:

The circle was ringed by sentries who threatened to shoot us if we moved outside. Beyond the ring were several British stores' vehicles loaded with clothing. I took my cap off and hid it in a thorn bush. Then I went up to one of the sentries, pointed to the sun and then to my head and asked if I could leave the ring to get a cap. The Jerry motioned me out and I shot into the back of one of the trucks like a rabbit going into its burrow. I grabbed a pack and loaded it with shirts, socks and a pullover. I couldn't find any food but in the driver's cab was the greatest prize of all—a carton of 200 cigarettes. I stuffed these into my pack and crept furtively from the vehicle. But in my excitement I had forgotten to get a hat. The Jerry was watching. He pointed to my head. I grinned sheepishly and muttered 'nix hats'. Fortunately I am very fair and rather Germanic looking; something which, although I didn't know it at the time, was going to stand in my favour when dealing with Germans. The Jerry let me go back. A few others tried the same dodge but it cut no ice. . . .

We stayed within the circle of stones for two days. German vehicles continued to bring in prisoners. Some were wounded. One poor chap had nineteen bullet wounds. His cries were terrible for he had been jolted over many miles of rough ground. But to give the Germans their due a surgeon operated immediately and removed each bullet, a process which took many hours. The lad lived and was transported by ambulance to hospital in Derna. The Germans were strictly correct in their behaviour towards us

* *Ils ne m'auront pas.* Op. cit., p. 53.

and there were no incidents of brutality on the part of the Afrika Corps. Rommel had no SS troops in his army, but we were to have many dealings with them in the years to come. The ordinary German soldier was a decent enough chap until provoked and then he would think nothing of clouting you with a rifle butt or his boots. We were soon to find out that the German soldier had some measure of respect for Britishers, Australians and Canadians but none for their allies the Italians, the French or any other Europeans.

We were marched to an airfield just outside Derna. It was only a few miles and my pack began to get uncomfortably heavy, consequently I started to straggle behind the main body, but a few 'raus's from the guards drove me along. No sooner had we settled down on the tarmac than we were ordered to get up again to go to Derna—and barracks which had once held Italians. . . . These barracks consisted of several stone huts, completely devoid of everything except space which soon got used up as more and more British, Australian and Indian prisoners arrived. The extent of the calamity in the desert was brought home to us by the numbers of men the Germans had captured.

A fortunate few of us had managed to bring some army rations like tins of 'meat and veg' and bully beef which we used to supplement the meagre Italian rations of weak macaroni stew and square biscuits as large and as hard as house tiles. After a few days there were some very hungry people about; a few tried scrounging *chapattis* off the Sikhs who prepared them on flat sheets of heated metal in the court-yards between the huts. . . .*

From Derna, Witte and the rest of his group was taken to Tripoli in Italian trucks. The 1000-mile journey lasted four days, and whenever the vehicles passed through small towns like Homs, Misurata and Sirte, the local populace emerged to hurl abuse and more solid missiles at the prisoners. The Italian colonists, Witte comments dryly, 'seemed to be well imbued with the Fascist spirit'. At night the prisoners slept fitfully in the sand, shivering in the low temperatures. After Tripoli the journey continued by train to Sabratha, near the French Algerian border, where a week was spent in another Italian barracks. This was the final staging post before the prisoners crossed the Mediterranean to Naples.

The crossing was made in an otherwise empty cargo vessel, escorted by an Italian cruiser and several destroyers. Conditions on board were reasonable and the prisoners' main concern was the possibility of being torpedoed by Allied submarines.

* Narrated to the author.

Fear of becoming involved in an attack by one's own side is a
common feature of this POW betwixt-and-between interlude. Geoffrey
Stavert, captured in Tunisia, recalls that his worst moment came
when a flight of Hurricane fighter-bombers flew in towards them. At
the moment his party of POWS was passing a column of German
troops, moving in the opposite direction on their way to the battle
front.

> The escorting officer said, quite politely: 'If we are attacked you
> may jump into the ditch, but if you try to escape you will be shot.'
> We scattered up the hillside among the German troops as the
> bombs began to fall. This is every prisoner's moment of truth,
> when he finds himself in the middle, shot at by both sides, wanted
> by nobody, a liability to friend and foe alike. Some of our own
> fellows even held up their yellow recognition squares, as if that
> would make any difference. Not so the Germans; instead of taking
> cover, every single man lay on his back firing off his small arm as
> fast as he could reload. Inaccurate maybe, but the volume of fire
> was tremendous; the RAF's strafing was half-hearted, and we
> were glad it was.
>
> That helpless feeling returned more than once: when Bizerta
> was bombed, even though they were well away from the cage, and
> more so when we were being shipped over to Naples in the hold
> of an Italian coaster, escorted by a single JU 88. If there were any
> Royal Navy submarines about, we unashamedly hoped that he
> would get them first.

Prisoners of the Japanese, transported in Japanese freighters
through Dutch East India and Malayan waters, were also apprehensive. But the appalling conditions under which they travelled,
battened down in the ships' holds in tropical heat, or packed together
on the decks, unprotected from heavy tropical rain, enhanced the
prospect of a quick and easy death. On these 'hellship' moves only
meagre rations of rice and fish were provided, sometimes not properly
cooked and there was rarely enough water to go round. Diarrhoea
and dysentery spread because the prisoners had to eat below decks
and the points from where the food was distributed were usually
sited near what served as latrines. Most accounts speak of the filth,
foul smells, lice and other vermin among which the prisoners were
forced to live, sometimes for journeys lasting a month. On one
voyage from Ambon to Java 21 died in a draft of 217, and it is small
wonder that the mortality rate was not higher on some of the longer
passages. Many of the prisoners did manage to keep an outward
show of cheerfulness, but the revolting conditions, the intense heat,
the endless waiting for food and water, and the nervous strain when

Allied aircraft passed overhead made the voyages seem like prolonged nightmares to the POWS who experienced them.

An artillery barrage or air attack by his compatriots often provides a salutary introduction to the ordeal which a newly-captured POW can expect to undergo. So far as his captors are concerned the sooner he is off the battlefield the better, and they will hustle him back regardless of the danger which exists until he is out of the fighting zone. If he has to move through a steel curtain of shells put down by his own side, that is his misfortune. In World War I the casualty rate among prisoners crossing No Man's Land after capture, in operations which triggered the defensive fire machinery, was very high— though not perhaps as high as might have been expected. When the Korean War settled into a static phase the circumstances were similar to World War I. Men captured during the epic defense of the Hook by the Duke of Wellington's Regiment in May 1953 were made to double through the hail of artillery fire plastering every avenue leading to the battle. Miraculously nobody was killed. After that the routine in Korea was similar to that which prisoners experienced in World War II—from the battle zone by stages to a camp where other prisoners were concentrated. Like their predecessors in the earlier wars, the prisoners in Korea got little food, little water, and precious little rest. Second Lieutenant N. F. Deaville of The King's Regiment was wounded in the Commonwealth Sector of the UN line, carried back to a Korean village, and kept there until he was fit enough to continue his journey to a POW camp near the Chinese border. He was lucky, said the Chinese commissar who interrogated him: under the New Lenient Policy towards POWS Deaville would not be murdered, tortured or have his personal belongings taken. His wounds would be treated and as a guest of the Chinese Volunteers he would come to learn the error of his ways.

We arrived at the village and I was put in a single room, where I remained for three weeks. Here I lived in the filthiest hovel I have seen anywhere. It had a sour farmyard odour, and was crawling with lice which lost no time in moving into their new home. . . .

I was put on a truck with some American POWS and taken north. The usual five- or six-hour journey developed into one of over twelve hours because of the dilapidated Russian truck and also because of our aircraft. Chinese soldiers are posted on hilltops to listen for aircraft and when one approaches they signal vehicles on the roads by loud bangs and all lights are extinguished. North Korean roads are extremely poor and our aircraft keep them that way. Some of their repaired bridges looked exactly like an Emmet drawing. For a fit man, a ride on the back of those trucks would be quite an ordeal; for a few of us who were wounded, it was indescribable.*

How long a man takes to recover from initial shock of losing freedom and having to accept the dictates of the enemy obviously depends upon the individual's resilience and the circumstances of his capture. Some men recover very quickly and start looking for ways of escape. The knowledge that one's own people are within walking distance provides the most powerful incentive; realization that opportunities for a successful break decrease with every step on the road back to the enemy's rear is an added spur. Where prisoners have been taken in large numbers—as happened in Poland, France, North Africa, the Soviet Union, and the Pacific and South East Asia during World War II—the captors rarely have time to do anything but assemble the prisoners and make a rough count before evacuating them from the operational area. Getting the prisoners away so that the forward troops can get on with the war is the captor's number one priority. Officers can be separated from other ranks, and groups of prisoners herded together. But military exigency sets a limit on the time available for classifying, recording and chronicling immediately after an engagement. Thus if a man can manage to slip away undetected, his absence is unlikely to be noticed—for some time, if ever.

The problem of escape is described at length elsewhere in this book. Here it is sufficient to say that by far the largest number of bids to escape are attempted during the capture-to-camp period. Few succeed. Why this should be so can be put down simply to the concentration of enemy troops in the area, the physical and mental condition of the escapers—tired, hungry and imbued with a determination to get away at all costs which leads them to take excessive risks. Boldness is always necessary, but fortune does not often favour the brave escapee. General Sir Frank Messervy who slipped out of the net twice can be considered an exception. Captured in May 1942 when his divisional headquarters was overrun by Rommel's panzers, Messervy ripped off his badges of rank and played the role of batman to one of his junior staff officers. The latter had been wounded and Messervy took him to a German ambulance for the wounds to be looked at by a German medical officer. The MO spoke good English and while he was dressing the wounds, he chatted amiably to Messervy: 'What a bloody war,' he said. 'Thank God I'll be out of it in a month; no one over thirty-three serves in the Afrika Korps.' Then taking a closer look, he added, 'But you must be much older than that. What are you doing in the desert?' With an ingratiating grin, Messervy replied, 'Well, you see, Sir, I am an old soldier of

---

* *The Kingsman* (Regimental Journal of the King's Regiment), October 1953.

World War I, and I joined up again for this. But at my age I wasn't considered to be much of use for anything other than officer's batman.' The German doctor expressed his admiration for the old soldier's sense of duty, and said he hoped Messervy would soon be out of the firing line. Messervy earnestly assured him that he would be equally glad. And when the fighting flared up he set about putting this wish into effect.

With other prisoners Messervy was hustled into a truck to be driven out of the battle area. As they pulled away, British 25-pounders shelled the road, and Messervy urged the German driver to drive on out of range. The driver needed no further encouragement and Messervy's vehicle sped away from the other trucks carrying the rest of the prisoners. As it raced along the edge of a wadi, Messervy saw his chance and gave the order to jump. Until nightfall he and a tiny group of other British officers hid in the wadi, 200 yards away from a German armoured car. Then when the battle rolled away and Rommel's panzers pulled back to refuel, Messervy led the way across the desert, back to where the Eighth Army had re-established a defensive line.

Two years later Messervy was commanding the 7th Indian Division in the Arakan when the Japanese launched the offensive which was intended to carry them to Delhi. Again Messervy's headquarters were overrun, and for the second time in his hazardous life he managed to escape through the enemy's ranks. When the fighting was at its height, he and 15 others dodged into the jungle and slipped through the attacking force.

Tony Farrar-Hockley was not so lucky in Korea. After his capture below Gloucester Hill, he and about 50 other prisoners were marched north, past the scene of their recent battle. Having pondered on the problem of slipping away, Farrar-Hockley had concluded that his best opportunity would come when the column crossed the Imjin River. And when the time came that night, he slipped down into the black waters of the river while the column passed. Surfacing about 30 yards downstream there was no sound of alarm or pursuit, and he swam on downstream until he found a hole in the river bank which appeared to offer shelter. Next morning he walked back up the valley dominated by Gloucester Hill and eventually reached the point where he had been captured. From there, the UN lines and safety were about eight miles distant. But this was the battle zone and the Chinese were deployed in strength. Farrar-Hockley managed to get past a number of sentries and Chinese working parties, but the inevitable confrontation came in the middle of No Man's Land. There, less than a mile from the UN line he stumbled on to a North Korean soldier and his bid for freedom was over.

On the Russian front starvation often motivated an attempt to escape. The Germans expected—and got—short shrift from their Russian captors if they were caught, but there were times when it seemed they had nothing to lose even if they were shot. In January 1945 the 17th Panzer Division was overrun near the Vistula River and the victorious Red Army rolled past. On this occasion the prisoners were not moved, but rounded up to bivouac on the battle-field, surrounded by the debris of their defeat. For a week or so they were able to survive on scraps of food and reserve rations foraged from their disabled vehicles. After three weeks one in four of the prisoners had succumbed to starvation and cold. And it was then that Obergefreiter Muller, Feldwebel Penzlau, Gfr [L/Cpl] Kudritzky and Gfr Fahrmann decided to run for home. They didn't get far, and when they were picked up by a Russian patrol they were so cold that the prospect of being returned to the bivouac area or even being shot seemed attractive. In the event they were not shot, nor returned to their old camp. Fahrmann's ability to speak Russian probably helped to save their lives—as indeed it did to the easing of their problems in the years that lay ahead.

A three-week journey took the four men from Poland into the heart of Russia. Two thousand German prisoners set out on this particular move and Kudritzky—the only one of the four escapees to survive captivity—reckoned that about ten per cent of this figure died en route. The journey alternated between rail and road. For the moves by rail the POWs were packed into freight-trains, so that there was no room to sit or lie down. When the doors of the wagons were slammed shut and padlocked the only light inside was that which filtered through cracks; there were no washing facilities and a small hole in the floor provided the only toilet. The latter was soon clogged and the dead had to be eased down from a standing position to lie among the excrement, under the feet of the living. Meals were few and far between; what food there was being issued to the prisoners when the trains stopped at a station. When the guards opened the doors at these halts the prisoners erupted out of the wagons like a horde of wild animals. Many were suffering from dysentery, others had diarrhoea and they had been unable to relieve themselves properly in the crowded wagon. Lines of men unashamedly dropping their trousers and squatting by the side of the platform apparently left Russian spectators unmoved.

Muller who had been shot through the arm when he was recaptured, suffered excruciating pain in the early part of the journey, and it became obvious that his wound was septic. Penzlau, who had had some medical training, realized that gangrene would set in and Muller would die unless something was done quickly, and Muller—a butcher in civilian life—reluctantly agreed that his arm would have to come off. Fahrmann appealed to the guards, but they could not or would not help, so the Germans were thrown back on their own resources. In the event the arm was successfully amputated in the crowded carriage with a knife borrowed from one of the guards— disinfected in the dregs of some schnapps. The improvised anesthaesia was reminiscent of Nelson's day, since Muller was reduced to a state of unconsciousness by beating him over the head with an iron ladle. Muller recovered from this crude operation (though he died later). But he probably owed his salvation to Fahrmann's pleas to the guards, which eventually produced a sympathetic Russian doctor who bound up the stump.

Asked about thoughts of escape during this period, Kudritzky said that no one even contemplated trying to get away.

Up to this point the ordeals experienced by POWs during the capture to captivity process have focussed on the mass surrender following a great battle. What happens to men who are captured individually, or to small groups, will be somewhat different. To begin with opportunities for slipping away are less likely to occur, and the prisoners will be under closer supervision. This, of course, can bring benefits in the way of food, accommodation, transport and medical treatment. But if reprisals are in the offing, it may work the other way.

The first illustration of this point is taken from the Western Desert, shortly after the fall of Tobruk. During the fighting round Tobruk the New Zealand Division was encircled, and a night attack with the bayonet which broke the encircling ring was the cause of much high feeling among the German troops involved. The result was that a group of 92 New Zealanders captured next morning was roughly handled. Lined up, stripped of everything except their uniforms, the New Zealanders were told that they would be shot because they had shot prisoners and bayoneted the wounded. The situation was undoubtedly looking very ugly, when a captured British officer who was not included in the New Zealand party intervened. Speaking to a senior German officer in his own language, he pointed out that if the New Zealanders were shot there would be no more prisoners taken by either side. The Germans took some hours to consider this, and eventually the New Zealanders were reprieved. Meanwhile they had been kept standing in the hot sun without food and water, while sentries with Schmeissers forced back into line anyone who tried to fall out or lie down.

Miles away from the battlefield prisoners can still encounter hostility. In March 1941 the German submarine U-99 was forced to the surface by depth charges in the Atlantic. The submarine sank shortly afterwards, and the crew was picked up and taken to Liverpool by the corvette HMS *Walker*. On arrival at Liverpool, a car and escort were waiting to take the U-99's captain, Otto Kretschmer, to the interrogation centre in London. The rest of the crew were also destined for the interrogation centre, but there was no transport for them and news of their capture had preceded them. Thus, when the German sailors and an escort of Liverpool policemen marched out of the dock gates bound for Lime Street station, a sizeable crowd had gathered. Liverpool people were feeling the effect of the U-boat blockade, and they were closer to its effects than others. They had waited for relatives manning ships which never returned, and they had seen the dead and wounded brought from other ships which had been attacked by German submarines. In the words of one of the German sailors, 'We didn't expect flowers, but we didn't expect to run the gauntlet either.' Nevertheless that is what happened, when the crowd released its pent-up fury. Many of the mob were women, whose hatred turned them into vixens. Attacking with brooms, pokers, shovels and garden forks they belaboured both the prisoners and the policemen who tried to stop them. In the end the party had to take to its heels and run to Walton Jail. 'Sorry, old boy,' one of the policemen said to Petty Officer Leckenbusch whose nose had been broken in the fracas, 'they're usually very nice people.'

Similar incidents occurred in Germany. Caleb L. Reeder, an American airman, bailed out of his aircraft near Hanover in 1944. Captured by civilians, he was cuffed and beaten for nearly an hour, and then forced to run for about five miles with his arms tied behind his back. Preparations were then made for him to be lynched but he was rescued by a policeman who put him into the local jail.

Summarizing the treatment a POW can expect on his way to a prison camp is difficult. Past experience demonstrates that men can be treated with almost theatrical politeness and consideration, or left to starve and die through neglect and incompetence, or driven and tormented like beasts. What happens seems often to be ruled by nothing but mere chance. But the odds are that the captive faces an ordeal.

5

Interrogation

In any war, the gathering of military information has always been of prime importance, and attempts to wring it out of captives have been made. In 401 BC, during the retreat of the Ten Thousand, Xenophon tried to get two prisoners to tell him about the strength and dispositions of their forces. When they refused, one was 'punished in the sight of the other'. During Napoleonic wars, the American Civil War, and in the Crimea, all belligerents staged raids for the express purpose of capturing prisoners for interrogation. In every war, thereafter, military intelligence has been closely linked to the interrogation of POWs. Thus, in the early days of captivity, the prisoner can expect to be questioned about his identity, and—if he is thought to have information of a tactical or strategic value—for attempts to be made to extract this information.

But the matter may not rest there. Total war has aggravated the practice of seeking information which in the modern era does not necessarily relate only to military aspects of war. Everything which relates to a country's war effort is important, and knowledge on what might otherwise be considered non-military matters—economics, the location of industry, the source and transportation of food supplies—becomes as useful to the captor as the identification of units and their equipment, disposition and morale. Consequently the interrogation techniques have been developed to cope with the increased demand for information.

Up to the outbreak of World War I, the rules were simple: soldiers were simply enjoined 'not to talk'. Unfortunately this rule was easier to recite than observe, even before today's methods of inducing or coercing prisoners to talk were adopted. Considered objectively, both captors and captives are in a dilemma. On the one hand, the captor has a duty to acquire any information which will help his side to win battles and save lives. On the other hand, the prisoner is committed to withholding information which might cost a battle and the lives of his countrymen. By virtue of the fact that he is a captive the odds are all against the prisoner, and his refusal to talk inevitably invites some form of duress. Thus, when attempts were made to regulate warfare by ethics, resort to physical violence in order to extract information was outlawed. When the Geneva Convention was drafted the seeking of information was not prohibited, but interrogators were expressly forbidden to get information by subjecting prisoners to threats or exposing them to 'unpleasantness', or resorting to physical or mental torture.

In general terms this provision would appear to cover most contingencies. As the extraction of information was—and still is—permissible under certain conditions, unscrupulous interrogators had plenty of scope. While physical violence was to be avoided, it was considered quite proper during World War I to make a prisoner stand to attention for long sessions during his examination and to withhold food and water until he was prepared to cooperate. As the war progressed, ideas began to change. Getting information out of prisoners without mistreating them was preferable, but stripping a man of his clothes in public to compel him to talk was reckoned to be neither harsh, cruel nor unusual. Threats were acceptable so long as no physical violence actually took place. Deceptive practices such as the planting of microphones, the use of 'stool pigeons', or getting the prisoner drunk and then giving them false hope, became accepted tools of the interrogator's trade.

By the time the Armistice was signed in 1918 attitudes towards the treatment of POWs had deteriorated. And methods used to attain or satisfy political ends were found to be reflected in interrogation techniques. Confessions in open court by some of Russia's toughest Red commissars and no less a figure than Marshal Tukhachevsky showed that the Soviet authorities had developed a very effective method compelling individuals to talk. In effect, this special intensive technique, which nowadays often is referred to as 'brainwashing', was a combination of threats, physical violence, solitary confinement, restricted rations followed by hours of questioning. When the prisoner was utterly exhausted, there would be an abrupt shift from brutality to leniency to throw the victim off balance. If the 'kindness' failed there would be a return to punishment, and the cycle would continue. Months of such treatment could, and eventually did, crack even the toughest of men. Sensitive men would succumb to this application of psychological and physical pressures sooner rather than later.

During World War II the German Wehrmacht seem to have been fairly punctilious in their handling of POW interrogations. At least so far as the British and Americans were concerned; what happened to the Russians and some of the Polish prisoners is a different story. But there was none of the brutality like that which was evident in such Japanese camps as Ofuna and Ashio, where the crews of American submarines were tortured.

Airmen and submariners bore the brunt of Japanese interrogation ordeals. This was because they usually possessed information of more value to the enemy than that of a simple soldier. The name of the carrier or the location of the island base from which the captured airmen had flown was vital intelligence. Similarly the cruising range of American submarines, their armament and their radar and sonar equipment was equally important.* So pilots and submarine crews who were captured were subjected to interrogations which were anything but subtle. The Japanese did not employ the methods associated with 'brainwashing'; POWs were flogged and underwent Oriental forms of torture. One submarine captain was burned with cigarettes, and had bamboo splinters forced under his fingernails when systematic beatings failed to persuade him to disclose the diving depth of US submarines.

German methods of extorting information were more refined and seemingly more effective. After November 1941, all captured airmen (other than Russians) were sent to the *Auswertestelle West* (Evaluation Centre for the West) at Oberursel for interrogation. On arrival officers were separated from their crews. All prisoners were then stripped; searched and deprived of any weapons and escape kits they might have managed to retain; after that they were photographed and fingerprinted. Finally they were escorted to solitary confinement in wooden, soundproof cells fitted with microphones and containing nothing but a bare minimum of furniture. Within the limits of the Geneva Convention, this introduction to prison-camp life was as severe as the Germans could make it, and perhaps slightly beyond.

Within the next twenty-four hours each prisoner was visited by a German 'receptionist', whose task it was to persuade him to complete the so-called 'Red Cross form'. It was also the receptionist's job to make a psychological assessment of the prisoner. On the back of the 'Red Cross form' he might note 'heavy smoker' or 'very secure' or 'susceptible to flattery' so that the interrogator who was to deal with this particular prisoner would have some guide as to the best method of approach. To soften the prisoner's resistance he might be told at this preliminary interview that he would be sent to a comfortable permanent camp as soon as the interrogation was over—implying the sooner it was over, the better for everybody.

* One of the best kept secrets of World War II was the depth at which a US submarine could operate.

At this stage the POW's living conditions were not comfortable. His cell was about 13 ft by 10 ft by 6 ft 6 in, and contained nothing but a bed, a radiator, controlled from outside the cell, and two blankets. It was poorly ventilated and evil-smelling; there were no facilities for washing or shaving; there were no reading or writing materials; and it was sometimes heated to an almost unbearable temperature if it was felt necessary to add to the occupant's discomfort. The only breaks in the monotony and loneliness were meals brought in three times a day: bread, jam and coffee; soup; bread and water. Such living conditions were in fact designed to lower a man's morale and to induce mental depression.

When the centre first started to operate a prisoner would be interrogated in his cell. But the Germans then decided that better results came from transferring him to a comfortable, sometimes opulently furnished room—the contrast in surroundings helping to throw him off balance. In this room the interrogation officer—primed with all the relevant information about the prisoner which could be supplied by the extensive intelligence library at Oberursel—greeted the prisoner with a smile. The interview would be opened by the interrogator offering a chair and a cigarette. 'Now it is my duty to ask you certain questions. May I have your name, rank, and service number.' The prisoner would comply; only after he had established his identity did his own service regulations require him to maintain silence. The interrogation then proceeded along one or other defined paths. The question of proof that the prisoner was indeed an Allied airman and not a saboteur or spy might be raised. If so, it would be pointed out that the answers to a few queries could settle the whole thing and facilitate transfer to a permanent camp. On the other hand, failure to satisfy the interrogator might compel the latter —albeit reluctantly—to pass the prisoner on to the Gestapo. If he refused to cooperate, the prisoner was normally taken back to his squalid cell 'to think things over'. On his return after a few days, he was often at least willing to start a conversation.

This, the second phase of the interrogation, might start as soon as number, rank and name had been established. Much would depend on the prisoner's attitude. The more he talked the longer he would be kept for interrogation—with the grant of minor privileges, such as a wash and a shave, by way of reward. And although the average stay was two or three days, solitary confinement with intermittent questioning might go on for a month. During this period he might receive treatment ranging from simple neglect to mild third degree, with little food, no tobacco or books, 'sweat-box' treatment, and his sleep disturbed by switching the lights of his cell off and on. Meanwhile he would be told repeatedly that all this would cease as soon as the interrogation had been satisfactorily concluded. Thus, although the Germans were *Korrekt* to the extent that physical violence was rare and never employed as a policy, solitary confinement, privation, and psychological blackmail were considered fair adjuncts to the interrogation technique. Only when the prisoner was given up as 'stubborn' or 'exhausted of information' was he sent on to a conventional POW camp.

Any variations of the methods that have been described usually followed a morale-lowering week or so of hungry and solitary confinement. The prisoner would then be confronted by a polite and genial individual who would apologize for the way the prisoner had been treated. Such an interrogator would often tell the prisoner that he was not concerned with politics or national prejudices: all he wanted was to get a satisfactory answer to a few points and he would see that the prisoner was sent on his way to a 'proper' camp. Sometimes a quarrel was staged in the presence of the prisoner between the interrogator and another German who had expressed fanatical opinions about Nazi beliefs or the outcome of the war. The interrogator would then excuse himself and during his brief retirement the prisoner would have a chance to relax. A relaxed man may be caught off his guard, and when the interrogator returned he would pursue a new initiative. At Oberursel a mass of information concerning Allied air force units, airmen, and possible operational activity had been assembled. Thousands of dossiers had been built up from newspaper clippings, documents and the personal belongings of other airmen, and information gleaned in the course of previous interrogations. Armed with such information as could be assembled on the prisoner, the interrogator would return smiling to the contest. In a cheerful and bantering fashion he would reel off biographical details of the prisoner's background, and referring to other members of his unit by name—even using the prisoner's nickname perhaps. Nothing could be more disarming than this routine, and nine times out of ten the prisoner would be completely 'beaten' by the interrogator's apparent knowledge of intimate details of his family, friends and home. Not to mention the type of aircraft he flew, its armament and its operational performance.

After the opening breach, the interrogator's follow-up was usually easy. The prisoner might be taken for a stroll in the park, or even taken to a quiet beer garden for a glass of lager. A 'free' conversation would be started—friendly but not too friendly; with some apparent flattery. Then the trick question, shrouded with indirection and delivered in an indifferent tone with an off-hand manner, would be slipped in.

If the prisoner proved obdurate, however, and kept silent, one or other variations of the glass of water trick would follow. A pill would be slipped into the prisoner's glass, and ten minutes after he drank the water he would show all the symptoms of a very sick man. In the event he had not taken anything fatal or injurious; indeed he would really suffer nothing worse than a bout of acute indigestion. But the POW did not know this. As he doubled up in pain, sweating, the interrogator would appear most solicitous—suggesting a possibility of peritonitis and immediate treatment in hospital. Almost as an aside he would suggest that the prisoner would want his next of kin to be notified if whatever he was suffering from proved fatal. Other leading questions would follow. If a prisoner then continued to refuse to speak, he would be returned to his cell to be locked up with another POW. Either this man was a stool pigeon captured earlier in the war, or if he were genuine his presence would tend to encourage conversation, which was picked up by a concealed microphone. The latest listening equipment was installed in 50 of the 200 cells of Oberursel, enabling even a whispered conversation to be heard and recorded on magnetic tape. By 1944 the Oberursel interrogation centre had a staff of 300, including 70 officers, which processed an average of 2000 POWs per month—a peak of 3000 mixed airmen and paratroops being reached in July 1944. There were 55 full-time interrogators, carefully selected as native Germans of liberal background who had spent part of their lives in Britain or the United States, as violent Nazis were not a success at interrogation. Only prisoners of special technical interest were sent to Oberursel, but other interrogation centres were established in Holland, northern France, and in Verona, Italy, for the questioning of airmen captured in these areas.

In sum, most of the prisoners who yielded information were tricked into doing so; they were not tortured. By June 1944 the sweatbox methods had stopped—mainly as a result of strong protests through the Protecting Power to the German Government. Prisoners were baffled by the stage-craft, misleading geniality, and glib queries that were as fast as the jabs and feints of a boxer. The average POW facing the German interrogators at Oberursel was at an almost hopeless disadvantage, analogous to the position of a civilian brought to trial and compelled to conduct his own defence against a skilled and wily barrister.

The development of interrogation methods was not confined to the Germans, who entered World War II with experience gained during the growth of the Nazi regime. On the other side of the hill, most British interrogation teams were composed of veterans of World War I, with a sprinkling of experienced men from the Security Service and a few detectives seconded from police work. When America came into the war, British Intelligence personnel were sent to teach military interrogation techniques to their counterparts in the US, and American military men were sent to London to observe the arts of field interrogations. On both sides of the Atlantic a two-tiered system of interrogation was used: first a simple screening, where large numbers of POWs were dealt with to sort out the worthwhile from the worthless, and then the full interrogation. In Britain this role was handled by the Prisoner of War Interrogation Section (PWIS).

On the battlefield, the first aim of prisoner-of-war interrogation is to get hold of operational information—the strength, location and movement of enemy formations. And at a time when bullets are whistling round and colleagues are being shot, those who conduct interrogations are apt to give the Geneva Convention a broad interpretation. But the interesting information in such circumstances is of a local, limited and tactical nature. Only when the prisoners are evacuated does the question of extracting strategic information arise.

In Britain, nine interrogation centres were set up, each with a 'cage' where important prisoners were held and questioned before being sent to the POW camp. The most famous was the 'London Cage' —a large house on the corner of Kensington Park Gardens and the Bayswater Road, commandeered for the duration of the war. (In 1945 the London Cage became the War Crimes Investigation Unit (WCIU).)* Other cages were established at Catterick, Loughborough and Edinburgh, at Doncaster where the race-track was commandeered, and at Preston where the football ground was used.

Army Intelligence sergeants were employed to do the initial screening. Most of these men were German-Jewish refugees who spoke perfect German, and who understood the German mentality. Their job was to get the basic details—rank, name, home town, family, civilian job—and then make recommendations as to the best method of interrogation. Nine out of ten German POWs knew very little about their own troop movements or the siting of industrial plants and they were promptly excluded from further consideration. The remainder went on for a full inquisition. Wounded men were not interrogated until a doctor certified them fit and by then any information they might have could have lost its value. During the war crimes trials it became evident that the PWIS teams had achieved a remarkable degree of success in extracting information from SS officers, truculent Luftwaffe pilots and U-boat skippers whose fanaticism and military dedication was such that they could be expected to resist any form of torture. Colonel Scotland has denied that physical tortures were ever used to get these results, and Colonel L. St Clare

---

* Colonel A. P. Scotland who was in charge of the London Cage has described the work there in his book, *The London Cage* (Evans, 1957).

Grondona, the Commandant of the Combined Services Detailed Interrogation Centre (CSDIC) at Wilton Park, has emphasized that the methods used by his interrogators were processes of 'painless extraction' seasoned with legitimate guile.* Some of the highest-ranking German and Italian captives—Marshal-of-Italy Messe, Field Marshal von Rundstedt and General von Thoma—were interrogated at Wilton Park, and St Clare Grondona has described the interrogation techniques employed.

It is essential to give, here, a brief description of this establishment's lay-out. Our troop's hutments were spaced amid tall trees within a few hundred yards of a Georgian mansion—the White House—which was our officers' mess. The prisoners' compound, with its four long intersecting corridors leading to brick-and-cement cells, had been built within a 14 ft brick wall that had enclosed a two-acre vegetable garden and orchard; and its low roofs were so camouflaged as to merge into the surrounding landscape and be invisible to other than very low-flying aircraft. Cells were centrally heated and each had ample space for four spring-mattressed beds. There were no bars across the windows, but the several small panes in each were set in steel frames that would have baffled Houdini.

In the early stages of the war all our prisoners were survivors from either shot-down aircraft or destroyed submarines. They were a tough lot, cockily confident that it was only a matter of time before Hitler had complete control of Europe and had crushed Britain, with virtual world domination then in prospect. But many of these men possessed valuable information, and it was our job to extract from them as much as possible of this—always with proper regard to the Geneva Convention.

So it was that our interrogating officers had to be wily and resourceful. Our methods of interrogation were processes of painless extraction, and more often than not a guest was unaware that he had given us any useful information.

All interrogation officers spoke fluent German. Most of them had spent much time in Nazi Germany, perhaps as students or in business, and knew a great deal more about the real Hitler than did most of our prisoners. The opening gambit was likely to take the form of a discussion which bore no resemblance to an interrogation. Its first phase might be to sow doubts in a prisoner's mind about the propaganda that had been fed to him over the years.

* In correspondence with the author, and in a letter to *The Times* of 27 November 1971.

An interrogating officer could take his subject for walks through the nearby woods. But this was always done to a time-table which ensured that one prisoner seldom saw any other being similarly conducted. They would leave by one exit from the compound, follow a prescribed route, and return through another entrance. Along this, certain tree-trunks had been wired with electric connections to an indicator watched by an NCO in our orderly room. The conducting officer would press a button at each of these check-points so that his whereabouts were always known.

In the early stages of a chat the British officer might say something of this sort: 'What baffles us about so many of the Germans is that they knuckle down to a state of affairs which, if they allowed themselves to think, would be quite intolerable.'

Naturally there would be many interruptions and protestations by the prisoner, who could of course say what he liked. But what he would find most exasperating was the British officer's calm assurance that Germany was heading for disaster. In his efforts to get the better of the argument, a prisoner might say many things that could not have been elicited from him by outright interrogation.

When an RAF officer was taking a walk with a German airman, they might talk about the various aircraft that were so often overhead. It could be that the RAF man would find out quite a lot of useful information without his companion's being conscious of having given anything away.

Some British officers were able successfully to pose as Germans. A recently captured Luftwaffe pilot—whom we shall call Schmidt—would be put in a cell where two beds indicated that he could expect a companion. Perhaps an hour later the door was unlocked to admit a new arrival in the uniform of a German submariner who, brought in by a British officer, would be introduced as Lieutenant Brunner.

Both men would click their heels with formal bows, and the door would close upon them. Schmidt would be very much on his guard, and the attitude of Brunner would be similar. Each would hold the other at arm's length with that cold correctness which characterized German commissioned ranks. But with two men alone in a cell, silence sooner or later became intolerable. Schmidt might eventually tell Brunner where he lived in Germany. Our intelligence library contained scores of German street directories, telephone books and other reference books, one of which would often reveal the names of people living in a prisoner's home neighbourhood. It would be odds-on that some listed public official—or perhaps some medical man—thereabouts would be known to him, if not personally, at least by name.

In due course Brunner would be 'taken to the interrogation room', where he could consult the appropriate books of reference. Later he would casually observe that his sister had once stayed with some people called Muller who, he believed, had lived in Schmidt's home neighbourhood, and he seemed to recall that she had spoken of a family named Hoffnung. Did Schmidt happen to know those people? Both would now start talking a little more freely. The best thing that could happen, then, would be that Schmidt would make some remark that could possibly be construed as having some military significance. Brunner would at once rap out a whispered 'Shut up', and hastily turn on both taps so that the rush of water would smother their whispering, while he told Schmidt that the only safe place to talk in safety was the exercise yard.

After subsequent visits to the interrogation room, each would tell the other, when out on exercise, how he had rebuffed or misled his interrogators. In this way most of the information Schmidt was able to impart was soon in Brunner's possession.

Some of the information sought from prisoners was vital. Details of what was going on at Peenemunde were essential to the mounting of a counter-offensive, and if it had not been for information obtained by the PWIS, it could have been London and not Hiroshima which was devastated by the first atomic bomb.* Yet the methods used to get the information were mild compared with those of the Gestapo. St Clare Grondona writes: 'It is the simple truth that if one of our interrogators had suggested submitting any prisoner to *any* form of physical duress (which would certainly not have been permitted) he would have been a laughing stock among his colleagues.' But the POWs at Wilton Park were of a different calibre to those who passed through the London Cage, where it appears that some physical pressure was exerted to get results. One interrogator has stated:

> One fellow we had up before us was really cheeky and obstinate. We told him to undress and eventually he stood in front of us completely naked. That deflated him. Then we told him to start doing exercises. That killed his resistance completely. . . . Sometimes we would keep them standing on their feet round the clock. If a prisoner wanted to pee he had to do it there and then in his clothes. It was surprisingly effective. . . .

* Information elicited by CSDIC led to the RAF bombings of the heavy-water plant and other installations in Norway, where the Germans were developing their own version of the atomic bomb.

Another interrogator recalled a psychological ploy he used with arrogant, untalkative Luftwaffe pilots. These men would be taken by car to an interrogation centre outside London, through the West End, along roads which by-passed bombed areas. En route the prisoner would be asked what he thought about the effect of German bombs and Goebbels propaganda. The inability to equate what they saw with what they had been told in Germany was calculated to have a considerable effect on the prisoners' morale.

Playing on the German prisoners' fear of the Russians was another technique said to be successful. At the London Cage a Russian-speaking interpreter, wearing a KGB uniform, would sit in on the interrogation of recalcitrant prisoners. And if his presence failed to frighten the prisoner, the ostentatious stamping of the prisoner's file with 'NR' usually did. To the prisoner's query as to what 'NR' meant the reply was '*Nach Russland*' (to Russia); and this was calculated to have a frightening effect.

Some of the allied powers whose 'free' governments were based in London had a reputation for rather less concern about the correct and gentlemanly treatment of German POWs than the British. The interrogation methods used by Deuxième Bureau of the Free French, the Poles and the Czechs, reflected the attitude of people who had suffered and were suffering under the Nazis. In consequence the British War Office insisted that a British officer should always be present whenever they questioned a POW in the UK. Such interrogations were usually conducted with the utmost propriety. Sometimes in spite of circumstances which might have provoked physical violence being used against the wretched prisoner. As an illustration, the case of a German colonel of the Wehrmacht's legal department who had been captured in Paris when the French capital was liberated and taken to London may be cited. A preliminary screening suggested that Colonel Koenig knew a great deal about the French Resistance, so it was suggested that the Deuxième Bureau might like to interrogate him. Escorted by a British liaison officer, Koenig was taken to the French interrogation centre where he was confronted with a French army colonel and a French naval commander. Koenig was told to sit down and offered a cigarette; then the questioning began. The interrogation focussed on the fate of a number of the Resistance leaders and Koenig was able to say what had happened to most of them. This one had been shot; that one had escaped; another had been sent to a concentration camp, and so on. Finally, towards the end of the interrogation the fate of a certain French lady was raised. Koenig said that she had been sent to a concentration camp and died there. There was a brief silence, before the French colonel stood up and said curtly: 'Thank you; that was my mother.'

The interrogation methods employed by the Americans in Europe were generally similar to those of the British throughout World War II. In the Far East their attitude was coloured by the brutality of the Japanese towards their prisoners, however. One US interrogator has admitted that a man might be subjected to physical assault if he had to be made to talk:

Sometimes, in extreme emergencies, you would find it expedient to extract information as quickly and as accurately as possible. In such circumstances you do not have the time to use normal methods. Maybe a time-bomb has been placed on an American ship, and lives depend on you getting the information without delay.

Then we would use extra-curricular methods. We found that a sure way of loosening a man's tongue without quite cutting it out was by using pressure points to work him over. Its not as bad as water torture, but there are certain parts of the body that can be very persuasive: in the neck and around the arms and in the thoracic abdominal areas, all the way down to the toes.

Before you can use violence you would first try to determine if, by that method, you could extract the information. You can pretty well judge your subject. Some would not talk if you strung them up with a toe-line to the ceiling and kept them there all the afternoon. You have to be able to judge a man's resistance to giving that information. The only justification in using violence is knowing that a person is particularly afraid of physical pain. It's not done just to torture him: it's a method he will be susceptible to.

After 1945 technical devices continued to be developed for interrogation purposes. Buttonhole microphones and bugged rooms superseded the primitive recording devices used during the war. Yet interrogation techniques have tended to concentrate more and more on the use of physical pressures in order to extract information. The reason given for inflicting any form of coercion on POWs is invariably that of expediency, and the military argument in justification of torture is one which has always been put in times of unrest: when guerillas are using horror tactics, and when many lives are at stake, the assault upon a single person's body and dignity is justified.

In 1948, the interrogation of captured guerillas (CEPs) and 'surrendered enemy personnel' (SEPs) was a powerful instrument in the suppression of a Communist revolt in Malaya. These prisoners provided details of the movements of the terrorist units, of their camping places in the jungle and—most important—of where and from whom they were being supplied. Under the Emergency regulations which were invoked, the security forces had a good deal of latitude in dealing with guerillas or those who were suspected of helping the guerillas. Semi-physical pressures like depriving a man of material comforts and sleep, while questioning him for hours on end, were not specifically forbidden, although most CEPs and SEPs proved surprisingly willing and even eager to supply information which often led to the death of the captive's former comrades.*

The Prisoners of War Convention drawn up in Geneva in 1949 to define higher standards of treatment for captured enemy personnel does not prohibit interrogation, but lays down that 'No physical violence or mental torture, nor any other form of coercion may be inflicted on prisoners of war to secure from them information of any kind whatever. Prisoners of war who refuse to answer may not be threatened, insulted or exposed to unpleasant or disadvantageous treatment of any kind.' Fifty-seven nations signed the new Geneva Treaty, and the ink of their signatures was barely dry before its intentions were being put to the test in the Korean War.

Until the end of 1950 the term 'brain-washing' was virtually unheard of. Following China's entry into the Korean War, however, it became synonymous with the horrors of North Korean prison camps. In effect, 'indoctrination'—which is described elsewhere in this book—more accurately describes the process to which the United Nations POWs were subjected. It is sufficient to say here that interrogation is an important adjunct to indoctrination and 'war upon the brain'. During 'simple' interrogations—i.e. those which were undertaken to obtain military information or to maintain security in their camps (as distinct from those whose alternate aim was to effect a permanent change in a man's opinions and character)—'simple' physical tortures were the normal treatment. A corporal of the Gloucesters who refused to give information to the Chinese was compelled to stand to attention, stripped to the waist, and savagely beaten. According to the British Government Report on the treatment of POWs in North Korea some British prisoners were made to stand to attention for hours on end, with Chinese bayonets to promote their obedience. Another British prisoner was made to kneel on two small jagged stones and hold a large rock over his head. Fusilier Kinne, who was interrogated about the uncooperative attitude of other prisoners of war, was severely beaten, tied up for periods of 12 and 24 hours, standing on tip-toe with a noose round his neck which would throttle him if he dared to relax.

During the civil war in Algeria in the 1950s the French resorted to

---

* In the author's own experience, an SEP led an army patrol back to the camp from which he had deserted less than 24 hours previously. This resulted in the death of a man who had been the terrorist's closest friend right up to the time of his desertion.

the same interrogation techniques as they had used in Indo-China. Henri Alleg, an Algerian journalist arrested by French paratroopers in 1957, wrote an account of his experiences at the hands of his Army interrogators. Alleg's book was banned by the authorities in metropolitan France, but it was published in Britain.*

Alleg was a radical who had gone into hiding when orders were issued for his internment by the French authorities in Algeria. Apprehended by paratroopers of the 10th Parachute Division after seven months on the run, the purpose of Alleg's interrogation was to get him to betray his colleagues and reveal details of the underground organization to which he belonged. 'Les Paras' had already acquired a reputation for using Gestapo-like methods to extract information so Alleg knew what to expect. In his account he stresses that his experiences were daily occurrences in Algeria, and as a European he considered that he probably got better treatment than the local population. For a month he was subjected to brutalizing treatment. First came the electric torture: for this Alleg was stripped and strapped down to a plank. Electrodes were clipped to various parts of his naked body: first an ear lobe and a finger. A magneto was used to provide the current and when this was cranked Alleg felt a flash of lightning exploding in his ear. From the ear, the electrode was then moved to his penis. 'Suddenly I felt as if a savage beast had torn the flesh from my body. . . . The shocks going through me were so strong that the strap holding me to the board came loose. They stopped to tie them again and we continued. . . .'

When Alleg still refused to talk, one electrode was fastened to his chest and cold water thrown over him to increase the intensity of the shock. When this treatment failed to have the desired effect, the current was increased again, and '. . . a greater pain took possession of all my muscles and tightened them in longer spasms'.

Then the interrogators turned to the water-pipe torture. Still strapped to the plank, Alleg was propped up against a sink. One end of a rubber tube was fastened to a tap and the other inserted into his mouth which had been wedged open. When the water was turned on: 'I tried, by contracting my throat, to take in as little water as possible and to resist suffocation by keeping air in my lungs for as long as I could. But I could not hold on for more than a few moments. I had the impression of drowning and a terrible agony, that of death itself, took possession of me.' When Alleg lost consciousness he was kicked and pummelled awake. After that he was hung upside down from a beam. 'They amused themselves . . . swinging me like a sack of sand. . . . I could see Lo-, who slowly lit a paper-torch at the level of

* Henri Alleg, *The Question* (John Calder, London 1958).

my eyes. He stood up and all of a sudden I felt the flame on my penis, and on my legs, the hairs crackling as they caught fire. . . .'

Other permutations of these tortures continued in the days to come, and Alleg also claims to have seen the subjects of other interrogations—one man with severe leg burns, another whose tongue had been cut, and women who had been stripped, beaten and assaulted. The electric torture and water-pipe seem to have been priority treatments presumably because they produced quicker results.

Compared with the French, the interrogation techniques used by the British during the 1950s would appear to be comparatively innocuous. Beatings with truncheons or kibokos (rhino-whip) cannot be classed in the same category as the agonies of electric shock treatment or the water pipe. Nevertheless Britain's post-war record of rule in internal security operations is not without blemish, and the methods of interrogation that have been used have outraged the Geneva Convention on a number of occasions. Inevitably the argument that has been used in mitigation has been that the security forces have been compelled to fight fire with fire. In Kenya the atrocities committed by the Mau Mau justified extreme measures to get the information without which the security forces were at a great disadvantage. Most of the ill-treatment seems to have been inflicted in prisons where the Mau Mau detainees were held after capture. But some 'roughing-up' undoubtedly took place soon after capture.

In Cyprus, where slaughter and treachery were daily occurrences during Britain's struggle with the EOKA underground movement, the record of the British security forces was not a happy one. Allegations of torture by the British forces were poured out daily by the Cypriots during the Cyprus emergency, and in 1957 the Greek Government charged Britain with 49 cases of 'torture or maltreatment amounting to torture'. Most of the allegations turned out to be without foundation, and where isolated cases of misconduct were proven, they were usually exaggerated and distorted for political reasons. In the Cyprus White Paper, Field Marshal Harding dismissed the possibility of torture because it was not in the character of the men concerned. Yet it was conceded that 'it would be unrealistic when men are fighting terrorism to exclude the possibility of occasional rough-handling of terrorists in the heat of the moment when their capture is being effected'.

'Occasional rough-handling' is probably an understatement of the treatment afforded suspected EOKA terrorists. In the early days of the Cyprus troubles a captain of the Intelligence Corps and a captain of the Gordon Highlanders interrogated a Greek Cypriot detainee, a certain Christos Constaninou. This man was asked the whereabouts of an EOKA terrorist, on whose head there was a reward for capture of £5000. When Constaninou said he had not seen the man for six months, he was told to strip to the waist, and beaten up. Subsequently both officers were court-martialled and cashiered on charges of assaulting Constaninou and conspiring to pervert the course of justice. This was one instance of a brutal interrogation in Cyprus; in January 1956 an Athens newspaper wrote: 'EOKA states that British interrogators examining suspects subject them to tortures such as flogging, or force them to stand on nails or on ice and inject them with narcotics.'

Whether or not the interrogations of EOKA terrorists did include brutality, they were not particularly successful. The main purpose of the interrogation campaign in Cyprus was to catch the EOKA leader, Colonel Grivas. With him out of the way the revolutionary movement could be expected to collapse. Yet it failed because the interrogators failed to get results, and were misled by false and improbable leads.

In Cyprus the police were largely responsible for interrogations. (In Cyprus, as in Malaya and Kenya, when the British Army was called in to aid the civil power, the intelligence system was left in police hands. Army Intelligence officers were infused into their system but the police remained in control.) Why the police interrogations failed can be attributed to a number of reasons, not least the Greek language barrier which few were able to overcome. But the Army concluded that the police were just not up to the job and when Britain assumed emergency powers to maintain law and order in Aden, the Army were given control in Intelligence matters.

During the summer of 1965 an interrogation centre was set up at Fort Morbut, staffed by interrogators all of whom—with one exception—were Army personnel. As in Cyprus it was not long before stories of tortures began to circulate. The International Red Cross sent a delegate to Aden on an enquiring mission, but he reported that he was unable to see any of the detainees held for questioning. A year later Amnesty International—an organization concerning itself with Human Rights—sent its own investigator, Dr Salahaddin Rastgeldi, a Swede, to Aden to look into the allegations of torture. And Rastgeldi's findings—or rather the lack of collaboration given to him by the Aden authorities—aroused a tremendous furore in Britain.

Ten principal allegations were made:

- Detainees were stripped and forced to stand naked during their interrogation.
- Between interrogations they were kept naked in cold cells with air conditioners and fans running.

- A state of exhaustion was induced by not permitting them to sleep.
- Hungry detainees were offered food, which was taken away as soon as they started to eat.
- Detainees were forced to sit on poles 'directed towards' their anus.
- Their genital organs were hit and twitched.
- Cigarettes were extinguished on their skin.
- They were not permitted the use of a lavatory, compelling many to soil their cells.
- Locking them in filthy lavatories on other occasions.
- Compelling them to run round in circles to the point of exhaustion.

In effect an official British Government investigation subsequently concluded that the allegations were not substantiated, and affidavits from interrogators all emphatically denied any maltreatment at the Interrogation Centre. Unfortunately any rumours that torture is being used in the interrogation of guerillas—who as freedom fighters consider themselves to be prisoners of war rather than detainees—rapidly gain ground. For the revolutionaries such rumours are ideal material with which they can fan the flame of the cause and provoke the sympathy of the uncommitted masses. In an 'emergency' situation this inevitably leads to an escalation of violence. The use of physical violence in an interrogation campaign is therefore to be condemned, since the success it may bring will usually be more than offset by the destruction of the cause the campaign is committed to save.

So far most of the examples of the methods used to extract information have been confined to those used by the Germans, British, Russians and Americans. But there is ample evidence of the use of physical violence by many of the smaller nations. Greece, whose Government complained about the treatment of EOKA terrorists in Cyprus, has been accused of using electric shock treatment, mock executions and bastinado to frighten or beat information out of prisoners. The Israelis have been accused by Amnesty International of flogging Jordanian POWs to get information about Jordanian guerillas. In Brazil army interrogators are alleged to have poured water down a prisoner's throat almost to the point of suffocation and to have thrown snakes and rats into the cells of men detained for questioning.

The conclusion is that the prisoner in an interrogation centre is a fly in a web. The enemy has all the say. The simple fact is that it is virtually impossible for anyone to resist a determined interrogator. All the prisoner can hope to do is to evade loaded questions.

6

Life Behind the Wire

Once he has got over the shock of being captured and uncertainty about his future treatment, the prisoner of war starts to adapt himself to his life behind the wire. For many POWs who find themselves living in close confinement with a herd of fellow men, with less food, less space, less privacy and considerably less freedom than they have enjoyed previously, the adaptation process is a long and unpleasant business. Nor does it really begin until the prisoners reach a permanent POW camp, although desultory friendships created by the need to share food or to take turns in preparing it on a journey from the battlefield to the camp will have set the scene.

Once inside the camp, however, the group mentality begins to operate, and men will start to 'muck in' with people of similar interests. Background, locality and regimental ties may draw people together initially but the social pattern which eventually emerges is one which is stratified by mutual interests rather than origins. Intellectuals tend to get together with other intellectuals, as do the sports-minded and those interested in amateur theatricals. C. S. Stavert, writing about life in Campo 49 Fontanellato in 1943, says:*

> The camp had its inconveniences: the rooms were too big; there was a complete lack of privacy, the water failed to run when it was most wanted, the toilets were squatters, and so on, but things were relatively tolerable. You joined a clique according to your temperament and social background, and passed the time as may be. We had all the types there. The hearties, who played rugger in mid-July on a gravel pitch in long woolly underwear. The keep-fit maniacs, forty times up and down the stairs at the double, morning and evening. The body worshippers, burning themselves black in ever-diminishing loincloths until even the sentries com-

* Letter to the author.

plained of their indecent exposure. The alcoholics, who bartered their cigarette ration and even their share of Red Cross treacle pudding ($\frac{1}{4}$ tin per man) for extra Vermouth tickets. The entrepreneurs, managers of the highly developed bartering system. The old-timers, two years and more in the bag from Wavell's time, wandering about in shorn-off greatcoats and carpet slippers, muttering gravely into their beards. The sex-starved, mostly the married men, who lined the windows every evening gazing fascinated at the local girls parading two by two in the street below. The writers, not many of them, starting novels which never finished; Michael Gilbert was one of the few who did succeed—his *Murder in Captivity* was born in Campo 49. And the bridge players—I'd recommend any man going into action to include a pack of cards in his emergency kit.

On the whole the students were the happiest. Intellectual exercise is one of the most convenient to indulge in, provided you have the basic materials—it needs no teams or competitors. I was one of these. Mostly we took up subjects in which we had not been specialists previously. Any subject is attractive enough for the first chapter or two; when it starts to get hard, you move on to something else. I was doubly fortunate in having a smattering of musical ability, and could get my fun from bashing the piano in the cellar (never mind the fellows up top, they're probably sunbathing anyway) and working with the band. . . .

Complete disregard of one's fellow prisoners in the pursuit of one's own interests is, in fact, rarely possible. Living cheek by jowl in cramped conditions, day in day out, for months on end, necessitates a curb on selfish activities. Bullies are soon taken care of; stealing from one's fellow prisoners brings savage reprisals from within the POW community; cleanliness is regarded literally as being next to Godliness. J. V. Webb, working with an *Arbeitskommando* (see p. 98) employed clearing up bomb damage in Munich, was quartered in a hut with five men from the Guards Armoured Division. One, a pre-war regular soldier, who was very conscious of his lack of education, spent most of his spare time proving his strength and fitness and demonstrating his physical prowess.

Not surprisingly, with six of us in a small room about ten foot square, we got on each other's nerves, and small matters assumed an overwhelming importance. On one occasion the jazz lovers were discussing various bands, and the question arose as to what was the signature tune of a particular band-leader. This minor question became the centre of a colossal argument, which at times reached almost the state of physical violence.

Captivity breeds increased irritability in all men; some suffer a little more, others a little less. This is the so-called 'barbed-wire disease' which is not particular to any nationality. Russians and Chinese, Japanese and Nazi prisoners, soaked in ideological beliefs, have all displayed the same symptoms as British and Americans. In a POW camp it can be observed daily in the most ridiculous trifles, beginning with friction between the early risers and the later ones, about the extent that a window should be opened to ventilate a room, or a discussion about the wash-basin, or—as in the example quoted— in a quarrel over a band's signature tune. Other typical manifestations reported from a POW camp in Germany were absent-mindedness, silliness like that of a British officer who would go around with a theme song, 'Pom-pom, tiddly pom-pom, pom-pom!'; or nocturnal symptoms like 'wind-sucking' while sleeping or getting up at ridiculously early hours in order to kick the furniture. In a German POW camp in England signs of '*gefangenitis*' were seen in tensions between various groups of prisoners—one group watching another to see whether it was issued with more soup than itself.

To a prisoner of war barbed wire is the one unchanging feature of his life. On occasions it may not exist in fact, but it is always there in fancy—from morning till night, and from day to day, through interminable weary months and years. Through it the prisoner has tantalizing glimpses of the great free world beyond; by it he is held back in his own drab and hated camp. The mere presence of the wire is a persistent irritation.

> We live in a kingdom of thorns . . . it is like a man pointing a revolver at you, in such a way that wherever you look you stare down the muzzle. . . .   *(French prisoner in World War I)*

Not only does the barbed wire shut the prisoners out from the world of activity, it also shuts them in with the herd of fellow prisoners. There is no privacy and no solitude.

> . . . huddled in the tiny huts, the Americans had to lie down twenty to a side, with their booted feet interlaced. There was so little room they had to lie hip to hip pressed tight to each other. Before the night was over their hips and elbows were raw, and they discovered that if a man wanted to shift his position or turn over he could not do so without waking every other man on his side of the room. . . . They slept. Men who had been fed only a ball of cracked corn a day, and who had had only fistfuls of dirty snow to drink, pressed against each other and went to sleep. Most of them were ill . . . some of them were already a little crazy.
>
> Still, they were Americans and still men. But here in this dirty

mining camp that came to be called Death Valley, the Chinese took away their manhood little by little. (*American POW in Korea*)

Invariably an intense irritability, a hatred of fellow prisoners, and a habit of suspicion has developed from such indiscriminate herding. Fresh from battle and pleased to be alive, the newly captured POW will often throw himself enthusiastically into prison camp activities. But as time passes surliness and introversion set in; this is regression:

> The best of friends quarrelled with each other and without cause. . . . None of us were in a fit condition to argue good-temperedly. . . .
>
> (*British POW in Germany during World War II*)

Where the captors' veneer of civilization is thin, or where ideological considerations influence their attitude towards their prisoners, the process is likely to be intensified. The effect is a progressive deterioration of morale, and as morale goes, discipline goes with it. In places like Korea, where the captors and captives were separated by an enormous gulf of culture and standards of humanity, the situation which developed destroyed many Americans' hopes of survival. In Death Valley, for instance, there was no one to give the POWs direction except the Chinese. One of the principles of the so-called 'Lenient Policy' which the Chinese People's Volunteers instituted in their POW camps was equality of rank—no officers, no NCOs, everybody equal. The result was that there was no one to bully and chivvy the wretched prisoners but the Chinese guards, and the result was that men dissolved into individuals governed only by their individual consciences. And as fear, cold, sickness and starvation deepened, conscience diminished.

> Most of those who could adjust and who wanted to live on, lived. It helped if a man could hold on to something. Some lived simply because they came to hate the Chinese so much.
>
> And there were some, determined to live, who took food from the sick and dying, and there was no one to say to them nay.

Without discipline there was, in this extreme but not unusual example, no effective way of helping the dying or giving aid to the faltering. No man would accept orders from another, and no organized effort appears to have been made. Few officers showed any willingness to take council and organization broke down completely. At this camp the prisoners had been starved and sickened into a disorganized, slack-faced mob, more animals than men.

Where there are no counteracting influences, utter listlessness and an opium-like lethargy are the more usual physical symptoms of 'barbed-wire disease'. But the dull resentment, heartache and feelings of oppression that cause this are also reflected in other ways. In some of the Japanese POW camps, and again in Korea, it was noticed that 'every trace of adult sexuality tended to disappear from conversation and obscene jokes were made, which sometimes caused everybody to titter like children when one of them expels wind'.* General degradation and coarsening of manners is usually accompanied by concern with animal functions—not even trying to restrain wind, and disregarding laws of personal cleanliness. All this can be explained as a return to childhood reactions, and the primitive infantile stage of humanity.

A combination of fatigue, hunger and watery food with a high carbohydrate content is believed to be the cause of the high incidence of bed-wetting and bed fouling in POW camps in the Far East. Colonel I. G. Thomas remembers the routine and meals in the Jinsen camp in North Korea.† Breakfast at 7 am was a bowl of hot daikon soup‡; for lunch at 12.30 there was 2–3 oz. of cooked rice; and there was a little more rice and another bowl of soup for supper. POW rations in the Korean War were almost as scanty—a basic diet of rice, occasionally leavened with vegetable soup. According to the Chinese and North Korean authorities this diet conformed with the rules of the Geneva Convention—that a prisoner should receive the same food as the soldiers holding him captive. Oriental soldiers are, of course, inured to a rice diet but the average European cannot stomach such fare. In recent years Americans in Vietnam have suffered accordingly, and gone hungry. It is nothing new.

In Andersonville Americans fought each other for scraps of food and let each other die. In 1917 a visitor to one prisoner of war camp in Germany found '600–700 men, none weighing over 75 pounds, lying listlessly on their cots all day, too exhausted by hunger to do anything else, while 10 to 40 of them were carried to the graveyard each day'.§ A little of a quarter of a century later tough panzer grenadiers of the Wehrmacht went listless in Communist pens and 'died for no reason', while British and American soldiers in Japanese prisons retreated into dream world from which some have never properly returned.

When POWS went hungry in World War I, Britain and Germany both argued that the literal fulfilment of the terms of the Geneva Convention was just not possible. The Allied blockade of Germany and Germany's submarine campaign reduced the available food supply. Rations were short everywhere and it was maintained that feeding their respective prisoners on the same scale as their own

---

* Coloco Belmonte, *Ervaringen mit gevangenkampen op Java en in Japan.*
† Jinsen was 'Inchon' in the Korean War.
‡ Daikon is dried turnip.
§ Conrad Hoffman, *In the Prison Camps of Germany* (New York 1920).

troops might have put the prisoners far above the civilian living standards. Indeed the civilian population was always afraid that this was the case, and on both sides the Press periodically claimed that captive alien enemies were living on the fat of the land. As the politicians could not disregard the clamour caused by such statements, officials were compelled to avoid any appearance of pampering the POWS. In consequence the prisoners' standard of living tended to decline towards the lowest civilian level.

The prisoners were also the victims of reprisals and counter-reprisals. All sorts of stories about ill-treatment were circulated on both sides, and prisoners of war were seen as the nearest objects for retaliation. Such prisoners were not responsible for the ill-treatment of the other prisoners, but they suffered because they were the only lever that could be used to move the situation in the enemy's camps. As always happens, counter-reprisal followed reprisal.

Prison fare fell off steadily as food became scarce. The caloric content declined and what was served to the prisoners of war became less and less appetizing. By 1917 prisoners in the German camps had to depend on supplementary supplies for a full meal, and the Germans in British camps were little better off. Fortunately for the wretched captives the Germans, French and British kept up a steady flow of food parcels. Men of other nationalities were not so fortunate, however. The Russians in Germany represented by far the largest national group in captivity. But they received entirely inadequate supplementary supplies; their government did little for them and the difficulty of transportation combined with the ignorance of the Russians in general denied them help from relatives. The populations of other nations such as the Serbs and Rumanians were already on the verge of starvation and even if they had had any inclination to do anything for their men in distant prisons they had no resources.

In World War II history repeated itself. Rations in German and Italian POW camps were more suited to the taste of their inmates than the food dished out in Japan. And there was usually more of them. Nevertheless a man could starve in staging camps between the battlefields and the regular camps in Germany and Italy. In North Africa, for instance, conditions in the POW camp at Derna were both primitive and chaotic. Food was scarce and what there was of it was almost inedible. Biscuits, reputed to be the size and texture of roofing tiles, and tinned meats which would have offended English dogs, were the staple fare. The only way to eat it was to soak the biscuit—a process which took precious water, add the meat and then boil the whole revolting mess in a pan. (As pans, tins and other cooking utensils were in short supply this was not often feasible anyway.) Food on the Italian mainland was slightly better. Italian army rations* of bread, macaroni and rice were supposed to be issued but the prisoners seldom got them in full. Bill Armitt, captured in the Western Desert, recalls his hunger:

> No one knows what it is like to be hungry until they've been without food or water for 36 hours . . . then you begin to feel your throat's cut. After that, you begin to think of all the food you've had before and what you would do with it if you could get it again. . . . When you're hungry, really hungry, you'll eat anything put in front of you . . . I've heard people say they dislike this and dislike that. But when they're hungry they'll eat anything —anything at all. I've eaten grass, I've eaten acorns, I've eaten cat, I've eaten dog . . . I've eaten anything there was—anything to keep alive. . . .

G. S. Stavert was 'hungry all the time'—even with Red Cross parcels—'and had no thoughts below his stomach throughout his captivity'.

German rations issued to POW camps up to June 1941 were estimated to provide about 1500 calories per man daily. Even when this was supplemented by small amounts of fresh vegetables purchased by the prisoners, the food was not enough to meet the rigours of a German winter, and the men were continually hungry. But for the Red Cross parcels in Italy and Germany, writes Witte, 'we should practically have starved to death'. Yet when supplies of Red Cross food were established on a regular footing, the Germans cut back the official rations.

In almost every POW camp everywhere food has been the prisoner's major concern.

> I had many misgivings about mucking-in with Hill [says Witte], because he was such a gannet. Our first issue was Canadian, the parcel containing corned beef, spam, tinned milk called Klim (milk spelled backwards), biscuits, coffee, tea, chocolate, raisins,

* Italian daily ration scales for POW (in grammes):	Officers	Other ranks (non working)	Other ranks (working)
bread	150	200	400
macaroni or rice	66	66	120
fat	10	13	13
sugar	16	15	15
cheese (cooking)	10	10	10
cheese (table)	when available	30	43
meat	14	34	34
tomato purée	15	15	15
egg	(1 a month)	—	—
peas and beans	15	30	30
coffee substitute	7	7	7

cheese and prunes which were inevitably eaten last. At first we mucked in, eating the spam one day and the corned beef the next and so on. But after about the third issue Hill wanted to eat the corned beef the same day as the spam, and in fact, eat the lot, and then wait round to the next parcel day. Hill had in fact joined the ranks of the parcel-bashers; we tried dividing everything out but when I caught him cheating on the Klim I opted out and looked for another partner. In the end all the parcel-bashers got together leaving the steadier kind to form fresh partnerships. I joined a foursome which worked well, because my three companions—from Yeomanry regiments—were good-natured, easy-going and fond of lying on their beds reading. Each day we took it in turns to brew up. We divided our eatables between four, making everything last round to the next issue, and we made superb cakes from biscuits, raisins and prunes which the cooks baked on payment of a few cigarettes.

Soon a pattern emerged in our barrack-room. Some people would eat their parcels in one go and then not shave or wash even until the day of the next parcel issue. When that day arrived they would be up with the lark, washed, shaved with clean shirts and ready to collect their parcels. The contents of English parcels were not uniform so merchants sprang up in the barrack-rooms who traded in commodities for a small cigarette percentage. Anyone wanting to exchange a meat loaf for a tin of spam went to one of the entrepreneurs; anyone wanting to buy a Yorkshire pudding, for example, also went to them. Each had a list of current prices attached to the door of his barrack-room which the buyer consulted when he wanted to buy something, but like London's Leather Lane, prices were much of a muchness.

Shortages of food—and the black markets that develop in the prison camps as a result of them—aside, there is another aspect to hunger which is something more than the mere craving for calories. Scarcity of food and the conditions of prison life throws the question of eating up into a central and unnatural position. In modern civilized society meals are social functions; for all except the very poor a pleasant feature of the day's activities. But when hungry men have nothing to do but wait for meals which are neither satisfying nor appetizing, the consequences are unwholesome. In Russia the NKVD moved in among the German prisoners with food as a bait for information; in some Japanese camps extra food was given to those who would help the Japs to keep order. (The other ranks' camp at Lintang Barracks in Sarawak was virtually run by British military police, who received treble rations for 'controlling' the camp.) After the Korean War, 192 Americans were found guilty on charges of misconduct while prisoners of war. Most of the charges involved the exploitation of other men's hunger. One officer, who allegedly courted favours of his captors as soon as he reached his POW camp, was recorded as saying: 'The more men who die here, the more food for the rest of us.' For extra food he signed peace petitions, made propaganda broadcasts, and 'ratted' on other prisoners. There was no evidence he was coerced. Many of the accused informed on their fellow prisoners with a view to getting extra food—with dire consequences for the victims who were usually severely punished. But as Bill Armitt said: a hungry man will do anything for food. 'The craving for food . . . created a drive . . .', writes Sidney Sheldrick, 'I was driven to digging under the wire at night and creeping down to the village to barter for food and tobacco with clothing I had got from the civilian men's camps. . . .'

If the weather is cold and men have insufficient clothing and are inadequately housed, the suffering is intensified. Accommodation, sanitation and clothing are fundamental items in living conditions. From war to war, country to country, and camp to camp, these obviously vary a great deal. Colonel Thomas describes his Japanese camp as:

> Dreadful. The camp was surrounded by a very high wooden fence, pitifully thin wooden barracks, and a bare straw-covered concrete floor to sleep on. Slit-trench type latrines which were cleaned about every three or four months. Rats abounded inside the huts. After the tropics the fierce cold of Korea was responsible for further diminishing our ranks. . . .

(Seven years later the very same words might have been used to describe the conditions in a North Korean POW camp a few hundred miles north of that in which Thomas was incarcerated.) On the other hand, conditions in the officers' POW camp at Sulmona towards the end of 1940 appear to have been analogous to those of a Butlin's holiday resort. The camp was set in a beautiful valley up among the Abruzzi, near a village with the romantic name of Fonte d'Amore; officer prisoners had individual bedrooms and a comfortable mess equal to that of the Italian officers. If an officer prisoner was short of clothes the *Unione Militare* would send a tailor to measure him for a uniform; if he wanted to go for a walk in the mountains he was allowed to do so. In sum the Italians were at this time doing everything possible to make the monotony of what seemed to them the unnatural life of a POW camp to be more bearable. Needless to say this was a state of affairs which did not last long.

Under the Geneva Convention, the clothing and footwear of prisoners of war is the responsibility of the captors. In World War II the Japanese and Russians largely ignored the problem, while the Germans and Italians would issue no clothing except to those whose uniforms were lost or in rags. All prisoners in Europe were entitled to receive a clothing parcel every three months, and many who were fortunate enough to get these parcels traded underwear with the less fortunate for tobacco and food. Uniforms were sent by the various belligerent Governments to the Red Cross in Geneva who redirected them to the prisoners. As the war progressed and the numbers of prisoners increased and with them the demands for more food parcels, more clothing and more amenities, the problems of getting the supplies to and from Geneva grew at a geometrically progressive rate. In Geneva every available warehouse was crammed with relief supplies and the Swiss were hard pressed to find extra accommodation and men to deal with them. In 1942 POWs working in German labour camps complained that work in the mines and industrial plants was reducing their one and only uniform to rags, and asked to be allowed an extra suit. The responsibility for providing the extra suit was, of course, that of the Germans. But as they appeared to have no intention of doing so, and Red Cross delegates who had visited the prisoners recommended that a change of clothing was hygienically desirable, the British authorities decided to supply the extra battledresses and foot the bill. The propaganda value attached to the appearance of well-dressed British POWs, in a country which was already beginning to feel the pinch, would, they decided, more than offset the cost.

If a list of the needs of POWs were to be drawn up—food to supplement rations; clothing; recreation, entertainment, education and athletic equipment; books; gramophone records; films, facilities for religious exercises—it would bear a strong resemblance to a catalogue of an army training camp's requirements. Indeed, the suggestion has been made that a prisoner's needs are just the fighting man's needs intensified. Such a view is not very useful because it is the deep difference not the superficial similarity that is significant. The chief difficulties arise just at the points of divergence.

In the question of food, for instance, it was not the frills of diet that prisoners in Germany, Italy, the Far East, the Soviet Union and Vietnam lacked, but the very essentials. In almost every case the countries concerned lacked an adequate supply of fats, sugar and other staple elements; therefore the prisoners suffered not only from the monotony of diet but from its actual inadequacy. There was as much need for the tasty additions, such as the chocolate and tinned fruit. But it is a reasonable supply of the foundations of nourishment which gives point to the extra. The first need of the prisoner is food; next come clothing and accommodation.

But the other needs, though quite as real, present a marked contrast between the conditions of the prisoner and the fighting man. Unless men are put to work by their captors—as were many POWs in the German and Japanese camps of World War II—or compelled to attend long and time-consuming ideological indoctrination sessions —as was the case in Korea—prison camps are full of idle men. For such men time drags. Moreover, in Jim Witte's words: 'Those who stare into space end up going round the bend. *It is vital to do something.*' As a rule prisoners of war are in fact eager enough to do something, and to help themselves. With the best will in the world, however, work cannot be carried on without material. Much can be improvised, and many camps have been thoroughly organized before anything appeared from outside. German prisoners in Russia whittled chess-men out of wood they brought from the forest, and played football with balls made from old Russian lorry inner tubes. Any copies of *Iszvestia* and *Pravda* that came into the camps were used as cigarette paper and were, in any case, unsuitable for writing on, and so writing was done in pencil on birch bark also brought in from the forests. Farther east, Colonel Thomas remembers the Japanese were 'amazed at the native skills and crafts of our men who turned "everything" into "something" with no tools and very crude materials'. The Germans in Britain were no less enterprising, as J. L. Rice recalls:

> A local pig farmer was issued with a large quantity of chocolate from a bombed factory. This disappeared by the sackful. The POWS were boiling it up, putting it into Cadbury's cocoa tins where, when set again, it was removed in a roll shape with the name 'Cadbury' printed on the top from the tin's lid! These rolls were sold in the camp and elsewhere.

Devising occupations for men facing a long, dreary, empty day and persuading men to develop their talents of making something out of nothing puts a premium on leadership. In exceptional circumstances and in the appalling and demoralizing conditions which have prevailed in POW camps in the Far East it has to be leadership of a very special kind. Strict 'military' discipline cannot work because it is too easily equated with enemy—Japanese, Korean, Chinese, Vietnamese—orders, as an anecdote of Sydney Sheldrick will illustrate:

> ... within our other ranks' camp we had also yet another enclosure and this was run by the Military Police whose ideas of discipline were rather unorthodox to say the least as they tended

to follow Jap Army rules of law rather than that of the British
Army, with the result that at least two British Tommies died as a
result of the heavy handling by these redcap thugs. I clearly recall
the one and only time I came into contact with these laddos. It was
early summer of 1945 and by means of our camp secret radio
(secreted in a messtin and never found by the Nips) we all knew
that the War was almost at an end so being, as ever, starving
hungry I and two comrades whipped a handful of sweet potatoes
and their leaves to make up a bit of a meal and just as we were
doing this along came one of the MPs and we were doubled along
the block that was used for a guardroom and as was the custom
we were judged guilty until such time as we could be tried and
that was that . . . so for about ten days we were given extra work
in camp plus extra drill and every movement at the double and
made to stand to attention facing the wall for several hours when
it was too dark to work.

In the absence of military discipline it is clear that self-discipline
is of high importance, and this has to be subtly encouraged. In the
Japanese and North Korean camps much could be and was achieved
by example rather than orders and rules and regulations. 'Inevitably
there were rebels and villains', writes Owen Greenwood on his
captivity in the Dutch East Indies,

> and their activities were more than usually difficult to suppress
> but again this, being a prisoner seemed to bring out the best in
> men far more often than the reverse. This may have meant that
> the need for the enforcement of discipline was reduced in some
> respects but leadership was called for in a high degree in the
> maintenance of morale, especially when it is remembered that
> sickness and privation were constantly at work undermining
> morale as a whole.

It is not hard to suggest activities that will fill up idle hours.
However the POW camp problem is something very different from
this. Provision has to be made for both a man's work and for his
play, with a clear understanding of the fact that life will continue on
its artificial round behind barbed wire for an indefinite period. Chess
and football are allies of health and sanity in the case of men in
confinement, but it does not require imagination to understand how
a man might come to loathe the very sight of a chessboard after six
months and that a football might in the end stir up only an ardent
desire to kick it over the wire once and for all. Plans for all activities
have to take into account two active enemies—the sense of monotony

and the sense of futility. 'Monotony,' writes Lionel Renton, 'is the main danger':

> In every [German] camp, [in World War II] the Senior British Officer encouraged the formation of every possible type of education and recreation, mental and physical. Personally I taught French ... and learned Spanish. I also studied history and heraldry, the necessary books being sent by the Red Cross and the International YMCA of both of whom I cannot speak too highly. If you have never had the experience you can never imagine what it is like to get up in the morning to face a long empty day with nothing whatever to do except what you invent yourself. Those who did not take part in games, classes, etc., stood a very good chance of becoming 'wire-happy', and in fact two people committed suicide in my last camp. ...

In World War II recreation was promoted on a large scale in the British, German, Italian and American camps. Quiet games and outdoor sports were encouraged; athletic contests were organized to give point to the activities and there are many ex-POWs who hold diplomas of merit, designed by their fellow prisoners and printed on lithographic presses in their camps which record their prowess in the field. As might be expected the gramophone served well, and where and when film shows were permitted they were intensely popular. Amateur theatricals and concerts were universal favourites. Probably the most remarkable feature of all the camps in Europe and America, however, was the intense enthusiasm for education.

> We had many able men among us drawn from all walks of life. This was a Godsend as it made it possible to set up an organization on the university lines and all sorts of subjects were taught. At first there were no books so everything was oral ... I started to learn German and French as well as going to other lectures ... ,

writes Colonel Cyril Whitcombe, who was imprisoned in Oflag VIIC at Laufen. 'Quite a number of people obtained professional qualifications,' says Lionel Renton, 'quite a feat when one considers the amount of study that had to be done in the most difficult surroundings and on very little food. ...'

In effect the difficulties varied. In the working camps in Germany serious study was clearly not feasible. On the other hand the serenity of some of the Italian camps, where nine months of fine weather allowed the prisoner to find a quiet outside corner in which to concentrate on his books, might be considered the Mecca of any university student. Allan Goodger, a prisoner in Oflag VIB at

Eichstatt, considers that he was one of the more fortunate POWs since he enjoyed

> a very well organized way of life.... As with many others, my usual day consisted of study in the mornings, sport in the afternoons and music in the evenings, with some cooking and other chores in between. I was successful in passing some exams which stood me in good stead in my future career, learned to play the double bass, after a fashion, and in fact played in the Wimbledon Philharmonic Orchestra for eight years after the war....

In a communist POW camp, a prisoner is unlikely to have the time to learn to play a musical instrument—let alone the inclination. Officer prisoners are offered no privileges by virtue of their rank: indeed, the reverse may well happen. Regardless of service, background or rank, prisoners in North Korea were organized into companies of about 200 men; three to seven companies would occupy one camp. Each company would be divided into three or four platoons which, in turn, were subdivided into squads of six to fifteen prisoners. These squads were the work units of the 're-education' programme which constituted the prisoners' work.*

The POWs' day started at 7 am and ended at 7 pm when they went to bed. Five of these 12 hours—from 9 am until noon and from 2 pm until 4 pm—were spent listening to lectures or attending discussions. (Men who wanted more time for study were given an extra two hours out of bed, i.e. until 9 pm, to be spent in the camp's library. The latter was well stocked with Communist reading matter, and run by 'progressive' prisoners appointed by the Chinese.) The lectures pursued one of two themes: the first criticized the attitude, behaviour and conditions in the capitalist western world; the second told of the idyllic life under Communism and eulogized the advantages enjoyed by those behind the Iron Curtain. Long passages from the writings of Lenin and Marx, and Chairman Mao's thoughts punctuated the programme, and prisoners were expected to take an active interest in the study and discussion groups. The difficulties which resulted from this stemmed largely from the fact that most of the prisoners knew very little about current affairs, Western politics or history—and cared even less. Some had never even hard of Karl Marx. Those who asked critical questions generally had to make public amends with long self-criticisms or accept punishment. A few POWs, who may have believed what they heard, cooperated with their captors and these were set against those who remained loyal to their 'capitalist' ideals. In some American camps this situation was aggravated by

---

* It is interesting to note that the size and organization of UN POWs in North Korea was almost identical with that of the German prisoners of war in the Soviet Union at the end of World War II.

officers refusing to assume leadership responsibility. In the event the organization in these camps deteriorated, and morale decayed.

In modern times it seems that all prisoners of war are condemned to be subjected to propaganda of one sort or another. In World War II the newspaper *The Camp* which was circulated among Allied POWs in Germany is perhaps the best-known propaganda sheet. The Italian equivalent, *The Prisoner of War News*, was a half-hearted affair compared with it. *The Camp*, printed and published in Berlin by a German staff assisted by one or two renegade British, purveyed the Nazi version and interpretation of the war news. Publication started on 8 July 1940 and the editorial of the first issue announced that *The Camp* would:

> make up to British POWs in a modest way for your having to go without your *Daily Express* or whatever paper may have been the joy—or the curse—of your breakfast table at home. This is not to say, of course, that *The Camp* will be conducted strictly on the model of either the said *Express* or the *Daily Mirror* or even *The Times*; no doubt you will understand that your German editor has come to look at all these papers with a certain feeling of reserve. *The Camp* will, however, true to its name, serve you the news, good or bad, in a simple and straightforward manner.

And serve the 'news' it assuredly did, only the news was never good nor was it served in a simple and straightforward manner. It was contained in a Weekly Military Survey, a column called World & War News, a Home News column, and in columns that consisted of quotations from Allied and neutral papers. Then there were many miscellaneous items which appeared from time to time, articles on German institutions and the social services (invariably favourably compared with the British), full-length reports of the speeches by prominent Nazi and Fascist officials (but not *in toto* of those by Mr Churchill and Allied statesmen), and so on; not forgetting 'the crossword puzzles and other entertaining matter' promised by the editor. Among the entertaining matter were included pirated extracts from modern English authors: P. G. Wodehouse, Jerome K. Jerome and Somerset Maugham being the editor's favourite choices. (The creator of Jeeves, although prisoners of war did not realize it, was residing in a suite at the Adlon Hotel, Berlin; so there is reason to believe that the Wodehouse extracts were not in fact *pirated*.)

Eventually about half the space of the weekly double sheet came to be filled by contributions from its readers. Most of these contributors seemed only too keen to break into verse or worse—although it would be more charitable to believe that prisoners who submitted poems, detective stories, cartoons and the rest, did so with the best intentions, hoping to entertain their fellow captives while helping to kill their own boredom. Without the cooperation of these voluntary free-lances, the paper might well have died an early death. In addition to the textual matter the camera was also used. When, however, *The Camp* reproduced a photo purporting to depict British reinforcements disembarking in the Mediterranean theatre of war (as proof of the greatly superior forces of the enemy being massed) and one of its readers recognized himself on the occasion of landing in England on leave some six months before this could have happened, faith in the veracity of *The Camp*'s editorial staff was not strengthened.

Probably only a small minority of prisoners who read *The Camp* believed much of what they read in it. Men soon came to realize that the paper could be trusted even less than the tabloid press in England —which, by comparison, was activated by harmless motives. Later on most POW camps had secret radio receivers, which obviated the need to rely on German sources of information. Compared to Communist indoctrination programmes *The Camp* was a puny effort, which at best could achieve only marginal results in discouraging POWs and lowering their morale.

The most effective antidote to propaganda measures is undoubtedly news from the prisoners' own country, and in World War II the BBC news bulletins—to which most camps in Germany had access through a secret radio—were sufficient to nullify all the German propaganda disseminated in publications like *The Camp* and by other means. Captain A. T. Casdagli, who was captured in Crete, was

> too long in the tooth for more active attempts at escaping, but was kept busy at other subversive activities, such as mapping and forging, and looking after the 'canary' or smuggled radio on which we heard the BBC news. This probably did more to keep up morale than anything else. . . .

Captain C. T. Collett, captured when his ship the MV *Chilean Reefer* was sunk by the *Gneisenau* in March 1941, spent the rest of the war in the Marlag und Milag Nord camp at Westertimke. Collett's self-education programme centred on learning shorthand, and after some time he had acquired a proficiency of 110 words a minute.*

> All this was highly gratifying to us in our captivity; the constant practice kept us on our toes and the occasional reporting of a communal argument, when read back to the participants, was most diverting. However, one day we heard that in exchange for a certain number of cigarettes and tins of real coffee, it was possible to get hold of a two-valve 'Peoples' radio set from German farmers who were willing to risk their necks over such transaction.

* Letter to the author.

Our outside contacts with the farmers produced one of the sets, and George Shaker, a Canadian wireless operator who was also a shorthand student, broke down the radio into smaller proportions so that it fitted exactly into an empty carton of Winchester cigarettes with room for four full packets on top. I kept the set on the shelf above my bunk, and, in spite of many searches, it was never discovered. The Germans would open up the carton, see the four packets on top, and remark enviously, '*Ach, viel cigaretten!*'

During the winter months the Germans used to cut off the lighting to the prisoners' huts at 8 pm to save fuel, but the camp library was on the same circuit as the German administration barrack, so we enlisted the help of the camp librarian—another prisoner—who used to lend us the library key. At a quarter to nine each evening I would tuck the carton containing the radio under my arm and walk casually across the parade ground to the library, closely followed by Lawrence Chisholm and George Shaker. Once inside we would attend to the blackout, then switch on the light. George Shaker would connect up the set and tune in to the BBC and then the three of us would stand by for the news.

Immediately the news was over we would dash back to our room where several longhand scribers waited with pencils and pads. There was just enough light from the candles made from German margarine for our purpose. A map would be spread out on the table to help us decipher our squiggles (names like Skoplje and the Marquesas Islands not being too easy for shorthand) and the three of us could usually produce a fairly accurate report of the news. The longhand writers would then make a few copies to be passed round clandestinely the next day. Somehow we never worried or even thought about being discovered by the Germans; had a guard burst into our room whilst we were reading back our notes with a large map in evidence, bread and water and solitary confinement would surely have been our lot.

Had a Japanese guard caught prisoners with a radio in one of the POW camps in the Far East, the punishment would have been death. But there were only few radios; in any case the Allied broadcasting stations were generally beyond the range of tiny home-made sets. In the absence of authentic reports of the war the yearning for news encouraged rumours—'Boreholes'.* Sir John Burns relates how he was the recipient of one of the few authentic ones:

It was towards the end of the war—not that we prisoners of war in Thailand had any knowledge that this was so or of the suddenness

---

* The basis of a South East Asian latrine is a borehole: the slang for rumour derives from that.

with which the war would actually end. We were being moved from our camp at Chungkai to a new camp in the north of Thailand. This had entailed a journey in open wagons from Chungkai to near Bangkok. The wagons were loaded with stores and billets of wood and we sat on top. The Japanese engine drivers had a trick of manipulation so that the wood-burning locomotive from time to time at their instigation blew out a shower of sparks which descended upon the hapless prisoners causing us so to arrange ourselves that each had a watchdog to beat out the sparks as they fell on our clothing, both that on our backs and in our packs. We were kept pretty fully occupied. The loss of clothing was a serious matter indeed as it was irreplaceable. The Japanese looked back and laughed at our discomfiture— vastly amusing for them but a distinct menace from our point of view.

However, we reached the river which debouches into the sea at Bangkok and upstream from Bangkok we transferred from train to river craft. These were covered barges to be towed by a tug in sixes in line ahead. There were, of course, far too few barges and we were shepherded on to them at the point of the bayonet so that eventually all were accommodated. This meant that we stood like vertical sardines in a tin except that we were not head and tail. Unfortunately, the tug broke down during the journey and we tied up to the bank for the night. It was a stinking hot night and the covered barge was sheer purgatory but we eventually reached Bangkok and there we bedded down for a few days in the godowns in the docks. Our journey now continued by the usual cattle truck—I never cease to marvel as to where all the cattle trucks used in war time come from. There were some twenty of us with all our pitiable belongings herded into a truck. Outside Bangkok there was a marshalling yard and there we stopped and there we waited for some hours. We were permitted to leave the trucks and walk or sit in the outside air. Most of the other occupants of my truck had taken advantage of the opportunity and were outside. Another train was parked on a line to our right and two Japanese armed sentries were seated on the running board of this train. I was sitting at the open door of our cattle truck when a little Thai boy appeared on the other side of the tracks just above the train on which the Japanese sentries were seated. He gesticulated and attracted my attention. When he was sure that I was watching him and that the Japanese were not, he raised his hands above his head and brought them fluttering down and this he repeated several times. Then he pointed to the Japanese and thereafter put his hands up in the conventional attitude of surrender.

I was now more than a little interested and I quietly slid further back into the truck so that I was out of sight of the Japanese but still in sight of the Thai boy. I raised my hands above my head and brought them fluttering down and this gesture I repeated two or three times. I pointed to the Japanese and then I raised my hands in surrender. The boy grinned and nodded his head vigorously several times to indicate that I had correctly interpreted and repeated the message he had passed on to me. Of course, I knew nothing of atom bombs and my interpretation was simply that Japan had been bombed and had surrendered. Much too good to be true.

His message delivered, the boy unobtrusively melted away. Inwardly greatly excited but I hoped outwardly calm, I got down from the truck and sought the senior British officer of my party. Quietly I told him of my experience. We agreed to keep it to ourselves. It had all the appearance of being genuine but did nothing that would help us at that moment in time. But it did turn out to be true. After a 24-hour train journey and a march of 45 kilometres (28 miles) in 24 hours we reached our new camp and boreholes had become authentic rumours finally to be confirmed the next day. I ate my rice and stew and physically weary but mentally happier than I had been for 3½ years I slept for 12 hours.

For readers who may think that incarceration in a POW camp may be an unpleasant experience but one which must ultimately show some financial benefit, mention must now be made of some aspects of the question of pay. Such consideration must be based on prisoners in the hands of a belligerent state which respects the Geneva Convention. The 1929 version of the Convention laid it down that officer prisoners were entitled to receive the pay of their equivalent in their captors' army—provided this did not exceed the rate paid by their own country. In World War II the rates paid in Italy were high compared with those in Germany (though not as high as the British), and there was often an insufficient balance left in officers' home accounts to provide for their dependants, or even to pay the necessary expenses such as subscriptions and insurance premiums.* Moreover the rate

* The comparative rates of pay for officers were:

	Italian	German	British
Second-lieutenant	£10 8s 4d	£4 16s	£16
Lieutenant	£13 3s 11d	£5 8s	£18 10s
Captain	£15 5s 7d	£6 8s	£22 15s
Major	£18 1s 2d	£7 4s	£32 10s
Lieutenant-colonel	£19 8s 11d	£8 0s	£48 15s

At these rates a second-lieutenant prisoner in Italy would have only £5 10s a month left in his home account. The Italian Government had agreed in principle to remittances of pay to the prisoner's home country, but no definite arrangements had been made.

of exchange of currency agreed by the governments concerned invariably seemed to work to the disadvantage of the individual officer.

Captain K. Williamson commanded a squadron of naval Swordfish which attacked and inflicted a mortal blow on the Italian fleet in Taranto in November 1940. Williamson's aircraft was one of the two shot down in the operation and he spent 3 years as a prisoner in Italy and 18 months in Germany. His financial plight is best told in his own words:

In Germany the Geneva Convention was observed, except that we would have starved had we had to live on German rations without Red Cross food parcels. My pay at this time was about £50 a month. This was sent to my bank, where I had a joint account with my wife, after income tax had been deducted and a further £5 which, by arrangement with the Germans, was given to me in 'camp currency' to buy things at a canteen; but you could remit this money home if you wished. I did, and it all got home. In short, in Germany I was not financially penalized for being a POW.

In Italy the Geneva Convention was not observed, and my three years in Italy cost me between £500 and £600. I found on arrival that I would be given in 'camp currency' the basic pay of an Italian major—1500 lire a month subsequently reduced to 1300 lire a month. This sum was deducted from my pay at home at a fixed rate of 72 lire to the pound. In 1943 the true rate of exchange was about 450–500 lire to the pound.

The Italians gave me nothing. We had to pay in advance for all our food, fuel, everything. In 1942 I was sent to the 'bad boys' camp at Gavi, north of Genoa. The camp was about eight miles from the railway station, and I not only had to pay for my own transport there, but also that of my guards!

The majority of the officers in captivity came from the then Dominions and Empire. They had to fall in line with the British, but in every case their Governments recognized the illegality of the proceedings and paid the money out of public funds. In other words, these officers did not have to pay for their captivity. I suspect our Treasury collected the money—and kept it. We thought we would get our money back after we had won the war. . . . Since this money was deducted at source and ultimately found its way to the Treasury it must be termed a tax . . . levied . . . without any reference to Parliament. . . .

Repeated efforts which have continued to the present time have failed to secure Captain Williamson any refund.

Prisoners of the Japanese received token payments only, and the Japanese attempted to draw huge sums from the Allied Governments for payments which were never made.

Some countries like the United States do give financial and other compensation to prisoners of war at the close of their chapter of life behind the wire. After their hardships the prisoners themselves may consider they have a just entitlement—especially when they see compensation awarded to others. (As happened with the Jewish inmates of German concentration camps.) Many, like Williamson, are bitter because they feel they have been cheated by authority and so penalized by their own side for becoming prisoners of war.

7

Work

The Romans are credited with being the first people to appreciate the economic value of prisoners of war as a source of labour, and to have begun to use them as slaves. Enslavement continued into the Middle Ages, but declined as the practice of POW exchange became popular. By the middle of the nineteenth century, when major conflicts were involving increasing numbers of men, exchange cartels were the exception rather than the rule. Belligerents were encumbered with great masses of POWs, but none of them appear to have been aware of the tremendous potential of the economic asset which was in their hands at a time of urgent need. But realization gradually dawned, and the Brussels code of 1874 included a provision, based on Professor Lieber's earlier code, 'that prisoners of war may be required to work for the benefit of their captors' government, according to their rank and condition'. The Brussels code was not ratified, but this article was one of those which was carried forward and embodied in the regulations adopted by the Hague Convention in 1907. International Law now permitted POWs to be put to work while in captivity. It was not until 1916 that their labour was used to any extent, however.

World War I was the first major conflict in which there was total economic mobilization, and in which there were more men held as POWs and for longer periods of time than during any previous war. Both the Allies and the Central Powers suffered from labor shortages. Nevertheless, it was not until 1916 that the British War Office could overcome opposition in the UK to the use of prisoners of war labour, and when the United States entered the war POWs were not usefully employed in America until the investigation of an attempted mass escape resulted in a recommendation that POWs should be compelled to work—primarily as a disciplinary measure.* Then when the

* Colonel Howard S. Levie, 'The Employment of Prisoners of War' (*American Journal of International Law*, Vol. 57, No. 2, April 1963, p. 321).

prisoners were put to work so many problems arose in the interpretation of the Hague Convention of 1907, a series of bilateral
agreements had to be negotiated between the belligerents during the
course of the war.

The inadequacies in this and other aspects of the 1907 Hague
Convention which had been revealed in the course of the war led to
the revised 1929 Convention. The latter was an improvement on its
predecessor; but in World War II it too proved inadequate. Practically all POWs were compelled to work, yet many of the protective
provisions of the 1929 Convention were either distorted or disregarded. Russia, which was not a party to it, considered that her
relations with the Axis powers on POW matters were governed by the
1907 Convention, and although Japan announced that she would
abide by the rules of the Convention, her violations are too well
known to warrant further account here. Germany's Nazi leaders
were acutely aware of the labour shortage in their country and
appreciated the importance of the enormous pool of POW manpower
that became available to them. Nevertheless it was a long time before
they permitted common sense and urgent needs to override their
ideological differences with the Communists. Himmler, speaking in
1943 of the Russian prisoners captured early in the war, deplored the
fact that at that time the Germans 'did not value the mass of humanity
as we value it today as raw material, as labour'. Russian prisoners in
Germany never did feed well, but their rations would have been even
less if the Nazis had not recognized that starving men do not make
good labourers.

Until the autumn of 1941 the Germans made little use of their
prisoners. During the Greece and Salonika campaigns working
parties of British POWs were sent out to bury the dead and clear up
the battlefields. Identifying the corpses was hard and unpleasant work
which many prisoners tried to avoid. But the other work was popular
because it afforded opportunities of picking up extra food. Many men
also made a break from the working parties, and escapes from Crete
and Greece were so numerous they constitute a notable feature of
both campaigns.*

It was about this time that the Nazi Government began to realize
that Germany had been landed on a long and exhausting struggle,
and decided to use its POWs to the utmost in any tasks that would
free Germans for a more active part in the war effort. *Arbeitskommandos*—work parties of up to 100 men—were formed at the

---

* It is largely guesswork even to estimate the numbers who broke from captivity
because it is difficult to disentangle evaders from escapers. Many of them got back to
Allied territory direct from Crete. Others made their way to one or other of the Aegean
islands and got back from there via Turkey.

Stalags and sent to work camps from which the POWs were pitched into farm work, coalmining, factory work and a variety of other unskilled tasks.* Some attempts were made to employ prisoners on military work, but the vigilance of the British camp leaders and the action of visiting neutral inspectors forced such projects to be avoided.

Conditions in the *Arbeitskommandos* depended very largely on the character of the German NCO in command and the employer for whom the prisoners worked, though living quarters were often quite good. A large party working on a dam at Lavamund was comfortably housed and enjoyed good camp facilities including hot showers daily. Eighty men working in a brick factory lived in the well-lit and heated rooms of specially built barracks. A party of 160 engaged on road work was lodged in a large converted house. Two hundred men working for an engineering firm had single-tier beds with three or four blankets, ample space for sport, flower and vegetable gardens— in the words of the ICRC delegate, 'a model camp'. Hours of work in the industrial plants generally varied between eight and nine and a half hours a day, with Sundays free—although laundry and camp fatigues took up a good deal of the free time. Prisoners were fed on the larger scale of 'heavy' civilian worker's ration, together with Red Cross food from the Stalag. On the other hand, with only a medical orderly in the camp and an often rather indifferent doctor paying infrequent visits, injuries were sometimes badly treated and illnesses neglected. And many of the prisoners were not used to the 'stand-over-you' type of foreman and the longer hours of work that are common in continental Europe.

Work in the coal mines was the least popular assignment. Living quarters were usually sited near the mine shaft and very primitive. Prisoners were made to work three shifts, so that with men in the same quarters coming in or going out to the mine, barrack lights were never off during the night. At first the German overseers were apt to shout at the prisoners and to lash out at them with pick handles; the civilian miners who worked alongside the POWs were also inclined to adopt bullying tactics. After a number of fights down the mines, however, the German miners came to realize that the British POWs were not to be trifled with, and hectoring German foremen found it expedient to change their technique if they hoped to get any work out of the *verdammte Englanders* whose standard response to any order appeared to be 'Fuck off'. With better understanding conditions of work improved. Nevertheless an appreciable number of prisoners reported sick in order to avoid the dangerous

* In March 1942 there were more than 260 *Arbeitskommandos* dependent on Stalag VIIIB alone.

and hazardous conditions below ground, which resulted from German haste to extract coal quickly at all costs. A few prisoners flatly refused to go down a mine and were given jail sentences for disobedience.

Work with the farming or *Landwirtschaft Arbeitskommandos*, which constituted about 20 per cent of all the working parties, was the most sought after. The hours of work on farms were much longer —sometimes 15–16 a day—but quarters were often warmer and more comfortable, and there was invariably more food to eat. Men working on farms received civilian rations, and when these were augmented with Red Cross food and eggs and farm produce the farm labour POWs could usually eat well. The outdoor work kept them tanned and fit; there was a certain amount of freedom to move around, and the farming folk for whom they worked were on the whole quite friendly after the first barriers had been broken down.

By far the great majority of *Arbeitskommandos* worked in industrial centres—in factories, or with picks and shovels on roads or canals and in quarries. Most of the small working parties had reasonably comfortable sleeping accommodation but primitive washing and sanitary arrangements. They did not have the recreational facilities of the Stalag but their day was often more interesting. Mr D. Ferguson, of the Black Watch, captured at the time of the fall of France, was sent with about 50 other prisoners to lay sewage pipes in the town of Poznan. Two months were spent on that particular job, and in that time, he said, he never saw a pipe laid although there was plenty of shovel bending and pick swinging which did nothing beyond ruining the trench that had been dug before the prisoners arrived. During these two months he and another Scotsman struck up an acquaintance with two attractive Polish girls who were not averse to carrying the friendship to fruition. An arrangement was made with a guard, and the two men slipped off to meet the girls in some woods about half-a-mile from the working site. Unfortunately the woods were a Wehrmacht training area and the two men were flushed from their rendezvous in the bushes and punished with ten days' solitary confinement.

Jim Witte's first work party took him to the railway repair works at Chemnitz, where his job was the seemingly senseless filing of a piece of metal:

> The minutes dragged by interminably; we scraped and scraped but never seemed to reduce the size of the metal. We kept on going outside to the toilet and as we had no cigarettes we rolled and smoked leaves wrapped in newspaper. The half-hour meal-break came at midnight when we downed files and ate the familiar

but revolting kohlrabi-soup. When the half-hour was up the
foreman came out of his office to get us started again. He didn't
get it all his own way; we called him every rude name we could
think of, so much so that he asked us quite mildly why Englanders
always said 'fuck this and fuck that'. In the end the Germans
believed that the English spent so much time fucking that they
were too tired to do anything else.

The weary night at last came to an end. The guard came for
us and we returned to our lager to sleep. The next night it was the
same and the next and the next. We decided to stage a revolt in
protest about the food, chiefly to break the monotony. We
downed files and waited. The foreman, not hearing any sounds of
industrious scraping, came out of his office and was horrified to
find the Englanders lounging about.

'*Arbeit*', he said, '*arbeit.*'

'Fuck off', we said.

The foreman was now plainly disconcerted. He didn't quite
know what to do. In the end he did the next best thing and
telephoned to a higher authority. Meanwhile we lounged on until
a railway official arrived wearing a hat covered in gold braid
which meant that he was quite important. After conferring with
the foreman, gold braid rushed into us shouting, 'arbeit, arbeit'.

We told him to fuck off as well.

He, too, was disconcerted, never having had to contend with
rank mutiny and open defiance. He stumped off temporarily
leaving the field to us. The poor foreman went back to his office
to await further developments. They soon came in the shape of a
railway policeman and a savage-looking Dobermann Pinscher.
No one said 'fuck off' to the dog which looked ready and willing
to bite chunks out of our legs. We took up our files and resumed
filing. But that wasn't the end of the matter for our own guard
returned and took four of the lads away. They spent three days in
solitary expiating our sins but the soup did improve so all was not
in vain.

Much was done in a low key to sabotage the enemy war effort.
Some of the sabotage was intentional, more of it resulted from a
combination of inexperience and bloody-mindedness. From filing
Witte graduated to the boiler-shop, to become a German welder's
assistant—pushing a trolley containing complex oxyacetylene gear to
where it was needed. Wheeling it over some compressed air-pipes
Witte managed to tip the whole trolley into an inspection pit. After
that he was sent to join a French riveting gang who soon discovered
that he was useless to them. Czech drillers took the same view, and

Witte was finally posted to an odd job gang composed of 'useless Englanders, Bolshie Frenchmen, and undernourished Russians' employed unloading wagons and sweeping up.

Under the Geneva Convention commissioned officers and NCOs of the rank of corporal and over were exempt from work. Much argument took place over German efforts to get these prisoners to work. The German authorities suspected—not without good reason —that some of those claiming NCO rank had merely assumed it for the duration of their captivity, giving themselves 'stalag promotion' in order to avoid having to work; and it was not easy to distinguish these from genuine NCOs. Pressure on the whole group took various forms: threats, long parades out in the cold, restricting the issue of clothes to those who refused to go out on working parties. Finally it was decided that if NCOs were not to work they must exercise instead; so they were marched round the sports field and drilled for two hours each morning and made to play games each afternoon. The lack of German guards to supervise the scheme and the winter months, when the weather made it impossible to continue, eventually brought about its cancellation.

Britain and the US had the same problem as Germany over POW 'camp promotion', and many duration Unteroffiziers were required to work. Whether it was teutonic discipline or the pressures exerted on them (the Americans adopted a 'no work, no food' policy) nearly all the suspect unteroffiziers were persuaded to work. The great majority of the Axis prisoners were employed on farm work in both Britain and the US. In America many of them were put to work harvesting sugar cane—hard and demanding labour ten hours a day, and the men involved saw themselves as a new race of sugar slaves. Living conditions and treatment sometimes left much to be desired. 'Many people still believe today that the German POWs in the US lived like maggots in the bacon. But even in God's Own Country there were camps which were hell . . .', was the bitter comment of one of these sugar slaves. Unlike Britain, where feelings towards the POWs mellowed as the war drew to a close, the American attitude towards their prisoners hardened. Reports of atrocities committed during the fighting and finally the revelations at Buchenwald and Dachau were largely responsible for this.

In Britain the prisoners lived in wooden huts close to their work. Mr J. L. Rice, who spent two years as a labour officer in charge of a mixed bunch of German, Austrian and Italian prisoners at Epping in Essex, comments:*

> Their conditions were first class, with adequate heating, good
> sanitation and facilities for cooking. Even so, the men suffered

* Letter to the author.

from 'barbed wire fever'. Many were homesick and apprehensive about their families at home. They were superb cooks of rabbits, etc., and made a syrup for sweetening from sugar beet. There was quite a bit of homosexuality—certain boys would be let off jobs. Some men always managed to get out of camp at night to find girls. Local girls fell over them! One of the Austrian boys, it was said, increased the local population by twelve! Two POWs, saying they were Polish, played in local dance bands, making, stealing or borrowing their clothes.

They all wore POW clothes—these had circles on back and legs meant to make clear targets in case of escape. In our camp few had any intention of escaping although they had plenty of opportunity. I have many times seen the POWs carrying the rifles of their guards! This often happened as we walked across the fields to our work. I can recall escorts being chased by POWs with paper bags filled with water.

In our camp there were four labour officers. Apart from myself they were ex-servicemen who had some disability. They had no training for the job whatsoever.

The camp had plenty of facilities for recreation, darts, etc. They produced first class plays and they had a group choir. They liked classical music in the main. They made their own sport. The camp commandant (a Jew) organized camp concerts. The men thought the world of him, by the way.

The POWs did many things to make a little money (they had no pay)—for example, they stole baling string, cotton, etc., from the farms, making these up in the evening into rope-soled shoes which they sold at the farms.

They also stole razor blades. I have never met anyone like the Germans and Austrians for smartness and cleanliness. The few Italians we had were a scruffy lot and couldn't care less.

When first captured the men seemed arrogant, but within a few months this attitude changed. Most seemed glad to be out of the war.

Allied prisoners of war in Italy were not compelled to work until the summer of 1942. Men were invited to volunteer for farm work or casual labour in the neighbourhood of their camps and double rations were held out as a bait. But German encouragement and the strain on POW camp accommodation brought a change in the system. Groups of 50 men or less were then sent to farms and vineyards to begin with. Then, as the Fascist Government began to realize the value of the massive reserve of unskilled labour they had in their hands, the Italian authorities set up work camps in areas where the prisoners would be employed to the benefit of the Italian economy.

The first of these work camps was Campo PG 107 at Torviscosa in the low-lying swamp country of the plain at the extreme northern end of the Adriatic. It is about 20 miles from the sea, with Udine about 15 miles to the north, and beyond the Julian and Venetian Alps. There was a large factory in the town for the manufacture of cellulose fabrics from cane that was grown on land reclaimed from the Udine marshes. POWs were used to drain and level the swamp, construct roads through it and later cutting the cane. They were paid by the company at the rate of 3 lire a day in addition to their normal pay from the Italian Army authorities, and received double the normal ration of bread and macaroni and cheese.

After an early morning drink of coffee substitute the men were counted out of the gate of the work camp by 7.15 am and marched along the road to the fields where they worked in parties of 100 men under a foreman and three or four overseers. In winter they worked 6 hours a day; in summer this was increased to 10 hours. The prisoners were not overworked and the overseers were usually willing to do an illicit trade in food and wine for cigarettes and soap, and to retail items of news they had heard over the BBC. As in Germany the British POWs quickly established a working arrangement, downing tools and refusing to obey instructions when their employers tried to impose any form of sanction or to speed the work beyond the limit the prisoners considered reasonable.

In the spring of 1943 new working camps were formed. Some were for farm labour; others, like an offshoot of Campo PG 57 about 20 miles north of Verona, were for more ambitious projects. This particular camp was intended to provide pick-and-shovel labour to build a canal which was part of a huge hydroelectric scheme using the waters of the Adige River. But in September 1943 the Italian Armistice brought an abrupt closure to this and all the other POW camps in Italy. (Of the 70,000 British prisoners held in Italian camps when the armistice was signed, 52,000 were transferred to Germany; 12,000 escaped to the Allied lines; 5000 got away to Switzerland. The official records do not reveal the fate of the remaining 3000.)

There was never any question of German prisoners of the Russians not being put to work. A man must eat in order to live, and the Russian prison camp system was operated on the donkey-and-the-carrot principle. If a man could do more work than the norm, he could win himself an extra ration. It was a vicious system which often defeated itself because, in driving himself to the limit, the prisoner often fell short of the norm in which case he was given less food. Embarking on a desperate attempt at furious physical activity which his undernourished body could not take, a man was eventually driven to commit suicide. In a temperature of minus sixty degrees Fahrenheit death is never far away.

In effect many of the German POWs who ended up in Soviet labour camps were surprised to have got so far. As many as 15–20 per cent perished on the journey back to the camps on the Volga; they had had precious little food en route; they had been stripped of most of their belongings; they had no medical aid of any kind; and they were riddled with sickness and disease—mainly dysentery, typhus and typhoid. One batch of 2000 German prisoners was sent to a camp at Elabuga between Kazan and Ufa where they were to be accommodated in a former Greek Orthodox monastery. Only 1300 arrived alive; the other 700 were taken from the train as frozen corpses. Initially there were no blankets, no clothing and no medical assistance and although the camp was kept up to a strength of about 1000 men with the arrival of new batches of prisoners from the various fronts, the death rate averaged 200 a week. With the passage of time conditions improved only marginally. Crowded together the prisoners slept on wooden planks or on cemented soil; one blanket often had to serve two men; food was barely sufficient to support life and few of the men weighed more than 7 stone. Writing of the conditions in this camp, one of the inmates—a German clergyman—said that hunger, rats, lice, bugs, spies and slave-labour drove men to despair and death. 'Burglaries into the bread store were frequent. A murder, in comparison, would have passed unnoticed.' Another prisoner has told how a man caught stealing bread was beaten to death by his fellows.

The Communists believe that no man is a human being until he does some productive work for the community, and this concept was applied to the POW camps. In the Russian wastes the most exhausting labour is fetching wood in winter. Standing up to their knees in snow, the POWs found it difficult to move. Huge tree-trunks, cut away with axes, sometimes fell on them, killing them on the spot. Clad in rags with no gloves and only thin boots on their feet, hardly able to stand for weakness caused by under-nourishment, their hands and bodies were frozen stiff in the bitter cold. The minimum daily task for four men was to cut, split and pile 4 cubic sajenes (a sajene is about 6 feet) and until they had done this they were not allowed to return to camp. Other prisoners were forced to haul sledges and carts piled high with the timber which had been cut. Day after day they dragged themselves across the country, harnessed to self-made raffia ropes. By the local Russian civilians they were nicknamed 'little Stalin horses'.

Any man who collapsed was allowed to rest for a few days. But there was no medical aid and his food was reduced to a non-worker ration. When, on one occasion, the prisoners refused to work in pouring rain without coats, the guards tied ropes round their necks and dragged them off to work. Faced with the choice of giving in or being strangled the wretched prisoners had to yield.

The Japanese treatment of prisoners in the Far East is comparable to that of the Russians. All fit men were liable to be called out for working parties and their biggest project was the notorious Siam railway. The idea of a railway connecting Moulmein with Bangkok had been mooted before the war and the Japanese decided to complete it with their large reserve of POW labour. Small advance parties of prisoners were sent from Singapore to Bampong in June 1942 to build transit camps to receive the main labour parties which followed. These were formed mainly in Singapore as battalions, each about 600 strong, from prisoners in the Changi POW camps.

After a week of travel in a steel goods wagon the prisoners were in poor shape. Herded 32 or more in a wagon, they could not lie down, and the intense tropical heat turned the wagons into ovens. Many of them were not fit therefore for the marches that followed. Eleven to thirteen miles a day over muddy jungle tracks through torrential rain caused most of the prisoners considerable distress. Stragglers were beaten up by Korean guards. ('They themselves were treated like animals, and who can blame them for treating us like they did—this was the first time they had been able to hit anybody for years,' wrote Colonel I. G. Thomas.*) Rations on these journeys were poor, and some who were at first thought fortunate in being taken part of the way by barge up the Kwei Noi River received no food at all while on board. The combination of poor food and physical exhaustion during these northward treks was the beginning of much illness that ended fatally for many of the men concerned.

They now found themselves in areas where the monsoon rains which had been pouring down for 5–6 months had converted jungle clearings into quagmires knee-deep in stinking mud. The camp-site clearings were on the east bank of the Kwei Noi River where the Japanese planned to lay the railway. Exhausted as they were from the march the prisoners were set to work to build coolie-type huts. These were bamboo structures about 100 yards long and 8 yards wide roofed with attap palm leaves and fitted on each side for the length of the hut with 6-foot wide sleeping platforms of lashed bamboo. The task of building such a camp, making it habitable for 1000–2000 men and ensuring sufficient cookhouse and latrine accommodation, was a big one. But the majority of prisoners in these parties were put onto road and railway construction work long before proper living accommodation was completed.

Water came from the river, and because much that was drunk

* Letter to the author.

could not be filtered and boiled men fell victim to infections carried down from camps further upstream. Rations were nearly always below official Japanese scales. Vegetables arrived in a rotting condition, most of the rice was maggotty and mixed with all kinds of fish. Supplies of fish, meat, oil, salt and sugar were meagre and men sometimes had to live months on end on little more than an ounce and a half of rice per day. The rice, the vegetables, and whatever else could be found to go with them, had to be cooked over bamboo fires in shallow 12-gallon containers. But there were not enough of these to go round. Nor were there enough cooks to do the work, because the Japanese would only permit one or two men for a hundred prisoners.

On this diet the prisoners were required to clear the jungle, fell trees, make embankments, lay rails, and bridge rivers and torrents. To complete their 'norm' the Japanese railway engineer drove the prisoners from dawn till dusk—demanding from each camp a certain percentage of its strength irrespective of the numbers of sick. To make up the quotas men quite unfit for work were driven out, sometimes even carried out to work. The line, boasted some of the Japanese engineers, would be laid over the dead bodies of the prisoners.

During the first 2 or 3 months officers went out with the working parties in an effort to safeguard the men's interests. But they were consistently ignored by the Japanese in charge of the work, and if they had occasion to remonstrate with the latter, were often made the object of especially spiteful treatment. By December 1942 the Japanese had decided that officer prisoners should also work on the railway and within a month parties of officers were labouring alongside the men and being treated as part of the POW labour force.

For those whose health broke down under these conditions of work there were only the most inadequate medical facilities. The region through which the Burma–Siam railway passes is generally regarded as one of the most unhealthy in the world. Yet there were very few Japanese doctors, and medical arrangements were left in the hands of Japanese soldiers who knew nothing of the hazards of the disease and sickness that ravaged the wretched prisoners. A hospital was created merely by setting aside one of the jungle huts and POW medical personnel with the labour force had to rely on whatever equipment they happened to have been able to retain and bring with them. Epidemics of malaria, dysentery and cholera could not be controlled because there were no drugs—or rather the Japanese would not provide the drugs. A great deal of essential medical equipment was improvised, but it was not enough to save many thousands of lives.

Early in 1943 the Japanese decided that the railway was not being built fast enough and 10,000 more prisoners were ordered up from Singapore. More were sent up from the Dutch East Indies, and tens of thousands of Tamils, Chinese and Malays—men and women— were pressed into service as labourers. Until the Japanese invasion of Malaya most of these unfortunate individuals had been employed by the rubber estates. The vast acquisitions of rubber by the Japanese were far beyond their needs, and the estate labourers found themselves without work or pay, hungry, forlorn and leaderless. Lured by Japanese promises they were packed into the trains that had taken the POWs up to the railway. Many were assembled prior to despatch in the Selangor Club in Kuala Lumpur, attired according to an eye witness,* in bizarre fashion wearing abandoned European clothes, flowered hats and coloured dresses—a sort of zany air of carnival preceded their Nemesis. In Siam they met and sometimes worked as fellow coolies with their former European masters. Mr C. H. Lee, a Malayan planter serving with the Straits Settlement Volunteer Force, recalls:†

The Malay from here who offered me tobacco (and samsu). The Tamil with whom I shared the sleepers and who found them as hot and uncomfortable under barefoot as I did, and consoled me, may be gone, but something else remains. Our perverted sense of humour met.

There was the occasion when our joint Korean guard was suffering from a complaint only too common on the line, and whose frequent excursions to the undergrowth, ending in final exhaustion and collapse, provided a neat opportunity for a joint 'bludge' and quite merciless merriment.

And here I should explain the word 'bludger' (spelling mine) which, coined in Australia with a rather more disreputable connotation, meant with us one who avoided work. And who did not some time or other?

When Winston Churchill—in his usual grandiloquent style— addressed the victorious Eighth Army at Tripoli, he said: 'You can tell your sons you marched and fought with the Desert Army.' For us nothing so Napoleonic, but we can tell them, if inquisitive, that 'we marched (or went by barge) and "bludged" with D Battalion', inglorious but indubitably true in my case.

In addition to bringing up more workers, the Japanese increased their pressure on the whole labour force. From April until November

* Mr R. H. Beins, a leading Eurasian in the Kuala Lumpur community.
    † Letter to the author, and extract of an article by Mr Lee published in the *Malay Mail*.

1943, the 'speedo' period, the Japanese engineers drove the Allied labour force mercilessly in an effort to complete the railway by the date set by their masters in Tokyo. In April conditions on the railway were hot and dry, with thick layers of dust everywhere; but May saw the onset of the monsoon, which continued until October. Ceaseless rain and thick mud soon made conditions for the workers doubly hard and turned their pitiful encampments of huts and tents into evil-smelling quagmires. Little account seems to have been taken of this in the demands of the Japanese: the daily task for one man could rise as high as moving 3 cubic yards of soil a distance of 300 yards through mud and then up an embankment 25 feet high. Tools and equipment were of poor quality and the earth had to be carried in bags or baskets or on stretchers. Work went on in some places until 11.30 at night, and for 2 or 3 months some working teams hardly saw their camps in daylight. After roll-call at dawn they were marched off to work, and they did not return to camp until dark.

In June 1943 a senior Japanese officer in charge of POWs in Siam expressed the general attitude of the captors towards the sick of their work force: 'Those who fail in charge by lack of health is regarded as most shameful deed.' During the 'speedo' period, owing to exhaustion from overwork and semi-starvation, few of the workers were free from some kind of sickness. But as the sickness rate grew the Japanese increased their pressure. The threat to turn out all sick from the camp hospitals led to only those being admitted who were seriously ill. Men were forced to limp out to work on sticks and some were even carried out on stretchers. Those who fell sick during work were liable to be severely and savagely punished. A prisoner stricken with a sudden attack of malaria might be stood up to his neck in a cold river; those who collapsed might be kicked or beaten; men with festering feet might be forced to work in the thorny jungle. Not until the railway was nearing completion were any of the seriously ill allowed to be evacuated to the so-called 'base hospitals' in Siam and Burma. There, in hopelessly overcrowded conditions and what was described as 'pools of infection and gangrene', only the devotion, skill and enterprise of the POW medical staffs saved the lives of thousands of sufferers.

Reckless disregard of the health of the POWs by the Japanese decimated the labour force for the railway so quickly that only a small fraction of its original strength remained at the time of its completion. In the space of a year deaths among Allied prisoners on the railway amounted to something like a third of their number—or some 20,000 men out of a force of 60,000 or more. Groups working under particularly bad conditions had an even higher death rate than this.* In addition large numbers of men were permanently disabled as a result of amputations or the after-effects of disease.

Elsewhere in Japan's 'Co-Prosperity Sphere', prisoners were used to construct airfields. Many of these were on small islands in the Dutch East Indies and no arrangements were made to accommodate or feed the POWs before they actually arrived. The treatment of a party of about 2000 officers and men which left Sourabaya in mid-April 1943 and spent 15 months in Haruku at Ambon takes its place with the worst examples of treatment in Burma and Siam. Many of the men were unfit before they left Java, and after a 2-weeks voyage in a 'hell-ship' they were totally unfitted to the heavy work of unloading the bombs and petrol to which they were set when their ships docked in the islands. Long hours of work on Haruku, inadequate food and no medical supplies rocketed the sick rate. By mid-May there were 700 patients in the improvised hospital on Haruku, mainly with dysentery and beri-beri. Besides reducing the rations for the sick the Japanese periodically drove out to work all those who were just able to stagger from the hospital and a policy of general intimidation was carried out with great brutality by some of the guards. In a little over 7 months some 400 of the prisoners were dead.

Elsewhere in the Dutch East Indies all who could crawl out of the gates of the POW camps were made to work 7 days a week from dawn to dusk. The tasks usually involved heavy manual labours, constructing airfield runways, building air-raid shelters, making roads, work in the sawmills and carpentry. Some of the few 'rest' days were filled in by compulsory labour in the camp gardens. Men who were considered to be idle were beaten, made to stand at attention in the hot sun for hours on end, hold heavy weights above their heads, or subjected to whatever other brutish punishment that sprang to the guards' minds.

Women POWs were interned in Sumatra, and although they were not compelled to do any work over and above that which the Japanese considered was related to their own maintenance and welfare, the latter was more than enough. It is also interesting to relate what the women had to do, with what could be expected of them under Article 49 of the Geneva Convention. The employment of POWs, the article provides, should be limited to those who are physically fit, and the work they do should be of a nature to maintain them 'in a good state of physical and mental health'. Age, sex and the physical aptitudes of the individual prisoner are supposed to be

---

* The most gruesome statistics relate to 'H' Force—men sent up to the railway in 1943 to speed the work. Of 11,500 men 6000 were dead within a year. In addition to the POWs uncounted thousands of the Asian labourers perished. (The figure has been put as high as 150,000.)

taken into consideration when determining what job should be carried out by whom. Women, for example, should not be required to lift and move heavy loads. At Palembang, a group of Australian Army nursing sisters captured on Banka Island soon found that the Japanese made few concessions for their sex.

> We always have to unload and carry in our own rice, but never before have we been asked to unload and store at least 200 sacks of rice while the Japs sat round and smoked our cigarettes. When the women could hardly stagger on their feet the Japs called it off and gave them a 'present' of a couple of tins of *paté de foie gras*. Rather ironical when it was taken from our own Red Cross boxes. . . .*

POWS transported to Japan were employed in shipyards and steelworks. In the Mitsubishi naval and shipbuilding yard at Yokohama the men worked from 7 am until 5 pm on all the heavy manual tasks connected with the building and overhauling of ships. In the Muoran Steel Works at Hakodate in the south of Hokkaido Island they worked similar hours for 13 days out of 14 shovelling coal and iron ore or in a repair shop for railway engines. Prisoners in a group of camps round Osaka in the South of Honshu Island were put to work constructing a dock. At Fukuoka other POWS were employed 11 hours a day in a factory making green carborundum, often working alongside high-temperature furnaces. At Zentsuji, on the island of Shikoku, the first batches of prisoners were employed on agricultural projects, but in 1942 they were switched to railway yards and docks, loading grain and heavy military supplies—the latter being work specifically prohibited by the Geneva Convention, of course.

Much of the other work done for the Japanese also fell into the prohibited category of the Convention, or was very close to it. Since the Japanese disregarded the Convention *in toto* the question is academic. Nevertheless the question of what is and what is not permissible employment for POWS is worthy of consideration. Under the 1949 Convention (Article 50) work 'connected with camp administration, installation or maintenance, farming and production of extra raw material' is permitted. Prisoners may also be employed on other work 'not having a military character or purpose' which is required for normal civilian consumption. The limiting phrase is, of course, 'not having a military character or purpose', for it is extremely difficult in modern war to exclude 'military character and purpose' from anything. Agriculture, long considered to be the least controversial form of labour, is often considered to be as important

* Betty Jeffrey, *White Coolies* (Panther, London 1958), p. 106.

to a belligerent as the production of small arms ammunition. Military traffic may use newly constructed roads, so POW labour used to build them is directly contributing to the enemy war effort.* Taking the analogy to its logical conclusion, it could be argued that a canning company supplying tinned food for military as well as civilian use cannot utilize POW labour because the prisoners' labour contributes to the war effort. Clearly there must be a limit if POW labour is to be employed at all. The Germans justified their use of POWs in coal mines on the grounds that the work did not amount to the production of munitions. Their employment of other prisoners in the building of the Atlantic wall was never questioned, and indeed the Nuremberg Military Tribunal held that the construction of fortifications by prisoners of war is not necessarily criminal.

If the purpose of the work stirs doubts about the legitimacy of employing POWs on it, there can be no question about work which hazards the prisoners' lives. Humiliating, unhealthy or dangerous work was specifically barred by the Geneva Convention of 1949. 'Dangerous' is, of course, a relative term. But the example leading to a great deal of argument among the Geneva delegates was that of POWs being used to lift mines. Many of the Allies used German POWs to remove German mines at the end of World War II. Moreover the British employed Japanese soldiers in military operations against Indonesian guerillas after VJ day. Under the 1949 Convention such employment could only be justified by international law if the prisoners were to volunteer for it.

In the Korean and Vietnam wars the question of POW labour did not arise. Indeed it was overshadowed by indoctrination. If it were to arise—as for example in a war between China and the United States—different standards of living might complicate the issue. Mention of this problem has been made in a different context in relation to Japan. In Western countries the local workers, and their unions, are often averse to foreign labour—more so when they are hostile combatants coming to their land and competing with them.†

Despite these complications the conclusion must be that the great majority of prisoners of any future war will be put to work. A few with special qualifications may find congenial labour commensurate with their skills. But the great majority will have to dig and chop and lift and carry.

---

* This question arose on the Alaska Highway, and POWs were debarred from working on it.

† This is best illustrated by an American speech during World War II: 'We will get them out of here just the minute any labor becomes surplus, and we won't allow them any grass to grow under our feet doing it. We are not going to prevent any American getting a job because of a prisoner. We do not and will not compete with free labor....' *Iowa Law Review*, No. 32, p. 73.

8

Religion

The question of religion is a delicate issue and essentially an individual one. Everyone who honourably becomes a prisoner of war is necessarily brought into pretty close contact with the final realities of life just before he is captured. A man's subsequent attitude depends largely on his background and upbringing. If he has strong religious convictions before capture, his faith might well be a comfort. Lionel Renton, a young officer of the Queens who was captured in France in 1940, observed that 'lots of people attended church services [in his POW camp] who never did so in civil live. In this connection it is interesting to note that the Roman Catholic and Nonconformist padres were far and away the best. . . .'

Frank Waddington, an RAF sergeant who spent a year in Stalag Luft III, was brought up as a Methodist. Captivity provided him with an opportunity to sort out his ideas and he built 'on the foundations of belief in God' which he had been given at home. On the other hand, Jim Witte contends that religion was 'no comfort at all. The only religion we believed in except for one or two religious maniacs was food and, when the stomach was full, sex.'

Mr H. O. Whiting, commenting on his captivity in Italy, observed that there was an upsurge of religious interest in the Catholic faith after a visit by a priest from the Vatican—'but due, I fear, to the fact that the participants received bread and wine at the services. At no time did I see any evidence of interest favourable or otherwise towards religion—just complete indifference.'

In conditions where life was most difficult religion might perhaps be expected to have its greatest influence. And Sister E. M. Hannah, the sole survivor of a group of Australian Army nursing sisters, maintains that her religious faith helped her to get through her years in Japanese captivity.* Lieut.-Colonel C. Gilbert, an Indian Army

* Sister E. M. Hannah, now Mrs E. M. Allgrove, served with the Australian Army's 2/4th CCS in Singapore. Of the original eight nursing sisters, three were shot, two were drowned, and two died in captivity.

officer, spent his captivity in Changi. He expresses a similar view and says that 'the work of the padres of *all* denominations in Changi was just magnificent!' Sidney Sheldrick found that religion was '. . . rather difficult, as the padre, who was, of course, an officer, was taken from us in the early days and so religion was a matter for a few extremely religious individuals and a few Jews in the camp who gathered on Saturdays and had a natter among themselves.' Owen Greenwood, a prisoner in Batavia, expresses a more positive view:

> Officially C of E on paper, I am not at all religious and, speaking personally, religion played no part in my life as a POW. Nevertheless, more than one man I could name became a convert to Rome, but, rightly or wrongly, I would attribute this to the exceptional qualities and dedication of the RC priest in one camp in Sumatra, as opposed to the ineffectual character of the C of E padre. Speaking broadly, and it is both difficult and imprudent to generalize, I am left with the opinion that religion played a very small part in the lives of most POWs. Such faith as we had seemed to be largely concentrated in Churchill and the British Army who would eventually 'get us out'.

Why religion has seemed to play a less important role in the lives of prisoners of war than might be expected may be attributed to two causes. The first is a comparatively simple explanation. At some prison camps in World War II many of the chaplains failed to meet the challenge of the time. There were notable exceptions, of course. And during the Korean War four magnificent parsons set a glorious example to thousands of UN POWs beset by the missionaries of Communism. (Three of these men, Rev. Kenneth L. Hyslop, Father Emil J. Kapaun and the Rev. Wayne H. Burdue—all chaplains of the US Army—died in captivity.) Credit for their work is best expressed by an officer who was a prisoner with them—Captain (now Major-General) J. H. S. Majury. In the dedication to a book of prayers used in the North Korean prison camps he writes: '[This] is a standing testimonial of the part religion played in upholding our morale, and the trouble men took to put their faith before everything in the face of the severest opposition.'

The second reason why religion may have failed to have any real impact on the lives of prisoners of war is more fundamental. Since World War I there has been a general tendency to break down old creeds and dogmas. In an increasingly materialistic world many people have rejected the traditional religions. A great deal that was obsolete and useless has been discountenanced, and possibly some things that are useful have been swept away also. In the event the result has been that although some men in captivity have found a desire to discover among the confusion of organized religion something which could be adapted to their needs, the majority have remained indifferent—or outwardly indifferent anyway. After a few days in a Japanese, North Korean or Russian POW camp on a diet of rice and watery cabbage soup barely sufficient to keep body and soul together many have found the Bible's words barren. When Communist propagandists say of the New Testament that 'it is the finest known piece of propaganda because it tells people exactly what they want to believe', the prisoners tend to agree.

It must be remembered that in most communist POW camps authority has refused to countenance religion; this in itself is an inducement to many captives to make use of it according to the simple law that what is forbidden is attractive. However, it may also be argued that as religion can lead to punishment men's interest in it must be, in part, genuine. Priests, more than other POWs, can, of course, expect their theological theories to be subjected to extreme tests. In Russia and North Korea priest-prisoners have been more savagely treated and disgustingly humiliated than other men. And there is no doubt that the Rev. F. Chambers' faith was pure. Among the POWs in Changi he was popular because he was always ready to lend a helping hand, even when it meant upsetting the Japanese. While trying to help another POW to lift a particularly heavy load Chambers ruptured himself. He was refused hospital treatment by the Japanese and died. Father Emil Kapaun was a heroic figure of the Korean War. In his camp Kapaun successfully fought indoctrination among American prisoners, ministered to the sick and dying of all faiths, and stole food from the guards to supplement the insufficient diet. By walking into a hut, laying his gains on the floor and asking all present to join in a prayer of thanks to God, selfish thieves were shamed into contributing their acquisitions to the common fund. Kapaun himself died of malnutrition, having literally killed himself by his unstinting devotion to others.

Between the different religions, Mohammedanism probably emerges as the faith with most stabilizing influence in World War II and the Korean War. It is not always possible, however, to dissociate faith from national character. How far the will of Turkish POWs in North Korea was strengthened by their belief that there was no God but Allah, and how far it was buttressed by their closeness to the soil and knowledge of hardship, is difficult to say. The Turks are barbarian-proud of their manhood and fighting ability, and although Turkish soldiers might realize, dimly, that economically their country is backward their faith in themselves and their country has not been lessened. The Egyptians are also Moslems, yet in four campaigns the Israelis have not found Islam to have been more worthy than Judaism on the field of battle or behind the barbed wire.

In this context Sheldrick's comment about Jewish prisoners in Sarawak is interesting. Few Jewish prisoners have acknowledged that their religious faith has helped them to bear their captivity, and as a religious group—rather than an ethnic one—they appear oddly disunited in POW camps. Minority religious groups, like Jehovah's Witnesses and Quakers, were much more united, militant and vocal during World War II.

In conclusion, therefore, it appears that belief, trust and faith in God is a paramount force for some POWs in some circumstances, and probably for many men during brief intervals. Much depends on religious upbringing and teaching; much more depends, as Witte and Sheldrick have both said in different ways, on food. When a man is really and truly hungry there can be no real and true religion beyond the preaching of an empty belly.

9
Guards and Discipline

Of all the exasperating facets of POW life it is the guarding and maintenance of discipline which can prove to be the most irritating. All too often the efforts to control the prisoners are a source of constant conflict between captors and captives. The reason for this is easily explained: on the one hand the prisoners resent being controlled and vent their resentment in strikes, conspiracies, attempts to escape and petty provocations; while the guards, on the other hand, are committed to suppressing such challenges to their authority and to seeing that their prisoners cause as little trouble as possible.

Various ways of overcoming the problem have been tried in the past; that of parole is probably the best known. In World War II the Germans attempted to ease their guard duties by offering extra privileges in exchange for parole. During the winter of 1940, officer prisoners crowded into the mediaeval castle at Spangenberg were permitted to go for walks twice a week if they promised not to escape. The system did not work. British officers were forbidden to give parole if taken prisoner, and so very few of them were prepared to accept the German offer. Moreover the commandant of Spangenberg camp insisted on guards accompanying those who did promise not to escape while out on a recreational stroll. This, he said, was 'to protect prisoners against possible insults from German civilians'. Some officers protested that they were prepared to take the risk of anything the German population might do; others complained that the imposition of guards under such circumstances was a slur on the honour of the officer who had given his parole. But no amount of argument was of any avail. 'No guard—no walks' was the German standpoint, and it remained so in most German camps throughout the war.

In 1942 the Germans also attempted to impose a collective stoppage of privileges afforded to prisoners in Spangenberg, and to reintroduce them only if parole were given regarding their use. This was strenuously opposed, and mail—both inward and outward—was stopped from the beginning of August. Two months later, doctors, chaplains and *grand-blessés**, were moved to another camp at Rotenburg, while those who remained at Spangenberg were subjected to rigorous restrictions. This was on the orders of the German High Command as a reprisal for the alleged ill-treatment of German officer prisoners en route for South Africa. British officers were denied the use of all books—except bibles—and other collectively owned property, their private effects were confiscated, they were deprived of soap, towels and razors, toothbrushes, knives and forks, and their badges of rank, medal ribbons and other insignia were removed. Not unnaturally this provoked resentment which did not make the guards' duties any easier.

The Japanese do not appear to have given any serious consideration to the use of parole in the accepted sense. In the early days of the war at least, POW camps were run according to strict Imperial Army discipline. Precise instructions were issued covering all aspects of camp routine and offences were usually punished on the spot by the culprit having his face slapped or being beaten for a length of time which depended on the seriousness of the culprit's so-called crime. Most Allied prisoners experienced face slapping at some time or other and although some men's eardrums suffered damage the punishment lay rather in humiliation than in physical injury. As Colonel Thomas put it,† 'The injury was greater to our dignity than to our persons'. After the capture of Hong Kong, however, the Japanese insisted that all prisoners in their camps should sign a pledge not to escape. All inmates of the Shamshuipo camp were paraded for a mass signing of the pledge, and the Japanese guards mounted machine guns for the occasion. British troops could not sign such an undertaking, the senior British officer said at the outset. But he was compelled to change his mind and the majority of the camp eventually signed the form 'under duress'. The few brave, determined or headstrong individuals who continued to refuse were taken away to the Kempetai barracks where tortures and deprivations persuaded most of them to change their minds and sign. When they returned to Shamshuipo they were physical wrecks. And of those who are presumed to have held out, nothing more was ever heard.

A similar attempt was made to extract an understanding not to escape from POWs in Singapore. When General Percival accepted the

---

* There were over 50 amputees and other seriously wounded cases in the camp at this time.
    † Letter to the author.

Japanese surrender terms in February 1942 the British troops were ordered to assemble at Changi, and 50,000 weary captives trudged along the winding road from Singapore city to the concentration area. At first the Japanese placed no restrictions on movement within the area designated as a POW camp, and the prisoners were allowed to roam over the whole eastern end of Singapore island. On 12 March 1942, however, prisoners were ordered to wire themselves in and a No-Man's land, separating the POW camps from the mainland was established. This area was patrolled by Japanese soldiers and turncoat Sikhs. With the passage of time the attitude of these guards hardened, and Sikhs in particular took advantage of their position to make increasingly absurd demands on the POWs.

In August 1942 General Percival and most of the other senior British and Australian officers were taken away to Japan, and Major-General Fukuye and a large administrative staff began to establish a proper POW camp regime at Changi. Hardly had Fukuye arrived than four escaped prisoners were brought in. Two of these had got away from Bukit Timah 5 months previously and had rowed 200 miles in a small boat before re-arrest. The Japanese reaction was an announcement that all prisoners in Changi would be given an opportunity to sign a statement: 'I, the undersigned, hereby solemnly swear on my honour that I will not, under any circumstances, attempt to escape.' As at Shamshuipo, the senior British Officer, Colonel Holmes, pointed out that POWs were not allowed to give their parole and he and his fellow officers refused to sign. To a man the other ranks followed suit.

Two days passed, with no sign of the next Japanese move. Then, on the morning of 2 September, the senior commanders were ordered to witness the execution of the men who had tried to escape. The victims were dragged to Selarang Beach and ordered to dig their own graves. Corporal Breavington, one of the two Australians from Bukit Timah, pleaded that his comrade should be spared, saying that he ordered him to escape with him. His plea was rejected, and the Japanese followed up this cold-blooded execution with an order that all the British and Australian prisoners apart from those in hospital were to assemble on Selarang Barrack square. This assembly, ordered at midday, had to be finished in 5 hours, and that night 15,400 men were crammed on the square with only two water taps and totally inadequate latrine facilities. There they were kept for 3 days until the British and Australian commanders ordered their men to sign the undertaking not to escape.

When it has not been possible to persuade prisoners to give their parole, some captor nations have tried to ease their control problems with reprisal punishments. Reprisals are prohibited by the Geneva

Convention, and in the twentieth century they may seem archaic; the truth is that more often than not they have been resorted to as a convenient cloak for disregarding the laws of war. Because some reprisals have proved effective in the past, however, POWs of the future will undoubtedly be victims to other reprisals. Sadly enough reprisals always evoke counter-reprisals, and the wretched POWs are always the victims.

What happened at Stalag IIIE at Kirchhain on the northern borders of Saxony, will serve as an example of a simple but brutal reprisal instituted because of an escape. In October 1941, Stalag IIIE was crowded with French, Belgian, Serbian and British other ranks. Guarding the camp was not easy and when 12 men managed to break out, the Germans decided to discourage other attempts at escaping. All the other inmates of the camp were deprived of their boots and compelled at rifle point to trot round a field in wooden clogs for nearly 3 hours. As most of the men involved were in a poor physical state this form of collective punishment was a brutal way of demonstrating authority. But incidents like this—though common enough— do not exemplify the real use of reprisals, which is to pressurize the captor's opponents. In October 1942 the Nazi Government decided to try to curb the activities of Allied commandos, and to do this they instituted reprisals against the POWs incarcerated in Oflag VIIB and Eichstaett.

Many of the most troublesome inmates of other German Oflags had been sent to Eichstaett, where their behaviour had led to a number of minor restrictions which had been termed reprisals. But none of these had any connection with what happened at the roll-call on 8 October. To their utter bewilderment 107 officers and 20 other ranks taken prisoners at Dieppe were fallen out, their hands were tied with rope, and they remained in this state for 12 hours daily. This, the commandant explained, was a reprisal ordered by the German High Command for British ill-treatment of German prisoners at the time of the Dieppe raid and also during a commando raid on Sark. Three days after this first announcement came a second. This said that, as German prisoners in England were now being bound, the reprisals would now apply to three times the present numbers. So more prisoners were marched off and placed in handcuffs, which had by then been substituted for the original rope.

It is fair to say that many of the German guards responsible for carrying out the reprisals were sympathetic towards the prisoners and disgusted with the whole business. And as time went on conditions were relaxed. The original tight handcuffs which raised callouses on the prisoners' wrists were replaced by police fetters which had a comfortable length of chain between the cuffs. Meanwhile many of the prisoners had found that the handcuffs could be opened with a nail, and a good many began taking them off while they were out of sight of the guards. The guards themselves began the practice of simply leaving the right numbers of manacles in each room, and leaving it to the prisoners themselves to decide who should put them on.

Eichstaett was not the only camp where shackling was imposed. On 9 October, 1500 British and Canadian prisoners in Stalag VIIIB at Lamsdorf had their hands tied with 18-inch lengths of Red Cross string. Four days later they were joined by another 800, and the issue of Red Cross parcels, and mail was discontinued; shortly after that all sports, concerts and educational classes were forbidden. All these restrictions entailed considerable hardship for the men involved, and if the restrictions had not been lifted in December, the prisoners would have had a dismal winter.

While such reprisals can never be condoned, it is obvious that punishment may well have to be imposed if discipline is to be maintained in a POW camp. Even in a society where captives and captors share a similar culture, the young and wildly frustrated among the prisoners will be inclined to do everything in their power to annoy their guards. At Laufen Cyril Whitcombe found that attempts to annoy the German guards often succeeded, but success did not always have the best results for others:

> The Poles before us had been far worse; unfortunately for us they had used the windows to shout rude remarks at the sentries and if possible drop things on their heads. The result was the sentries were apt to fire at anyone they saw near a window whatever they were doing there. Tragedy soon followed our arrival and of course it was an innocent who suffered. The top windows of one block (3rd floor, I think) gave a magnificent view of the country-side and distant mountains and our people were in the habit of going up there just to have a look and drink it all in. I, myself was yelled at by a sentry for being there and moved slowly but firmly away. A few days later one officer went up there to sketch and was sitting at the window oblivious of outside noises when he was shot through the head by a sentry in a box far below on the river bank. The Americans were then our protecting power and an appeal was sent to them. They were horrified at the fact that the sentries shot *into* the camp, but they were never as successful as the Swiss were later on in getting the Germans to do anything.

Where the ethnic, racial and cultural backgrounds of captors and captives are very different the imposition of discipline is likely to create even worse situations. Soldiers of the Imperial Japanese Army were brought up to believe that military honour dictated no sur-render, and training manuals of the Japanese fighting forces contained the warning that 'Those becoming prisoners of war will suffer the death penalty'. Men who were in danger of falling into enemy hands were instructed to attack, escape or commit suicide. Consequently the attitude of Japanese troops towards the prisoners of war of their enemies tended to be one of contempt, and this was reflected in the attitudes of the guards. Since POWs were little better than dead men their living conditions were of no importance. Moreover, as British and American POWs were members of enemy nations which in the past had been patronizing and superior, their loss of face should be made apparent to themselves and to the peoples of the East which Japan was supposed to be liberating. Thus the beatings, the mass punishments, the tortures, beheadings, callous neglect and murder of Allied POWs in the Far East could be explicable in terms of the military code, *Bushido*. Unfortunately the sadistic complexes of individual guards often played a part also, and the circumstances of some of the bayonetings and beheadings of recaptured prisoners suggest that those who took part in these dastardly crimes were motivated by something more than a sense of duty.

Strangely enough there appears to be a limit beyond which humili-ation loses its power as a disciplinary weapon.

The fittest survived [writes Colonel Thomas]* but each man, I am sure, was continually asking himself, as I was, how much longer can I go on being so lucky. Yet there was still a pact with oneself to survive but what the hell for then God only knows.

The humiliation which the Japs exploited fully, particularly as far as officers were concerned was of little importance long before. Once one has been so thoroughly humiliated as we all were very early on in our captivity further instances were relative and unimportant.

There was not very much brutality. I myself suffered 14 days solitary confinement and the Commandant made great play of presenting me with a fan at the conclusion of it. The Bushido spirit—we were sick of it and the deep, oriental insincerity of the Japanese officers responsible for our welfare. But stick a couple of hundred Britons in a shanty camp in North Korea, give them the absolute minimum of sustenance, plenty of hard work, no books, papers, news or letters and leave them to get on with it with no chance to escape and if they wish to continue to live under those circumstances then they must have faith in something—was it God or Winston Churchill? . . .

*Letter to the author.

1–2 The moment of capture. The expressions on the faces of these two PoWs are eloquent of their despair and hopelessness. The top picture is of a German taken at Stalingrad; the lower of a 16-year-old German youth who surrendered at Lemgo in 1945.

3–4   These men are soldiers, owing their lives to the sufferance of their captors, no longer effective in the business of war, and embarrassments to their captors.

5 *Turks captured in Mesopotamia in World War I tramping into captivity.*

6 *Exhausted by their recent shattering experience, hungry, thirsty and depressed, these newly captured French colonial troops have flopped down to rest.*

7   This photograph of recently captured German PoWs illustrates the magnitude of the problems of accommodation, feeding, guarding and control which face the captors. Men from this camp at Sinzig were sent to rebuild France.

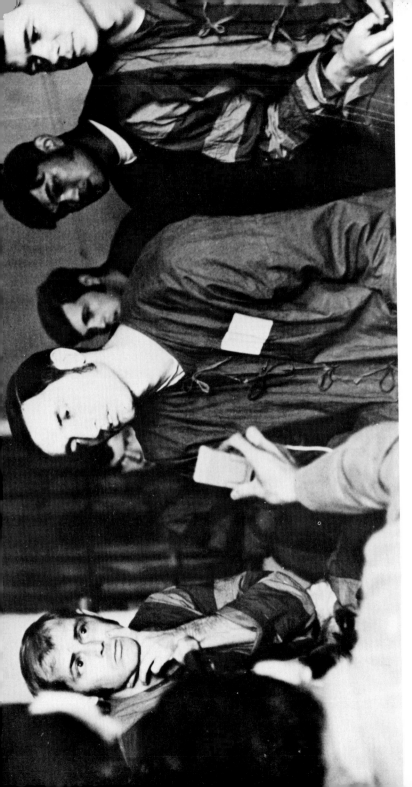

10 *Interrogation. These captured American pilots are being questioned for propaganda purposes at the 'Hanoi Hilton'.*

11 *American prisoners feeding pigeons in a Vietnamese PoW camp. Photographs like this were taken to support claims by anti-war activists in the US that PoWs were being well treated.*

12   Stalag VII A, a cosmopolitan, overcrowded and dirty camp in Bavaria.
The tub contains the daily rations for 360 PoWs.

14   Entertainment of Oflag 7D, Querum near Brunswick. This camp was surrounded by military targets and in air raids on the Brunswick area the PoWs suffered casualties.

n G. T. Valentine, a Canadian officer captured at Dieppe in 1942,
acles at Oflag VII B Eichstaett.

21   *German PoWs were used to lift mines after World War II. In Holland alone 210 Germans were killed, 200 were repatriated as cripples and 460 others were wounded in the course of this work—which is prohibited by the terms of the Geneva Convention.*

Communism, Chairman Mao, Ho Chi Minh or other appropriate dignitaries obviously substitute for God and Winston Churchill to sustain Communist POWs whose faith is not shaken by their contact with capitalist society. And this adds further complications to the problems of control and discipline. Ideological fanatics are unable to understand others, and so every act of those opposing them—however innocent or beneficial it may be—is considered perverse. The inevitable result is bitterness between captors and captives. As captives such men have been known to incite riots not only to undermine and disrupt the authority of their guards, but to discredit the captor nation in the eyes of neutral states. Such was the purpose of the riots on Koje Island during the Korean War. As captors the same sort of individuals, brought up to have little regard for human values in respect of their own nationals can hardly be expected to act differently towards the prisoners they take. Reconciling these two opposing views is a difficult if not impossible task.

When all is said and done however, prisoners of war must be kept under control, and they are subject to the laws, regulations and orders in force in the armed forces of their captors.* This requires them to show due respect for those senior in rank. In normal circumstances, of course, prisoners of war will organize and control themselves according to their own disciplinary code. After the fall of Singapore discipline and administration was quickly re-established in Changi. But POWs have a tendency to view the trappings of army discipline with mixed feelings and to many of the other ranks prisoners ceremonial parades, military lectures and a lot of the routine chores they were ordered to carry out seemed petty and irksome. The insistence of senior officers that the distinction between 'officers and gentlemen' and 'other ranks' should be preserved also rang hollow to many who had seen their comrades die in battle or captivity, and knew that heroism and cowardice were no respecters of rank. The same sort of situation has arisen among American prisoners captured during the Korean War and Vietnam. And in both of these wars the Communist captors have exploited a lack of discipline to promote their indoctrination programme. Sooner or later there is a day of reckoning, however. After the Korean War the behaviour of 565 American ex-prisoners was the subject of intensive investigation, and 192 were deemed to have committed misdemeanours; 21 others refused repatriation.† More recently it has been announced that some of the American prisoners in Vietnam face court-martial charges for making anti-war statements without per-

---

* Article 82 of the 1949 Geneva Convention.
† Some did eventually return home, but three are still alive in the Far East. The rest are dead.

mission (which was generally granted if the statement was made under duress).

Permitting prisoners to organize and administer themselves is a convenient method of easing the problem of guards and discipline, and in camps run by the Western powers there has been a tendency to encourage it. Apart from saving labour, 'indirect' control has much of the appearance and some of the reality of democracy. In practice however, the system is subject to serious abuses. Where men of conflicting beliefs are involved it is bound to work badly. At the British Cultybraggan camp in Perthshire, for instance, Feldwebel Wolfgang Rosterg was tried and lynched by other German prisoners in December 1944 because they believed that he had betrayed a group of ardent Nazis, who were planning an escape.* Similarly, in the Koje Island camps in Korea, fanatical Communist prisoners murdered non-Communist prisoners in order to establish Communist control of the camps. In other circumstances it is not difficult to appreciate that a racial majority may maltreat a racial minority. At best, the men who are favoured by their captors can be expected to gain control.

> At the Dulag [writes J. V. Webb†] the British liaison officer was an Airborne sergeant who had been captured on D-Day and who had by the beginning of September 1944 achieved a very powerful position. He was in charge of the distribution of Red Cross parcels, and always had unlimited cigarettes to exchange with newly-arrived prisoners for their gold rings, wrist watches or other valuables. It was said, with great bitterness, that he had dropped on D-Day with his Stalag disc in his hand! . . .

In Java, where Sidney Sheldrick was a prisoner of the Japanese a group of British military police ran the camp.

> . . . when the Nips decided to remove our officers [he writes‡] presumably because they wished to reduce our resistance, our discipline then depended upon our senior NCOs and whether we liked it or not, we had to have some form of self-control within the camp or the Japs would have taken over themselves within the camp and that would have been terrible. So anyway our senior Warrant Officer assured the Japs we would instill discipline. So as we had half a dozen Redcaps led by the notorious Sgt 'Bash' Vernon they took over control of the camp.

---

* Six of those who judged and executed Rosterg were subsequently tried and convicted of murder.
† Letter to the author.
‡ Letter to the author.

Quite frankly this was not a good thing as power went to their heads and to keep themselves in with the Nips they did indeed lean hard on us all. . . .

If there is any lesson to be drawn from these examples of self-government it is that a POW camp is not a normal town that can be left entirely to a normal and self-contained life. The ideal, of course, is to make life as normal as possible, and there are bound to be occasions when guards will have to enforce discipline. This is recognized by the Geneva Convention which specifies sanctions which can be imposed on POWs who get out of hand. Such sanctions include fines of up to half a prisoner's monthly pay, discontinuance of 'extra privileges', fatigue duties for other ranks and confinement. As in criminal law the punishment is supposed to fit the crime, and the scale of crimes has tended to vary according to the views of the captors. The Nazis, for example, were concerned about preserving their Aryan supremacy, and POWs who fell in German hands were warned that association with a German woman carried the death penalty at worst or 10 years in gaol at best. Italians, Russians, British and Americans took a somewhat more permissive view, and even the Germans were prepared to turn a blunt eye to POW romances with alien females of their slave labour force who sometimes worked in close proximity to the prisoners. But the punishments which have been described are obviously open to abuse.

The most serious punishments have usually been incurred as a result of attempts to escape. Escape itself is no crime; indeed it is generally accepted that it is consistent with military honour to escape, and the idea that a man is committed to gaol because he has done wrong cannot apply to prisoners of war. But captor states usually get around this by sentencing escapers for other acts committed in connection with escape. And in reality, punishment, even extreme punishment, for escape has been frequent. With the Japanese there was only one punishment for recaptured escapers—execution. The Russians were also prone to shoot escaping prisoners. The German attitude was generally more humane. Recaptured escapers were usually sent to a military prison. But many of the officers who came to be regarded as habitual escapers or constant trouble-makers were sent to Oflag IVC at Colditz, not far from Leipzig in Saxony. Colditz was not supposed to be a punishment camp but merely one that was escape-proof. But conditions in the old castle-like group of stone buildings were extremely bad, basically because it was overcrowded, and supervision was unnecessarily harsh.

Unfortunately the German record for relatively humane treatment of escapers was broken in April 1944 following a mass escape from

Stalag Luft III in the last week of March. Seventy-six prisoners broke out of the camp through a tunnel, before the alarm was given. Three of them eventually reached England, a few got to Danzig, the Czech, the Swiss and the Danish borders but the majority were caught within 50 miles of Sagan. All of them were wearing civilian-type clothing, and the Germans used this as an excuse for disregarding their POW status. Fifty of the recaptured prisoners were separately interrogated and then put in a car and driven out into the country. There, on orders signed by Himmler and Kaltenbrunner, they were executed by members of the Gestapo. The Nazis tried to keep secret the true fate of the Sagan Fifty. 'Orders carried out, prisoners shot while trying to escape', read the official report in every case. But the truth leaked out, and suspicion of murder quickly gave way to shocked realization of the tragic actuality.* Apprehensive of an uprising among the millions of foreign workers and POWs in Germany at a time when the Wehrmacht was losing the war on every front, the Nazis had decided to try to discourage attempts to escape from POW camps.

What happened at Sagan has come to be seen as a war crime—a subject on which much literature has been published since World War II. Despite this, few people are clear about the 'laws of war' which make POWs liable to punishment for crimes committed in violation of the rules and customs of international law. Many find the phrase 'laws of war' absurd. War, after all, sanctions acts that civilians label crimes—arson, murder, kidnapping. As C. P. Snow once remarked, 'More hideous crimes have been committed in the name of obedience than have ever been committed in the name of rebellion.' Some of the basic concepts of the laws of war have been expressed in the Geneva Convention. But many more are unwritten international undertakings respected by some countries and not others, and subject to different interpretations. The overall key theme, however, is that fighting men may not go beyond strict military requirements and their actions should be governed by humanity and chivalry.

Any violation of these somewhat vague principles of humanity and chivalry can therefore be dubbed a war crime. A soldier may kill an enemy civilian who attacks him, for example, but he must not harm those who do not. Defeated enemy troops, wounded, aviators who have parachuted from disabled aircraft and other helpless individuals must be well treated. Hospitals, churches, museums and coastal fishing boats are not supposed to be attacked unless they are

---

* Twenty-two men were subsequently put on trial in Hamburg as war criminals, and 13 of those directly responsible for the murder of the Sagan prisoners were hanged on 26 February 1948.

used for military purposes; torture, looting and political assassination are banned; reprisals against illegal enemy acts are permitted only on the highest authority—and never against civilians. And so on.

Behind the barbed wire, a POW who collaborates with the enemy or supplies information about his fellow prisoners may well find himself facing war crime charges when he goes home. After the Korean War six American soldiers were tried and convicted of war crimes perpetrated in prison camps in North Korea. In one case an officer was accused by 180 other POWs of making anti-American speeches, informing on fellow prisoners, hoarding food, taking classes on Communism, and ordering men to sign peace petitions. In another case a sergeant was accused of giving information about his fellow prisoners, beating a sick man, stealing a wallet from another, forcing yet another prisoner out into the snow and leaving him there to die, and drowning three UN prisoners crossing a stream. One US officer allegedly sought to curry favour with the guards of the camp to which he was sent. 'The more men who die here,' he is supposed to have announced, 'the more food for the rest of us.' At the time of writing, the behaviour of some Americans captured in Vietnam is being investigated. Mercifully the number involved is small.

'Confessions', oral or written, true or false, may well result in prisoners of war being indicted as war criminals—either by the captors or by the prisoners' own state when he returns home. The extraction of confessions is a comparatively recent technique used by the Communist Bloc countries who have made a significant reservation to Article 85 of the 1949 Geneva Convention. Under this reservation a prisoner of war who may be convicted of an alleged war crime under the laws of the captors loses the protection of the Convention. In Korea, UN prisoners who made and signed statement which would be interpreted as confessions found that they had provided evidence for a war crime charge to be brought against themselves. They also found that they had signed away any protection due to them under the Geneva Convention—including repatriation until their sentence was served.

How a confession is extracted may be as relevant to a prisoner's guilt as its substance. Under torture a man may eventually confess to almost any crime. Under normal circumstances it seems unlikely that prisoners would voluntarily confess their crimes, knowing that their captors were proposing to punish them on the basis of what they confessed. Moreover if a prisoner does volunteer a statement and it is used for propaganda purposes, sooner or later he will have to answer to his own side for what he has done. The conclusion is that any confession at all may result in him having to answer charges as a war criminal; so his best course of action is to keep silent.

Finally there is the question of the relations between captors and captives. Like so many aspects of the life of a POW it is not easy to generalize on this. At the moment of capture the transformation from fighting man to prisoner of war is bound to be abrupt and difficult; in an age of conflicting ideologies with propaganda machines blaring out messages of hatred and fear, the chagrin and distress are likely to be worse than ever. Right up to the moment of capture captors and their prisoners are trying to kill each other. Then, without any change in their loyalties the relationship between the self-same people undergoes a radical metamorphosis. Past hatreds still exist but both sides are expected to show forbearance with each other. Respect for the enemy, or regard for his ruthlessness perhaps plays a great part in proceedings. H. O. Whiting had little respect for the Italians guarding his camp at Capua.*

> Although I have never been able to forget the attitude of the Italian guards towards and their actions against the POWs, they changed towards the end of *their* freedom and baiting by the prisoners—always to the maximum within the bounds of safety—obviously increased. The Germans were found to be a different kettle of fish, however, and reinforced their discipline requirements with bursts of machine gun fire across the compound. No one argued. . . .

How the war is progressing will also tend to influence the attitude of the guards. Colonel Cyril Whitcombe noted that when he was captured in 1940

> . . . the Germans were infuriating—they strutted about in front of us and expected us to salute them whenever we saw them. We got over this by never wearing headgear, even if we had it, and told them that British officers never saluted when bareheaded. They told us that we were all privates—even the General—and that we must all salute very German whatever their rank. Needless to say we ignored this and them. The Adjutant, a large dugout Prussian subaltern came on parade in his very best uniform just to make us poor sods feel small in our tattered battledress, our shaved heads and our yellow faces. They can't have got much satisfaction out of it and it only made it more difficult for them to control us. . . .

By mid-1944, however, it was becoming apparent that Germany had lost the war, attitudes changed. '. . . it did seem to improve the guards' opinion of us, if they had suffered a heavy and successful

---

* Letter to the author.

air raid,' writes J. V. Webb, 'whereas they tended to become arrogant if they had been left in peace for a week or more. . . .'

Oriental attitudes do not vary in the same way. The harshness and brutality of Japanese guards at camps in the Far East persisted up to V-J Day; North Korean and Chinese guards did not soften their treatment of UN prisoners when the Korean truce came into being. In Vietnam the guards are said to have behaved consistently throughout the war, and the intensive bombing of Hanoi did not modify their approach to US prisoners either one way or the other.

Perhaps the last word on prisoner–guard relationship should come from a prisoner and his guard. Twenty-five years after his release from captivity, Cyril Whitcombe took his wife to the locale of his POW days at Laufen. Little remained of the old prison camp; the wire and fences had long been dismantled and an old people's home had been built on the site. But there were some relics:

> At a little tea-shop outside the entrance, we drank tea and ate buns. The proprietor, noticing foreigners, came round and I told him I had been here during the war. It turned out he had been a sentry though not when I was there. Anyhow he insisted on taking us over the place, marching us round the village and introducing us to all his friends. . . . Just before parting I said to him, 'You don't know how fed up I got, tramping round and round this green inside the wire." He replied, 'You don't know how bored I got marching up and down *outside* the wire.'

10
Consolations
and Diversions

That there can be any sort of consolation in a POW camp may seem strange, but it is a man's nature to seek consolation and most adaptable men can rationalize benefits from their situation. At the same time it would be inaccurate to give the impression that all such adaptability is merely rationalization; letters from some ex-prisoners of war seem to show a genuine conviction that imprisonment has its riches.

Writing about his captivity in Hong Kong, George Johnstone,* an officer of the Royal Army Dental Corps, said:

> I think I may be forgiven if I assume that a full appreciation of the circumstances of that life is denied to him who has not experienced it. How can the uninitiated know the thrill of writing from memory the full words and music of one of the Gilbert and Sullivan operas, or of recalling the lines of some classic in the realm of literature, or of making from empty cigarette packets and other scraps, the necessary properties and paper money for that excellent time-passing game 'Monopoly'? Or can they understand how, even at a time when morale was at its highest and life seemed to have relatively few snags, there was always that undercurrent of doubt as to whether our captors would appreciate our latest attempts to amuse ourselves, or whether they would read into our humble efforts all sorts of insults to themselves? Or how can anyone know the real joy of receiving a Red Cross food parcel without having lived on a diet of boiled rice and filthy green vegetables or stewed chrysanthemum leaves? . . .
>
> . . . It is rather amusing to look back on some of the more outstanding contrasts between the normal peacetime occupations and those brought about by necessity; the banker—nursing orderly,

* Captain (later Lieut-Colonel) G. Johnstone: letter to the author from Colonel W. B. Purnell.

the policeman—a patcher of shirts and shorts, the stockbroker—baker, the lawyer—boot repairer, or the shipping magnate—bricklayer. Everyone found something with which to occupy his time, either for the benefit of all or, in his leisure hours, to increase his knowledge.

Classes of all kinds were conducted, mostly in the open air—book-keeping and accountancy, motor mechanics, languages (about fifteen in all), elementary classes for medical students, history, literature, architecture, and many others. Some of these classes were in the nature of general lectures and perhaps ought to be thought of more as entertainment. In this field there was great variety, band concerts, musical shows, plays, camp farces, etc. It would be difficult to know who had more pleasure from this aspect of camp life, the players in rehearsals and performances, or their audiences; but certainly all were, for a time, transported from the sordid circumstances in which we lived to some better and more pleasant place. . . .

Amateur dramatics have provided recreation and consolation in POW camps throughout the world. Even in the primitive 'animal' camp at Yelabuga holding some 20,000 German prisoners during World War II the favourite recreation was theatricals. Plays by Chekhov, Gogol and Gorki were staged with the approval of the Russians. Texts translated into German were vetted and Russian censors attended the performances. Despite this the prisoners managed to get sly digs at their captors by the frequent use of a Russian word such as 'ponimayesh' ('Do you understand?'). Another favourite interpolation was 'zabrali' ('it was taken'), which was brought in at every possible opportunity to remind the audience of what had happened to their personal possessions when they were captured. Sketches written by the POWs themselves at this camp were also staged, and these were deliberately and blatantly pro-Communist because they helped the prisoners to get permission to continue their theatricals.

In difficulties analogous to those of the German POWs in Russia, theatricals were a consolation in the Japanese camps. Sidney Sheldrick, who has described himself as "a proper little Cockney runt of a Lance-Jack' was a POW in the Dutch East Indies.

We have some happy memories [he writes], such as the time when the Nips allowed us to put on a play. We had a fair amount of talent at that time and so *The Merchant of Venice* was put on, and the acting was very fair indeed. In fact so good was the lad who played Portia the Japs demanded an inspection on the spot as they suspected he was a bird . . . so much like a bird, however, that ever after during captivity he was known as 'Portia'.

Under the conditions in which POWs live a certain amount of homosexuality is inevitable, and in some camps dressing up as a woman turned out to be a perilous pastime. Jim Witte writes:

> The camp theatre was a great institution in Sulmona. Its production company put on many good shows from the *Belle of New York* to the *Second Mrs. Tanqueray*. The girls really looked like girls and anyone of them would have given Danny La Rue a good run for his money. Dutiful swains used to wait outside the theatre for the girls to appear after the show. They couldn't take them to dinner so they took them, instead, to quiet places in the compound. The trouble was, though, that there was very little privacy for love affairs of this nature. The boy friends used to get very jealous if you so much as glanced at their girl friends. There was a corporal in the Military Police who was violently in love with one of the actresses called Jerry. Both were missing during a roll call and were found snuggled down under a blanket in a corner of another compound. This amused the Italians who put them into solitary together for a week. They weren't so keen on one another after that.
>
> Another gorgeous piece was Frankie, who had the touch of the tarbrush about her. When she took a bath half the camp used to come and watch.

As a consolation, homosexuality served only a few. Like normal sex its impetus depended on food, climate, conditions and opportunity. According to Sheldrick:*

> The first thing to go was our sex urge. The craving for food was with us at all times . . . so low we were in vitality that had we seen a bowl of rice and a naked bird in a hut she would have got killed in the rush for the rice. . . .

Witte's experience in Sulmona was similar:

> During the winter months when Italian rations were poor and the issue of Red Cross parcels irregular, love took a back seat. But when summer arrived Cupid came into his own again. This was because there was a steady flow of parcels and the Italian stew thickened up.

In Yelabuga the Germans found the most effective deterrent against homosexuality was publicity. A senior officer or camp leader would pass the word round that Mr and Mrs so-and-so had been

* Letter to the author.

seen together again the previous evening. The culprits were tried and sometimes a silence ban imposed. Not being allowed to speak to anyone and not to be spoken to by anyone is unpleasant enough anywhere; in a POW camp it is a dreadful sanction.

Opportunities providing an outlet for conventional sexual activity are a rare feature of POW life. In an Eastern theatre of war they are less likely to occur than in the West, and when the captors are ideological fanatics the chance of men having any contact with women at all may well be zero. In World War II men who were prisoners of the Japanese had brief encounters with local women outside their working camps. But these were very rare. In Korea and Vietnam it is extremely unlikely that any illicit liaison ever occurred. In Europe, America and in the Soviet Union, however, the odd prisoner had sexual adventures. In some cases these could be said to have ended happily when they were legitimized in marriage after the war.

From the POW camp at Evansville, Indiana, almost all of the escapes attempted by German POWs had the same short term objective—the brothel area in the town. In Germany J. V. Webb recalls that one man in his working party attracted the notice of a good-looking German girl. 'She used to visit our working site several times a week; they would retire discreetly into a bombed building, and emerge an hour later with satisfied smiles, and filled with the bottle of brandy she invariably brought.' In Poland 'Jock' Ferguson remembered the adage attributed to Napoleon: 'The women are everything and the men are nothing when discussing Polish people.' In the factory, where Ferguson was set to work,

> The women came from every walk of life. There was Zoshia, who could trace her family back to the counts of the Polish kings—and there were girls all the way down the social scale until you came to a lady nick-named 'Two-fag Annie'. We all made the best of it, some more than others! Most of their menfolk were either dead or prisoners somewhere, so they were not averse to male company, especially males who seemed to have lots of scented soap. . . . After a week or so we all had a girl friend except the misogynist. . . .

Jim Witte also had his moments. Working in the railway workshops in 1944 he struck up a friendship with the German girl driver of an overhead crane. When attempts to consummate the friendship in the cab of the crane were thwarted, his affections were focused on a robust Belgian girl who worked in another part of the factory. A fellow Belgian worker acted as go-between, and for some weeks the two lovers ran a successful affair—terminated when Witte was seen climbing out of the factory window en route to a rendezvous with his girl friend.

In less prepossessing circumstances Erwin Herman also managed to have a series of love affairs in Russia. Captured at Stalingrad, he survived the initial trek back to a POW assembly area near the Volga, where all the German prisoners were stripped and their bodies examined for vermin. The examination was carried out by a blowzy middle-aged Russian nurse using an electric torch to probe the intimate regions of the men's bodies. Those whom she took a fancy to were segregated for duty in the Russian women's quarters. Escaping from this camp Herman lived for a time with the wife of a Soviet officer fighting in Germany. Finally his life in the penal camp at Karabas was eased by the attentions of another Russian nurse.

In the absence of normal sexual outlets masturbation is to be expected among those who found celibacy too trying and it appears to have been widely practised in the POW camps of World War II. Younger men who had little or only spasmodic experience, or perhaps had not even sampled the delights of sex before captivity were probably less prone to indulge than married men. The latter, when they had nothing to do and when their stomachs were full, would re-live their courting days, the wedding night, the honeymoon and Sunday afternoons on the carpet. Witte recalls that at Sulmona there were onanists who could not stop.

> Poor wretches who earned the contempt of their fellows in their huts which manifested itself in descriptive epithets like 'bishop bashers', 'mutton floggers' and 'wire-pullers'. The penis became 'the one-eyed milkman', and the hand 'the five-fingered widow'.

To the great majority of POWs, whose sexual outlets are restrained, the absence of women is reflected in songs and humour. Bawdy ditties were great favourites at camp sing-songs in World War II. Some, like 'When this bloody war is over', were revivals of Anglo-American songs of World War I. Others of a later vintage were given new verses to fit POW camp life. One of these concerned the advantages of 'My brother Sylveste'.

> Have you heard about the great big man?
> Who lives in a caravan? . . .
> That's my brother, Sylveste,
> What's he got
> He's got the row of forty medals on his chest,
> > Big chest,

He killed forty niggers in the west,
He takes no rest,
Big as a man,
Hell fire,
Son of a gun,
Don't push,
Just shove
Plenty of room for you and me,
He's got an arm
Like a leg, a lady's leg,

And a punch that'll sink a Battle ship,
                    Big ship,

It needs all the army and the navy
To put the wind up—Who?
Sylveste.

Now he thought he'd take a trip to Italy,
He thought he'd take a trip by sea.
So he jumped off the harbour in New York
And he swam like a man made of cork.
He saw the Louisiana in distress.
What could he do?
He swallowed all the water in the sea,
                    Big swallow,

He put the Louisiana on his chest
And took the whole bloody lot to Italy.
Now he rowed across the Med to Africa
And he landed on the beach at Li-bi-yah,
He ate up the desert in a gulp,
                    Big gulp,

And he mashed all the Nazis to a pulp,
                    Big mash,

He sang a song as he churned up all the sand
He's got a voice like the Royal Fusiliers Massed Band,
                    Big Band,

He's got a chest like a bloody armour plate
He's the boy that the Gerries love to hate.

Other songs were written around the time and place. The text and
the tune of *The Kriegie Ballad*, for example (written by the Scottish
poet Robert Garioch), told the story of the fall of Tobruk, and

captivity in Africa and Italy. Sung to a traditional Irish tune the words were as follows:

Tooralie Ooralie addy-ee-ay
Here's hoping we're not here to stay

Yes, this is the place we were took, sir,
And landed right into the bag,
Right outside the town of Tobruk, sir,
So now for some bloody stalag.

There was plenty of water at Derna,
But that camp was not very well kept
For either you slept in the piss-hole,
Or pissed in the place where you slept.

And then we went on to Benghazi,
We had plenty of room, what a treat!
But I wish that the guard was a Nazi,
He might find us something to eat.

With hunger we're nearly demented,
You can see it at once by our looks.
The only ones really contented
Are the greasy fat bastards of cooks.

We were promised a treat for our Christmas
Of thick pasta-shoota, all hot,
But somehow the cooks got a transfer
And shot out of sight with the lot.

So somewhere they wish us good wishes
That we're not all feeling too queer,
And while they are guzzling our pasta
They wish us a happy New Year.

Current hit songs also enlivened many a prisoner's hour. Sydney Sheldrick recalls the ones that were sung in Sumatra:*

Songs we sung?... Stone me yes!... you remember Vera Lynn singing *Yours*? well for nigh on four years that was our latest song and we wore it out more or less. A number of quite good songs were in fact composed by some of our more talented lads and I recall one entitled *When we sail down the river to the Sea*, a very good ballad with some excellent words but sad to say although every word seemed to be engraved upon our minds then, after so many years it is as much as I can do to remember half a dozen now. We did make our own amusements and we staged

* Letter to the author.

camp concerts once a month until near the end when even the effort of singing or laughing was almost too much for the survivors. I recall a Manchester lad whose name—damn it is on the tip of my tongue and I may recall by the time I finish this letter—singing so very good as Tom Jones himself . . . Ah I remember. . . . Tommy Burns was his name and I have never heard such a good voice in such terrible circumstances and that goes too for other amateur artists that did their best to cheer us up.

On the other side of the hill, Lale Andersen was to the Germans what Vera Lynn was to the British, and the haunting bars of *Lili Marlene* sounded in POW camps from the Volga to the Nile, and from the Rhine to the Mississippi between 1943 and 1949.

More recently, with the introduction of the ideological war, songs and doggerel attributed to POWs have become fashionable. Propaganda material like the 'Hanoi Hilton Song'

> When I crashed in the Red River Valley
> My Jet had been hit by a SAM.
> I was captured by a posse of peasants
> And my life as a prisoner began.
>
> I have moved to the Hanoi Hilton
> With its radio, close shaves and good books
> New clothes, twin blankets and tooth paste
> Hot soup, good rice from the cooks,

can hardly be classed as consolation material.

POW humour followed the same pattern as the songs. Much of it was bawdy, some was sadly nostalgic, and some was based on provocation.

Sir John Burns who worked on the Burma–Siam railway will always associate the solders' version of *Colonel Bogey*—'Bollocks and the same to you'—with an incident at one of the camps in Siam.

A British other rank had been caught by the Japanese outside the wire which surrounded the camp, trading with the Thais. This was not uncommon. The Thais would buy most things and the rewards were considered by many to be worth the risk. Unfortunately, it led to thieving within the camp which could be tragic when one's possessions were so few and those few so precious. The Japanese camp commandant was in benign mood. Instead of having the man beaten with male bamboo, or stood to attention for 24 hours in front of the guard room, or worse, he sentenced him to be paraded round the camp with a placard hung round his neck on which was written in large letters 'I have been caught trading outside the wire. I am sorry. I will not do it again'. It was a lesson and a warning to other prisoners. To draw attention to the man on his journey round the camp three British prisoner musicians were ordered to accompany him and the Japanese armed sentry, whose orders were to parade all four all round the camp. I forget the instruments the British carried—shall we say a clarinet, a saxophone and a violin. It was the 'yazmi' day, the half day's holiday from the railway which the prisoners were allowed each week. It was the afternoon and the majority of the prisoners were lying on the bamboo slats of their huts, sleeping perhaps, or re-reading old letters, or maybe just chatting. The first hut to be visited were aroused by the strains of Colonel Bogey played by the oddly assorted trio and, curiosity awakened, they crowded to the door or peered beneath the eaves. The strange sight of an armed Japanese sentry, a placarded prisoner and the band met their eyes. The strains of Colonel Bogey grew louder and were greeted by gales of laughter. Through everybody's mind ran the words 'Bollocks and the same to you, Bollocks and the same to you'.

Fortunately, no one sang them and equally fortunately, the Japanese sentry imagined the laughter was directed at the placarded prisoner. The one thing the Japanese cannot stand is to be made fun of, to be laughed at and had they suspected the truth of the laughter which met the little band, the punishment meted out to the three musicians would not have been benign and each of them must have known this as clearly as everyone else did. 'Bollocks and the same to you, Bollocks and the same to you.' Now the doors of all the huts were crowded and everywhere in their perambulation round the camp their arrival was greeted with great gales of laughter. 'Bollocks and the same to you, bollocks and the same to you.'

The three musicians would never know just what they had done for their fellow prisoners. An afternoon of laughter, true, free flowing laughter, something to be treasured, to be taken out from time to time in the dismal, weary months ahead from the pigeon hole of memory, to be talked about and smiled over and to draw strength from as one hummed to oneself 'Bollocks and the same to you, bollocks and the same to you'. Today, more than twenty-five years on, it is still a treasured memory and humbly I salute that British band of three. 'Bollocks and the same to you, bollocks and the same to you.'

So many aspects of POW life had a humorous side. German censorship forbade adverse criticism of prison camps but the captives usually beat the censor in the long run. In the early days of the war one man wrote home thus:

We are housed in comfortable quarters and not overcrowded. There is generous provision for sports and amusements. Food is good and plentiful and well served. Our captors treat us well in every way.

Tell all this to your friends in the Navy, the Army and the Air Force. And you can tell it to the Marines as well.

The Rev. J. S. Naylor who was a POW in Italy, has recorded in his diary an incident headed 'Toujours la Politesse' . . . . Overheard in the camp: 'Here, use my knife. Its quite clean—I've just licked it.'

Even escapes and the preparations made for them had a humorous side on occasions, as Bill Ashton, a POW in Oflag 7B recounts:

One day I was sitting on the latrines in company with about a dozen other officers. Opposite was a trough used as a urinal and in due course a kilted officer made his appearance and began to use the trough. But before he got under way a very young officer standing nearby said, 'Excuse me, but would you be kind enough to urinate in this tin?'

With the least hesitation and with only a vestige of a raising of the eyebrows the Scot lifted his kilt and, exposing a very manly pair of testicles, did as he was requested and gave very good measure.

The very young officer thanked him courteously and, carrying his tin of urine with the greatest of care, departed.

We all watched this scene with some interest and not a word was said among us. Only an amused smile here and there.

I happened to know what it was all about. The very young officer was a dyer in civilian life and had been given the job of dyeing khaki battle dress trousers to some colour more serviceable to would-be escapers and his only possible method of acquiring ammonia for his work was in this way.

How many of those watching knew this I do not know. We never discussed these things. There might have been a stooge present.

Ashton himself tried to escape on a number of occasions. All his attempts were unsuccessful, but a flash of POW humour is apparent in a post-war encounter with a fellow prisoner who in 1941 he had told to jump off a German train moving at 45 miles an hour. The would-be escaper was recaptured but Ashton did not meet him until after the war. In August 1945 however the two men spotted each other outside a tube station in London's West End. 'By Christ, Ashton,' said the other by way of greeting, 'that bloody train was going a hell of a lick when you told me to jump.'

Not all humour was confined to camp life as the story of a certain Captain Brown—a New Zealander captured in Crete—will demonstrate. Brown had been sent to North Africa and from there went on to Greece. Before embarking for Greece, however, he arranged for his heavy luggage to go to Cairo, and when he was captured the Army authorities sent it home to New Zealand. Whoever was responsible for forwarding it was unaware that Captain Brown's luggage contained 600 contraceptives—the official issue for his entire company, made on the presumption that the New Zealanders would be in Egypt for at least a year. The luggage was duly delivered to Brown's wife in New Zealand, and after he had been in captivity for some months he received a letter from her. In it she expressed with surprise: 'One normally expects a man on active service to have a few romances,' she wrote, 'but I never dreamed you were so virile.'

Provoking guards and sentries—variously termed guard-baiting, ferret-taunting, or Nip-bashing, according to the war and the place—has long been a source of humour. It is one of the more dangerous diversions, but among men imbued with the will to carry on the fight inside the wire, it has a purpose which transcends the fun associated with it. Dennis Glover, a sergeant in the Royal Sussex—captured in France in 1940 and a persistent escapee—was committed to ferret-baiting. Time and again in his camp in Poland the sentries were induced to go through the laborious business of taking off their gloves in near-Arctic conditions and undo their coats to look at their watches. This was done in response to cries of 'Fishpaste'. Shivering in their towers, many of them were old soldiers who were not antagonistic towards the prisoners. Some had been prisoners in World War I themselves, and most preferred amity to alienation. 'Fishpaste' sounded like 'Wie spät' (what's the time?).

Another play was frequently used at concerts at which the German camp staff were inevitable guests. Singing of Allied national anthems was forbidden, but the concerts often closed with 'God Save The King'. And to make sure that the Germans remained standing, there would be a pause while the Germans moved towards the door. Then the ranks of the audience would close, the singing would start, and the Germans would find themselves unable to move until it was over.

Humour in reverse could also be funny, as Sidney Sheldrick relates:

> I remember during a short stay in Changi one funny incident. It so was arranged that in Changi the internment area was split into two large sections and to get from one to the other it was necessary to fit a Jap armband on, that was obtainable from the camp office. But only for really needy people. . . . Anyway I knew this

fellow who wanted to visit the other area, and as it was only to see an old pal he couldn't get priority and armband for his journey. But he did know a bloke who had found an armband with the Jap characters on it, so he got this and proceeded to cross No Man's strip . . . along came a Nip guard and he glared at the bloke in amazement and took him to the Nip guardroom where the Nips, instead of giving him the usual beating, all bellowed with laughter. The interpreter was sent for and informed the bewildered soldier that the armband he was wearing stated that the wearer was a registered prostitute. . . .

Probably the greatest consolation to prisoners of war anywhere at any time has been derived from their letters. Letters from home and food parcels are the highlights of a prisoner's life, and he cannot provide either of these himself. Even the activities which keep minds bright and pass the time depend to some extent on those who think of the prisoners and wish them well. In their own letters home, prisoners usually try to give the idea of a life rosier than it really is. In two world wars complaining letters were few; men who felt downhearted just did not mention it. Emphasis was thrown on the good points in camps, and even small privileges were mentioned over-eagerly. If a man was having a rough time or doing work which his family might think dangerous he would not tell of it until later. 'I never told you what work we were doing because I thought it might worry you' is a phrase from one letter which is typical of many more.*

Running through the letters of course—expressed directly and by implication—is the longing for home. Some men will say right out how deeply they wish to see their families; others show that they are hungry for scraps of news of their friends and neighbours, office gossip, the antics of family pets—the seemingly trivial things that put colour into the pattern of life. The POW sees his time in captivity as a gap, a period of existence between life as he used to live it, and as he hopes to live it again. Time to him seems to be an almost personal enemy, something to be attacked and got rid of. So the phrase 'killing time' which occurs again and again in letters home from POW camps, has a live and forcible meaning in terms of consolation.

Men with paper and pen or pencil in a POW camp do not often confine their writing to letters home. Whether it is simply a wish to record their experiences for their family, or for history or an innate desire to justify themselves, the fact is prisoners of war compile

---

* Extract from a letter of a German POW who had been employed lifting mines in Holland.

more voluminous diaries and records than other servicemen. Some
turn from straightforward prose to poetry.

Ted Dyson, a POW of the Japanese, recorded his experiences
building an airfield on the island of Haroekoe in an ode which he
called by that name:

> 'Haroekoe!'
> A hastily consulted map.
> Moluccas; Ambon; Isles of Spice.
> Jungle a maze of chorded green,
> Repellent antlers, bodkins, fronds,
> Great roots, low greasy walls,
> Your bonds.
> Butterflies laughing, colour in the green.
> A river, Kali Pulau's sheen.
> The water flowing, audible,
> against its reefs of granite rocks;
> Stealthy, subdued, yet crystal clear.
> —you had no shoes, nor socks.
>
> 'The camp!'
> Dripping, flooded, misery in the mud.
> Animals in filth and squalor.
> *Gunso Mori—'Blood'.
> He of that strange unmoving race
> who brought you to this bitter place.
> A hospital of horror, where,
> with scarcely but a passing stare,
> you witnessed death;
> —And did not care.
>
> 'The Sick!'
> A dozen bamboo coffins lay
> awaiting those who die by day.
> You buried them at night.
> Filth, flies, a crawling slime,
> Men, crying in the dark.
> Four hundred stricken; one small hut;
> Soon all but ten—were stark.
> Your guards, afraid, came seldom by;
> Except for Mori—'Blood'.
> He, grinning, Hell's emissary,
> stalked evil through the mud.

* Gunso Mori: Sergeant-Major Mori, a Japanese nicknamed 'Blood'.

Merkwürdigkeiten
im P.O.W-Camp

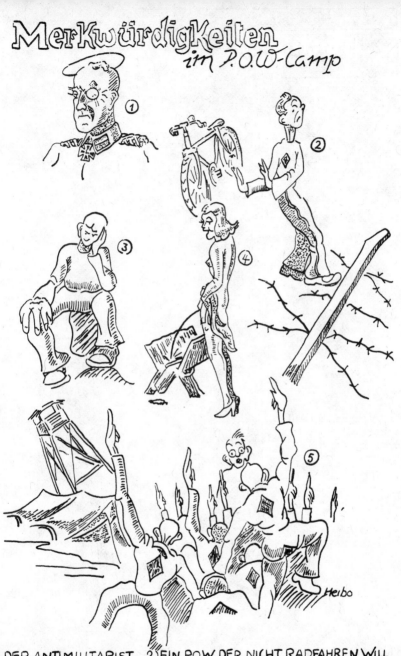

1) DER ANTIMILITARIST 2.) EIN POW DER NICHT RADFAHREN WILL
3.) EIN P.O.W DER NIE **ZEIT** HAT 4.) EIN MITGLIED DER THEATERGRUPPE
5.) EIN PENFÜHRER SUCHT FREIWILLIGE HELFER ZUM ARBEITS-
DIENST

Oddities in a POW camp
  1. The Antimilitarist. 2. 'The Creep'. 3. The POW with no spare time.
  4. 'The Actress'. 5. Calling for Volunteers.

Küchengerät wird beschafft!

Kitchen-equipment will
be provided!
(By courtesy of the
dustman)

'What's this? Having
been so long in captivity,
I've forgotten!'

Was ist das? Infolge der langen Gefangen-
schaft hat das Erinnerungsvermögen gelitten!

*'Mati Mati!'—'Many die!'
'Those men who work—may eat.'
Then silence as you groped your way;
mincing, on shoeless feet.
Shadowy horror, searing men's souls
with a loathsome, crawling fear.
Dysentery! Malaria!
'Oh God! Let death draw near.'

Brigadier Cooper, captured at Tobruk, expressed his regret about his first visit to Rome in a poem *The Road to Rome*:

I'd heard said when I was a youth that ALL ROADS LEAD TO ROME,
My sojourn there was short, foresooth, nor did I feel at home.
When first I girded on my sword and drew it for the fray,
I felt I really could afford my fancies to let play.

'Twas said the task was grim and hard that it might cost us dear,
And never did I disregard the risks nor at them sneer.
Those risks of bomb and shell I knew and was prepared to take,
Such, though they might be far from few, could not my ardour shake.

I never had the slightest doubt, I'd see THE APPIAN WAY,
Nor was I in the least put out when there was some delay.
But never had it crossed my mind as day by day we fought,
That I myself should ever find by our opponents caught.

THE ROAD TO ROME I visualized—one of triumphant joy,
And never had I realized how't would my pride destroy.
But now, alas, I must explain the wrong path which I took,
One I ne'er wish to take again—the road via TOBRUK.

When then, to enter Rome, I came—a prisoner under guard,
With head bent on the ground in shame,—it really was too hard.
THE ROAD TO ROME I trod that day gave me no feeling glad,
Although it took my breath away my heart was truly sad.

'Prisoners Laments' were a popular topic, and the following one was written by a Norfolk man, Mr Dick Pavelin:

The Guard says Aufstehen
and put on your clothes.
You must go and Arbeit
as everyone knows.
So fold up your blankets
and put them in line.
When I blow the whistle
just get out on time.

* Mati! Mati!: Die! Die! (Malay).

We've counted the days and
we've counted the nights
we've counted the minutes
we've counted the lights
we've counted the footsteps
we've counted the stars
we've counted a million
of these prison bars.

Drawing comes easier to some than writing, and a POW camp is a cartoonist's paradise if nobody else's. Many men develop fads and foibles in captivity; others cannot help a tendency to exaggerate habits and actions which would pass almost unnoticed in ordinary life. Thus it was that men like Ronald Searle, with his facile pen and eye for the curious in his fellows, was able to draw humour in World War II.

Shaved to the bone, all the intellectual and physical consolations and diversions pursued by prisoners can be seen as a mere making the best of the situation. There are so few moments of real joy in the life of a POW that they are magnified out of normal proportion. The happiness and humour which prisoners write about or sketch should be regarded in this context. Realistically there is no consolation in the life of a prisoner of war beyond the single one—the divine benevolence of there being 24 hours in a day, and not 25.

11
Escape

Most of the current literature about prisoners of war is concerned with attempts to escape. As psychological studies many of these adventure stories are fascinating, but the true escaper often finds they contain an intolerable amount of sentimental wash. Why does a POW try to escape? One reason that is overstressed is a sense of duty. But this never has been and never will be the fundamental reason for man refusing to resign himself to life behind barbed wire. The true escaper tries to get away because he is rebellious by nature, and objects to his liberties being restricted by a lot of bastards whom he despises. He also enjoys the adventure for its own sake, and the fact that considerable risks are attached puts escaping into the same class of amusement as big-game hunting under difficult conditions. The rewards of success are great and the penalties of failure are not usually excessive.

Even among those nations who have treated prisoners with neglect or even with downright cruelty, escape is no crime. The idea prevailing in criminal law that a man is in prison because he has done wrong and is therefore under a legal or moral obligation to serve a sentence does not apply to prisoners of war and the Geneva Convention of 1929 laid it down that no POW could be punished by more than 30 days' solitary confinement for a single escape. To a young man lately arrived in a prison camp from pleasant and civilized surroundings 30 days' solitary may seem severe enough, but to the hardened prisoner of some years standing, it appears insignificant and in the past it has even come to be looked upon as a welcome relief from overcrowded quarters. (Clearly this attitude is modified in circumstances where solitary confinement constitutes a form of torture, as in some Japanese camps during World War II, in the notorious North Korean 'Camp I', and in Vietnam. Solitary confinement usually entails short rations and no tobacco, but in some well-organized POW camps in Germany arrangements were often devised by which food, literature and tobacco could be conveyed surreptitiously to the inmates of the prison cells. In World War I very heavy sentences were sometimes imposed on recaptured prisoners, especially if they made a habit of attempting to escape. But in World War II the Germans generally followed the Geneva rules and on the whole imposed lighter sentences than the British imposed on Germans. (A normal sentence on a recaptured British prisoner was 5–15 days solitary confinement; the British sentences on Germans were more frequently over 20 days.)

In early March 1944, however, the Gestapo issued an order that prisoners of war other than British and United States nationals who escaped and were recaptured were to be shot, and the International Red Cross would be informed subsequently that the escapees had not been recaptured. Shortly afterwards there was a mass break-out from Stalag Luft III near Sagan, when 76 British officers got away from their camp by way of a tunnel. Three of the escapees eventually succeeded in reaching England, a few got to Danzig, the Czech, Swiss and the Danish borders, but the majority were caught within 50 miles of Sagan. On the grounds that they had been apprehended in civilian clothing those who were caught were put in civilian jails, and on orders signed by Himmler and Kaltenbrunner were eventually executed individually. In every case the victims were driven to a lonely spot and then shot as though they had again attempted to escape. Subsequently the Germans tried to justify the deaths in a note to the Swiss, in which they stated that mass escapes were a danger to public security in Germany, that special orders to guards were necessary in such cases, and that weapons had to be used against 50 prisoners who had escaped from Stalag Luft III. The Japanese made no attempt to justify their actions. Their policy was clear from the start: anybody who attempted to escape would be executed. They respected the rights of a prisoner to escape, they said; indeed, a prisoner who escaped vindicated his honour by doing so. But, so far as they were concerned, the punishment for an unsuccessful attempt was death. During World War II, practically all those who escaped from Japanese prison camps were caught and executed.

According to the Geneva Convention, a POW can be tried and punished for all other crimes, other than escape, under the military laws of the detaining power. Thus, if an escaping POW overpowers a guard he can be tried by court-martial for assault; if he kills the guard or anyone else in effecting his escape he can be tried and condemned for murder. If he steals a uniform in which to escape, he will be tried for theft. If he tunnels through the walls of his prison or cuts the bars, he will be up on a charge of wilful damage of government property. A simple escape is, therefore, not quite so easy to accomplish as some may think, and much depends on how far the captors are prepared to enter into the spirit of the thing. As most civilized nations recognize that POWs consider it their duty to escape, offences committed during escapes have generally been treated with considerable leniency—although commandants and guards must sometimes have had great difficulty in restraining themselves from reprisals on captured prisoners.

But past experience suggests that the situation could be very different if an escapee manages to acquire a firearm. Whilst it can be argued that a man has a right to protect himself—especially if he is likely to be shot for escaping anyway—if he is known to be armed those who are after him are likely to adopt a policy of 'shoot first and ask questions later'. When a fighting man surrenders he ceases to be a combatant and as a POW the Geneva Convention can give him some protection if he commits 'privileged' crimes—like stealing food, or trespassing—while he is on the run. But as soon as an escapee picks up a lethal weapon, he loses his POW status. But what should such a man do if he is shot at? Could he plead self-defence? What if an escapee shoots a would-be captor who is about to shoot at him? What if it is merely likely that the captor will shoot at him? What if a starving escapee levels a pistol at a farmer who refuses to give him food? What if he shoots at a little girl who sees him and is likely to report him to the authorities? What if the escapee shoots indiscriminately as a matter of precaution at everyone he runs across? None of these questions are easy to answer, and there is never likely to be international agreement on any answers that are given.

In Eastern theatres of war, where his colour, appearance and language of a European distinguishes him from the local population, an escaping POW is at a far greater disadvantage than in Europe. There have been no recorded instances of successful escapes by German prisoners in the Soviet Union, by UN POWs in North Korea, or by Americans captured in Vietnam. During World War II, in Korea, Vietnam, Algeria, the Middle East, men have succeeded in *evading* capture while in enemy territory, but the problems of an evader are very different from those of the POW. The basis for any analysis of the difficulties and problems facing would-be escaping POWs must therefore come from the experiences of those captured in the World Wars.

Although a far higher percentage of the Allied prisoners of World War II tried, and kept on trying to regain their liberty, the numbers who actually succeeded in escaping from Germany were considerably less than in World War I. In part this is due to the fact that between 1940 and 1945 both the prisoners and their guards had far greater knowledge than in World War I—much of the knowledge being gained from the numerous 'escape adventure' books which were published between the two wars. Some of the English and American books, translated into German and Italian, even became compulsory reading for POW camp commandants and prison guards in these countries. There was not much left untold in these books and so a new generation of POW guards had little to learn about the escape techniques used 20 years previously. The prisoners also read the books, as copies of some of the old escape stories found their way by various guises into their camps. On balance the guard probably gained more from the books than the prisoners, since the tricks which the prisoner can play, the disguises which he can adopt and the bluffs which can be attempted, are strictly limited by the conditions in which he lives—and to a large extent these conditions are controlled by his guards.

Given time and the requisite knowledge any set of captors should be capable of working out schemes to deal with most eventualities. The Germans and the Italians were no exception. They judged, quite rightly, that the barracks, forts, disused factories or other large buildings used as prisoner-of-war camps in the 1914 War were by no means the best type of prison from a security point of view. They offered many opportunities for ingenuity, and depended too much on locks, keys and stone walls. Long experience has shown that such obstacles are relatively ineffective as preventatives to a determined escapee. Furthermore each new type of camp presented a fresh problem for the guards and new opportunities of the prisoners. In World War I prisoners were able to escape from newly-formed camps with relative ease. Studying the problem from inside, they quickly learned the weak spots in the camp's defences and it was not until the prisoners had exploited these weaknesses that the captors were able to block the exits. But the process took time; the prisoners became experts and escaping knowledge accumulated, and the number of escapes from German POW camps steadily increased as the war progressed. From the German point of view, the obvious answer was to simplify the problem and as far as possible to confine all prisoners to one type of camp, so that the lessons and experiences learned in each camp could be made common property.

It is hard to imagine a type of camp more suitable for the purpose than the one they selected for standard use. The prisoners were housed in long wooden barracks, surrounded by a double-fence of barbed wire, 6–7 ft apart and wire 12 ft high. Rolls of Dannert wire between the fences often constituted an additional obstacle. At night the wire perimeters of the camps were flood-lit from pylons outside and 14 ft towers were erected at intervals along the fence. On each tower there was a machine-gun and a searchlight. Thus it was fairly easy to ensure that there were no blind spots. As a defence system these arrangements were extremely good. Nevertheless they were not absolutely impregnable. On at least two occasions prisoners escaped over the wire by making use of the floor of a tower to obscure the sentry's view—an incredible performance if one takes into consideration the disheartening noises made by a wire fence when one tries to climb it. On another occasion one of the most successful escapes of World War II was made by first short-circuiting the electric system and then storming the wire in the dark with scaling ladders.

Apart from escaping over or through the wire of the main defences, prisoners also resorted to tunnelling, bluff and change of identity. To take the last of these three first: it sometimes happened that officers and senior NCOs of all services were able to communicate with the large camps for 'other ranks'. From the latter working parties were sent out daily into the fields or factories and many an escape started by an officer or NCO changing his identity with a private soldier. (Airey Neave, now a Member of Parliament, was one who tried this method.) But even working parties were well guarded and months of preparation and waiting were often necessary before an opportunity arose. Nor was it easy to obtain the information and equipment needed—papers, food, civilian clothes—in an 'other rank' camp.

Tunnelling is probably more successful in the setting of a television drama than it has proved in practice. The few tunnels that succeeded in World War II have become famous—and rightly so, because the difficulties involved were enormous. Disposing of the earth is not the least of these difficulties. In Stalag Luft I, at Barth on a small peninsula jutting out into the Baltic, the prisoners of war made holes in their trouser pockets, filled them with earth and then walked around the compound gently shaking themselves. In due course a thin deposit of fresh earth was noticed by observant German guards and this resulted in a search for the location of the tunnelling operation. But tunnels are vulnerable in other ways. To make a long tunnel requires an elaborate organization, many workers, and months of labour. The opening and closing of the mouth of a tunnel is a perpetual anxiety, and, as the tunnel lengthens, the problem of supplying the workers at the face with fresh air becomes an engineering problem of considerable magnitude. Most tunnels are betrayed—sometimes by traitors, but more often by indiscretion among the prisoners, for not everyone is capable of guarding his tongue for months on end. Between 1940 and 1945 a great deal of energy was devoted to tunnelling operations, but relatively few were successful. Yet even unsuccessful tunnels are not necessarily a waste of time.

As has already been mentioned, if POWs are to retain their sanity it is essential for them to have an outlet for their mental and physical energies, and, if to this is added an element of danger and a large prize for success, so much the better. Planning and organizing a tunnel escape fulfils all these conditions.

But the best escaping dividends in the past have undoubtedly been paid by exploits depending on sheer bluff. One of the best instances of this in World War II was that of two soldiers in an 'other ranks' camp, who happened to find a pot of white paint and two brushes. There was only one exit from their camp—along a road past the Commandant's office inside the wire, through the main double gates to the camp. Behaving as if they were on a normal fatigue duty, the two men proceeded to paint a white line down the centre of the road from the top of the camp. The guards took little notice as they worked unhurriedly towards the exit. And when they reached the gate, where they stood chatting and smoking, someone opened the inner gate and told them to get on with the job. The same thing happened at the outer gate, and they continued to paint a line down the centre of the road outside, until—seizing the opportunity at a convenient corner—they unobtrusively disappeared.

As a comparison, the escape of Second-Lieutenant Marcus Kaye, of the Royal Flying Corps, in World War I is interesting. It is far more elaborate, but the principle of bluff is the same.

The prisoners of war at Schweidnitz were quartered in a large building which had been a workhouse. For exercise they were allowed to use a sunken rectangular courtyard, which was bounded on one side by the main building, by high walls topped with barbed wire on the opposite and one adjacent side, and by a 30 ft high vertical brick-faced embankment on the fourth side. As the courtyard was sunk below the general level of the ground, the top of this embankment rose only slightly above the countryside on that side, and from its cliff-like face gardens and allotments sloped gently away from the prison. Guards were posted on platforms above the building, the walls and the embankment, so that the whole prison was under constant surveillance. On the embankment there were two platforms—one at each end, from where the guards could look straight down into the courtyard. These guards reached their posts be means of ladders reaching from the courtyard to the two platforms. An opening in the face of the embankment led to a latrine hollowed out behind the wall, and a 6 in ventilation duct ran up the wall from the latrine.

Both guards were relieved at midday, and on the day he made his escape Kaye paid several visits to the latrine prior to the new guard coming on duty. Each time he went to the latrine he took an item of his escape, and secreted it inside the latrine. His last visit was timed for two minutes to twelve, when he entered the latrine in his uniform. At two minutes past the hour, when two different guards had taken over, Kaye emerged from the latrine dressed in the nondescript clothes of a German workman and with his face smeared with dirt to fit him for the part and to prevent recognition. He was now carrying a small bag containing mostly odd lumps of metal which were intended to simulate tools.

Kaye stopped, set down his bag with a clink, opened it, took out a wrench, and proceeded very deliberately to take down, examine, clean and finally replace the last two sections of the ventilation duct.

The sentries watched him with mild interest. Having finished the first part of his work, Kaye nodded to the sentry, indicating that he must do the top part of the pipe as well. The guard nodded back; so Kaye collected his tools and climbed slowly up the ladder. The guard spoke to him as he passed, and Kaye grunted a few words of German in reply. Then he repeated the operation of dismantling and re-erecting the duct, taking some 20 minutes over the job. By now the guards had become accustomed to his presence and when he finished his work, collected his tools and walked off through the allotments they ignored him.

It will be noticed that in both of the foregoing escapes full use was made of psychological defects in the guards' attitudes. In both instances too, the timing was all important. In circumstances like these any precipitate action gives a guard a reason to think, and this has to be avoided at all costs. But to prolong operations as these escapees did, doing everything in slow time, required very considerable nerve.

Clearly the POW's first problem is to escape from his camp. And if this proves difficult it is certain that the next step, the journey through alien territory will be even more arduous. Between 1940 and 1945, travelling through occupied Europe was made more hazardous by the existence of the Gestapo, whose network of agents regulated everybody's movements.

Frequent searches and 'check-ups' were intended primarily to control the millions of foreign workers in Germany. Consequently, when he had successfully avoided his own man-hunt, an escaped prisoner was quite liable to run into that of someone else. Unless one's papers were perfect—and a man had to have a baffling number of passes to justify his existence—the effect of this was the same— arrest and an examination which usually terminated the escape. Luck played a big part in such adventures, of course, and some escapers missed all searches and controls. Provided one could buy a ticket, which in itself entailed a degree of fluency in the language of the country, travelling on the railways was usually easier than walking through Germany. The Germans were themselves wary in their dealings with the Gestapo, and tended to keep themselves to themselves. This meant that boldness often paid a handsome dividend. Sergeant Nabarro, for instance, made an astonishing trip through Germany, by train although he knew only a few words of German. He changed trains several times and bought tickets without apparent difficulty. His method was to give the name of the station and thump down the money. The most dangerous moment occurred when he was sitting in the corner seat of a carriage full of German civilians. To his utter consternation the old lady in the opposite seat leaned forward, tapped him on the knee and spoke to him in German. To Nabarro whatever she had said was quite unintelligible. But when he failed to react she repeated her question, and the rest of the occupants of the carriage began to take interest. Realizing he had to do something, Nabarro reached up to the rack for his hat, glanced round the compartment, and said obscenely '*Scheisse*!' ('Shit'). The whole carriage gasped with horror. Nabarro stalked to the door, pulled it back, and then turned to glare round and repeat one more word of his limited German vocabulary. '*Schweinehunde*', he snarled insultingly, as he went out to stand in the corridor. There was no response; it was all too clear to the rest of his compartment that Nabarro was a most unpleasant individual and his fellow travellers preferred to leave him alone.

Considering the number of foreign workers in Germany walking through Germany could have been expected to have presented few difficulties. Sometimes this was the case, and several escapees tramped long distances without hindrance. More often the reverse was true, and most escapees ran into control posts and were picked up. For some obscure reason, few escaping prisoners seem to have considered using bicycles. There was no shortage of bicycles in Germany, and 'liberating' one of them was not likely to be beyond the ingenuity of a man who had been capable of getting out of a POW camp. Moreover a man on a bicycle does not attract the same sort of attention as a man on foot; head down and pedalling away, there is a vague purposefulness about him which militates against his being stopped and asked for his papers. So far as speed was concerned, a man on a bicycle could travel almost as fast as on the German railway system. And he could vary and change his route, whilst a rail journey imposed strict limitations on his initiative. One sergeant in the RAF stole a bicycle from a village in the middle of Germany and rode hundreds of miles to the Baltic without being stopped once. In the course of the journey he exchanged his bicycle several times and often stopped to talk to British POWs working near the road. Finally he stowed away on a ship and eventually reached

Sweden. But this man's case was unusual; either he was exceptionally lucky, or he had a natural gift for dealing with the sort of situations which arose.

In considering the difficulties of escaping from Germany it must be remembered that it was only by crossing into Northern Holland that a would-be escaper avoided a formidable water crossing, since the western frontiers of Germany are bounded by the Rhine and the Maas. In 1914 Holland was neutral, and although crossing the border between Germany and Holland was by no means easy for a tired man, once he was over an escaping POW was welcomed by the Dutch and sent back to England.

In World War II the barbed wire frontier between Germany and Holland was loosely guarded by towers and sentry posts about one kilometre apart. The space between these towers and sentry posts and the surrounding terrain was patrolled, but few escaping prisoners seem to have had any serious difficulty in dodging the patrols or getting through the wire. (Those who did run into trouble did so in wooded country where the Germans had a habit of posting standing patrols under cover.) Once in Holland, however, the escapee's troubles were far from being over. Proximity to Germany, mutual trade and economic interests, and intermarriage in the border region made it inevitable that the apparent success of Hitler's regime should attract many young Dutchmen to the doctrines of the Nazis. And after 1940 some of these Dutch Nazis were drafted into the Dutch police force. Because they knew the difference between a Dutchman and an Englishman—which the normal German sentry did not— these men were a menace to escaping POWs. Holland's canals presented a further problem. The terrain is criss-crossed with waterways, the bridges are easy to guard, and swimming canals is not an easy matter when it has to be undertaken by a tired and half-starved man —which is what an escaper usually was.

The following story of an RAF pilot who baled out over Holland illustrates the sort of difficulties that were encountered. His aircraft was shot down and he landed in the first light of dawn not far from his burning machine on an island about three miles long and half a mile wide formed by the canals. When he had recovered his wits, he found that he was in a field with a herd of cows. At the far end of the field was a gate, and as he started to walk to it he noticed that he left a trail of footprints in the heavy dew. With the burning aircraft in such close proximity he knew that the Germans would soon be looking for him, so he rounded up the cows and drove them with him to obliterate his traces. Near a house he hid in a hedge, and eventually attracted the attention of the occupant. The Dutchman was too frightened to take him into his house but he did give the pilot some food and civilian clothes. Thus equipped, he reconnoitred one or two of the bridges but found them all guarded, so he approached a house and knocked on the back door. When he explained his circumstances, the occupants were anything but pleased to see him, but when he pressed them for help they advised him to leave the island by a certain bridge. The pilot left the house feeling uncertain as to whether these Dutch had given him the advice to assist him or to betray him. Half an hour later, when he observed several lorry loads of German troops racing towards the bridge they had indicated, he realized his doubts were justified.

In condemning the action of these particular individuals, it is well to remember that the penalty for helping an evader or escaping POW was likely to be death for the head of the household and deportation for his family, and that the dangers in Holland were far greater than in France or Belgium. In favourable circumstances the Dutchman in question would probably have been fully prepared to help. But in this instance he may well have considered that the airman's plight was hopeless, and all he would be doing would be to bring German vengeance on himself and his family.

As it was obvious that all the bridges near the one he had been told to cross would soon be impassable, he made his way to the opposite end of the island. There he got his opportunity. Many of the smaller bridges in Holland can be raised at one end to allow barges to pass under them. At one such bridge the pilot saw a group of civilians, together with a few German soldiers, waiting on his side of the canal for the bridge to be lowered. There was a control post and a couple of German sentries on the far side, but as it was still early in the morning, he thought that there was a fair chance that not all guards had yet been warned to look out for an English airman. In any case the longer he stayed on the island the more certain he was to be captured. So he joined the crowd. No one took any notice of him except a young woman with a baby and a pram. She glanced at him, turned away, and then looked again. The pilot guessed that she had realized who he was, so he moved up to the pram and played with the baby while the bridge was being lowered. No word was spoken. Then when the time came to cross, he took the handle of the pram and she linked her arm in his. Then helped by a bright smile from the woman to the sentry, they crossed the bridge. Ultimately this particular airman reached home, after a long journey through France and Spain.

Another way out of Germany was through Switzerland. But Switzerland was entirely surrounded by countries allied to Germany, or by an unfriendly Vichy France. Where the Swiss frontier juts out north of the Rhine, the line between Germany and Switzerland is as complicated as a jigsaw, and it is very easy to walk into Switzerland and then walk out again into Germany without knowing it. In both World Wars many POWs have made this heart-rending error; many more have used the Swiss salient as a means of entering Switzerland. When the Rhine is the frontier, there is no friendly or easy crossing, for the river runs swiftly with many swirls and eddies. Furthermore on those places on the Swiss bank where a swimmer would most naturally choose to land, barbed wire had usually been put under the water.

Nevertheless the Swiss frontier itself was probably as easy to cross between 1940 and 1945 as it had been in the 1914–1918 War, but the approaches to it were more difficult because the Germans near the border were constantly on the look-out for escaping prisoners. The Baltic outlet to Sweden was, for some unexplained reason, exploited more successfully in World War II than in World War I. If the practical difficulties in both wars were roughly the same the successes of the 1940–1945 generation of escapees must be taken as a measure of their greater skill and ingenuity.

One thing that is certain is that the skippers of neutral shipping trading between German ports in the Baltic and Sweden had a very lively fear of the Gestapo. Only on rare occasions are they known to have willingly accepted an escapee on board their ships. Considering each ship was subjected to a close search—in which tear gas was sometimes employed to smoke out the places where escapers could hide—this is hardly surprising. The result was that an escaper who reached a Baltic port not only had to find the means of boarding the right ship from a heavily guarded quay, he also had to find a place in which he could stow away until the ship was at sea. It was also advisable for him to select a ship which was about to sail, and to have with him sufficient food and water to see him over the next few days. The Blue Peter, the flag flown 24 hours before a ship leaves port, was a great help but in wartime ships do not always leave at the appointed time.

Even outside the 3-mile limit it was not always advisable for an escaper to declare his identity. There is the story of one man who, when half dead from hunger and thirst, received a very poor reception when he presented himself to the furious captain. Only his exceptional powers of persuasion enabled this ex-POW to induce him not to turn the ship back towards Germany.

Every escaping POW or evader has, with few exceptions, at least one moment of acute anxiety when his fate hangs in the balance. One hears of those ruses which were successful, but seldom of those which failed. In general it may be said that many who have relied implicitly on bluff, and on the stupidity of guards and sentries often had their reward. When dealing with officers—and even more with the German Gestapo—a nimble tongue and an unusually quick wit have been needed. Nevertheless British soldiers with no knowledge of the language, the country through which they were trying to escape, or its customs, have succeeded in disguising their identity even when faced by an intelligent German officer backed by interpreters. The classic example is that of the three 'other ranks' from a unit of the 51st (Highland) Division. After the fall of Calais these three changed into civilian clothes and tramped the whole length of France to cross the Pyrenees and eventually get home. The crisis in their escape came early in this remarkable trek.

In appearance they were typical Scottish gillies—broad, strong, thick-necked and taciturn. They bore no resemblance to the French peasants, and they spoke not one word of French. At one place they were stopped by a suspicious German officer who asked them who they were, and where they had come from. According to a pre-arranged plan, the three Scots refused to understand and gabbled back in Gaelic. A series of interpreters were called, who tried the highlanders with every known language. Finally, in despair, the German produced a map of the world and indicated by signs that they should point to their country of origin. After careful study one of the Scots slowly and deliberately placed his finger in the middle of Russia.

The German was delighted; the possibility of the three men being Russians had not occurred to him. And, as this was the period of German–Soviet collaboration, the three were released, and allowed to continue their march south.

During World War II escapes and evasion were considerably more difficult from Germany than from the occupied countries of Europe. This is also true of Italy during the period the Italians were allied to the Germans. In the Far East escape and evasion were virtually impossible when the Japanese had overrun a country and fewer than 50 British (excluding Indians) succeeded in escaping from Japanese hands during the whole of World War II. Of these escapes that of three British officers—one of whom was a New Zealander—illustrates the difficulties which European POWs faced in an Asiatic environment. In the early months of 1942 the three officers were able to slip through the wire of the large overcrowded Hong Kong camp at Shamshuipo near Kowloon harbour. As it would have been difficult to conceal themselves in the city they had decided to make their getaway by boat. So a local Chinese had been bribed to sail his sampan past the breakwater at a certain time. When Japanese guards opened fire the escapers took to the water and swam for about 20 minutes across Laichikok Bay. They then eluded a Japanese patrol while crossing a brilliantly lit road, and walked for some hours well into the surrounding hills. The party kept heading north, hiding by day and travelling by night over hills and through swampy valleys, and eking out their scanty food supply. They were attacked by two different parties of Chinese bandits, and on one occasion were beaten up and robbed of their valuables but finally released. Seven days after their breakout they reached a South China guerilla band which looked after them and gave them guides to take them through the Japanese outpost line to the regular Chinese forces. After crossing the main Canton–Kowloon railway, they made their way from village to village until they met a unit of Chiang Kai-Chek's troops. Sixteen days had elapsed since their escape, and it was another six weeks of travel by river, rail, lorry and air before they eventually reached safety in Calcutta.

In the Korean War it was the same story; and in Vietnam only prompt and daring rescues by helicopter or speedily mounted patrol sorties have succeeded in recovering evading airmen whose aircraft have been shot down. Soldiers whose units were overwhelmed, or airmen who were shot down have managed to get back to their own lines during the Arab–Israeli conflicts but those who were actually made prisoners of war rarely escaped. In all these cases the reason is that the conditions for evasion, and still less for escape, were exceptionally unfavourable. In occupied territory in Europe and in Italy when the Italians ceased to be Hitler's allies, the population was not hostile. Nor was the countryside swarming with enemy troops as many people seem to imagine. Only in the frontier regions where the escapee had to make his first bid for freedom were control posts established. In France, for instance, the Gestapo concentrated on main line stations, and routes across the Pyrenees. To discourage the locals they also reacted brutally against anyone found helping escapees. In the event the control points, manhunts and brutality were matched by courage and cleverness—and they only served as temporary checks. As time passed a network of underground resistance—whose *raison d'être* was the rescue of evaders—was built up in the occupied territories. This resistance movement was particularly strong in Belgium and France; it existed under greater difficulties and danger in Holland; and in the latter part of the war, the Danes showed themselves especially courageous and ingenious in the same perilous work.

On the other side of the hill, the Italians showed remarkably little desire to escape once they had been taken prisoner. Their hearts were not in the war, their conditions in captivity were not too arduous, and it meant that their survival was assured. According to Israeli sources, many of the Egyptian soldiers captured during the Six-Day

War had a similar philosophy. In Korea the last thing many of the
North Korean POWS wanted, was to return to North Korea. Among
these men, therefore, there was no question of escape; and the dedicated Communists constituting the bulk of the remainder had no
wish to escape because they had a job to do *inside* the camps—
dealing with their recalcitrant comrades, and stirring up trouble
which would reflect on the course of the armistice talks. Not only
were there few attempts to escape, but the flow of traffic was in the
reverse direction, with agents from North Korea deliberately getting
themselves captured so that they could infiltrate the POW camps.
Once inside the camps these agents took control planning, organizing
and staging incidents, and maintaining contact with their headquarters through refugees, civilians and local guerillas.

Organizing and undertaking an escape necessarily calls for very
individualistic efforts, and these demand the sort of flexible outlook,
which many nationalities do not seem to possess. Experience suggests
that the requisite individualism will be found among the British, and
the French; the Russians do not seem to have it, nor do the Germans.
In the case of the Russians, the reason seems to stem from deliberate
suppression of individual initiative—first in Czarist times, and now
by Soviet authoritarianism. With the Germans it is the love of rule
and order which makes them basically unsuited to escape from POW
camps. Organizing an escape from Britain should not have been
beyond any German who was determined to get away. Boats were
constantly crossing between England and Ireland, and with probably
forged papers and good English—such as any POW could learn in a
year—an escape should have been reasonably easy. Certainly it
should have been well within the capacity of the British prisoners
lodged in Colditz. Yet only Hauptmann Von Werra, an airman
shot down in the Battle of Britain, can be classed among the great
escapers.

After a couple of thwarted attempts to get away, a truly magnificent effort of bluff almost enabled him to fly off home in a Hurricane.
Had it not been for the actions of a quick-witted RAF duty officer,
he would certainly have succeeded.* As it was, the British authorities
decided to send Von Werra to a prison camp in Canada. There, his
persistence eventually paid off. Following a successful breakout, he
succeeded in crossing the St Lawrence in the depth of winter, without
a boat—an incredible feat which few have accomplished—and reaching the then neutral USA. Rescued from an American prison by the

---

* In World War II only one other man is known to have escaped by stealing an
aircraft. He was a Norwegian who absconded with a German seaplane during the
invasion of Norway. An American pilot, Lieutenant Kelly, of the USAAF nearly got
away with a FW 190, but failed because he was baffled by the instrument panel and
could not start the engine.

German Consul, Von Werra travelled back to Germany, where he was awarded the Ordre pour le Merite for his feats and the information he had collected in the course of his escape.*

In November 1941 two other young German Luftwaffe officers, Lieutenants Wappler and Schnabel, also very nearly got away from England. Escaping from an officer POW camp near Penrith in Westmorland, they made their way to a nearby airfield, climbed into a training aircraft at the edge of the field, taxied out, and took off. No attempt was made to stop the aircraft and there was no pursuit; as the airfield was a training centre the air control officer probably assumed that the escapees' plane was carrying a pupil on a routine instrumental circle and bump. Wappler and Schnabel set a course for Germany, but the plane's petrol gave out over Yarmouth and they were compelled to land at an RAF base near the station. But their luck had not yet given out. Posing as officers of the Netherlands army in Britain, they were taken to the officers' mess to be given a meal and a bed. Next morning, however, their exploits caught up with them. All RAF stations had been warned to look out for a plane stolen from Penrith, and the two 'Dutchmen' were awakened by the military police who were to escort them back to their prison camp. It had been a gallant effort, which led to the tightening of security at British airfields and a stricter surveillance of the prisoners at Penrith.

Hijacking an aircraft enabled Lieutenant Ted Strever of the South African Air Force to escape. Strever was shot down in April 1942 over the Mediterranean. Picked up by an Italian destroyer Strever and his crew were taken to Greece, and subsequently put on an Italian flying boat to be flown to Italy. On the way they overpowered their guard and prevailed on the Italian crew to fly them to Malta.

One tragic unsuccessful attempt to escape deserves mention because of the peculiar circumstances which prompted it. On 27 August 1941 the German submarine U-570, under the command of Kapitanleutnant Rahmlow, was spotted on the surface of the Atlantic south of Iceland. Attacked and disabled by a Hudson of RAF Coastal Command, the U-boat captain hoisted a white flag and in due course the vessel surrendered to a British destroyer. Rahmlow was separated from the rest of his officers and crew and sent to a different POW camp. The rest of the officers were imprisoned together and when they got to their camp they faced a barrage of criticism from their fellow countrymen. The Fuhrer's orders were that disabled naval vessels in danger of falling into enemy hands should be scuttled by their own crews. In the absence of Rahmlow the onus of

---

* Von Werra was killed later on the Russian front.

blame for not carrying out this order fell on the two officers of the watch and the chief engineer. Inside the camp, unbeknown to the authorities the POW '*Ehrenrat*' (Council of Honour) convened a court of inquiry which exonerated the engineer and one of the officers of the watch. The third officer, Oberleutnant Bergmann became the scapegoat. Ostracized and fearful of the eventual outcome of his alleged negligence Bergmann asked for permission to commit suicide in order to redeem his honour. The '*Ehrenrat*' refused; there was an alternative. From some of the camp staff the Germans had learned that U-570 was lying at Barrow-in-Furness, and it was proposed that Bergmann should undertake a suicidal mission. With the help of others he would escape, make his way to Barrow-in-Furness and sink his old ship. In the event he was seen getting through the wire, challenged by a sentry, and shot when he failed to obey the order to halt.

Because of their proximity to Spanish territory, some of the prison camps in North Africa may have seemed to offer better opportunities for escape than Britain. Attempts were made but there is only one recorded success, that of a Hauptmann Kindshofer. In 1943 Kindshofer was imprisoned at Camp Geryville in Algeria. With eight others of Rommel's Desert Foxes he got away through a tunnel which they had dug under the wire. A thunderstorm and the end of Ramadan which the Moslem guards were celebrating provided unusually favourable conditions for an escape and all nine men got clean away from the camp. By morning they were 12 miles away. Progress after that was slower and one by one they dropped out, gave up or were captured, unable to cope with the hard conditions of the near-Sahara countryside. Following a sample of the treatment doled out by the Bedouins on the Goums, the escapees were glad to get back to their camp. Kindshofer was almost caught as well, but 800 miles of hair-raising adventures eventually took him to Spanish Morocco and freedom.

At the end of the war one and a half million German prisoners were transferred from POW camps in America, Canada and Britain to France. In America and Canada, as in Britain, few of the prisoners had attempted to escape. Conditions had been relatively good, Germany was a long way off, and transport seemed an insuperable obstacle. After D-Day the chances for getting home seemed even less rosy, and the urge for freedom was generally restricted to short term escapades into towns, where wine and women might provide a brief solace. But France was different. Five years of occupation had left a burning hatred in French hearts, and the reputation of French POW camps had reached the German transferees long before they set foot on French soil. With home so much nearer, many POWs were tempted to escape; some got away; many more were caught and severely punished. Others were offered the alternative of punishment or joining the French Foreign Legion.

Of those who did get away from French camps, some ended up in Luxembourg where their reception and lenient treatment did much to bring about a new friendly understanding which has paid dividends in the post-war era. Like all the occupied countries Luxembourg suffered under the German jackboot. Four thousand male Luxembourgers who were conscripted into the German Army did not return, and another 7000 were deported to work in Germany. But it seems that the people of Luxembourg were prepared to overlook the past and to treat the German prisoners with humanity.

Few escapes were attempted from POW camps in Holland. As in France the German record of occupation was not a happy one. But as long as the Germans behaved themselves, the Dutch—with an eye to the future like Luxembourg perhaps—treated their prisoners well.*

In Russia, as in the Far East, it was the physical conditions imposed by geography and climate which were the limiting factor. With all the initiative, determination and luck in the world, it is doubtful whether any but the most able and persistent escapees could have got away once they were on their way to the prison camps in the Russian hinterland. The story of four men of the 17th Panzer Division whose unit was overwhelmed near the Vistula in January 1945 illustrates the point. Like most men who become POWs, these four were tired to the point of exhaustion, hungry, and demoralized, when they were captured. Nevertheless they decided to make a break for it and try to rejoin the German rearguard. After a few days dodging Russian columns, and sleeping out in bitter cold, with no food and no prospects of finding any in the denuded countryside which had twice been subject to the ravages of a scorched earth campaign, they were only too ready to give themselves up. Crammed into battered cattle trucks which took them deep into Russia, the icy winds and lack of food suppressed any further display of initiative. Finally the prospect of escape was killed by sheer distance, a continuation of exhaustion arising from incessant hard labour plus the savage treatment of those who refused to work. When survival is the prime concern, thoughts of escape are discarded. Hunger takes precedence, thoughts are focused on food, and as men grow listless their escapes are to a world of dreams.

* Off duty, that is. The prisoners were employed clearing the mines which littered the Dutch coast. In this operation 210 POWs were killed, 460 wounded, 200 of whom were eventually repatriated as cripples.

12

Indoctrination

One of the innovations introduced by the Germans in World War I was the process known today as political indoctrination. They did not employ it successfully or on a large scale. But they set a pattern for the future.

At Limburg and Zossen, the Germans set up what were known as 'political camps', to which were sent prisoners who seemed likely subjects for subversion. The inmates were quartered in comfortable barracks, fed on special rations, and issued with tobacco and cigarettes. During the first 18 months of the war most of the POWS sent to these segregated camps were Irishmen, who were told that the Kaiser regarded captives from 'the down-trodden state of Ireland' as being in an especially deserving category. Sir Roger Casement, the Irish rebel who was executed for treason in 1916 and who was in Germany trying to raise a brigade for service against England at this time, gave a series of lectures at Limburg. But his attempts to enlist Irish prisoners of war were a pathetic failure. 'The lectures were poorly attended and as soon as the real purpose of them was disclosed serious trouble developed in the camp whenever Casement appeared; in fact a guard had to be sent with him to protect him from the indignant Irishmen. After every inducement had been held out for a long time, including freedom of the prison camps, and especially the privilege of having an Irish regiment of their own with green uniforms and a harp embroidered on the coat, only 32 men volunteered for the new regiment from 4000 captives. The 32 were despised by their compatriots.' *

When Casement's recruiting campaign failed, '. . . the Irish captives were subjected to rigid discipline and limitation of liberty. The leaders in this antagonism to German diplomacy were removed from

* Major H. C. Fooks, *Prisoners of War* (Stowell Printing Co., Federalsburg, Maryland 1924), pp. 193–195.

the main camp to others, among which were working camps where they were forced to live on the camp foods without receiving their packages and letters which would normally have been forwarded to them. Bitter complaints were made to the effect that men too ill to get out of bed were ordered to leave in violation of the orders of the medical officers . . . Reprisals by the Germans were not uncommon. . . .'*

Similar attempts to persuade prisoners of war to change their allegiance were used by the Turks. Addressing Muslim captives of the Indian Army, Mustafa Redin Bey, a member of the Turkish Parliament, said: '. . . We bring you the greetings of our rulers and our Sultan, who are brothers of the same faith. For a soldier it is a great misfortune to be taken prisoner. You, however, have not the justification that you have fought for your faith and your race. You have been drawn into the struggle by force. Thanks to the extraordinary goodness of the High German Government, they have taken cognizance of your religion, your customs and manners . . . they have called special teachers to give you special instructions . . . we hope you will prove thankful for this. . . .'

Such appeals terminated in a suggestion that Muslim POWs should join the Turco-German crusade. In the event the response was similar to that of the Irishmen.

When World War I ended, indoctrination to alter a man's attitude without upsetting his character continued with political prisoners in Soviet Russia, Nazi Germany, Fascist Italy and Falangist Spain. Techniques of 'brainwashing'—a process by which a subject's personality and character undergo a permanent change—were also perfected. For the 'purge-trails' of the mid-1930s, the Russians used brainwashing to change individuals so that they would not only believe in their guilt, but help to provide the evidence against themselves—where no such guilt or evidence existed. By 1939, these two techniques of psychological indoctrination and brainwashing had been advanced to a leading place in the Communist arsenal.

Compared with the Soviet programme the German efforts were puny, and their indoctrination was about as successful as it had been with the Irish POWs. Anti-Semitic pamphlets were distributed at Stalag IXC (Bad Sulza) and others on atrocities committed by the Poles were issued at Dulag Luft (the transit camp at Oberursel). For general distribution to POW camps there was also a small four-page newspaper in English—*The Camp*—which in the autumn of 1941 was pointing out to its as yet 'unenlightened' British readers the solidarity of Germany and Italy and the exploitation of the 'Anglo-Saxons' by 'world Jewry'. Over the camp radio loudspeakers came the voice of

* Fooks, *Prisoners of War*, pp. 194–195.

Lord 'Haw-Haw' expatiating British losses and difficulties in England. Camp leaders took a firm line in combating such propaganda, and for the vast majority of British prisoners the printed and broadcast propaganda became matters for derision. Food parcels from the UK were a great help in the propaganda war. To a German officer who told him that Red Cross parcels for British prisoners were merely sent as propaganda, a prisoner retorted that at least you could eat British propaganda.

In 1942 the Germans rubbed in the apparent hopelessness of the Allied position. The fall of Tobruk, the German advance into Russia, and Germany's claim to have repulsed an invasion at Dieppe had set men wondering, although the majority of the POWs gave no sign of it. A year later *The Camp* and Lord Haw-Haw were having a struggle to appear convincing, and they began to concentrate on the denigration of Russia. From 1942 a series of articles in *The Camp* entitled 'The German Point of View' endeavoured to prove what reasonable and civilized people the Germans were. Articles and photographs depicting the Russian massacre of Poles and their burial in the Katyn ditch appeared in 1943 issues of *The Camp* and attempts were made to persuade a number of British officers to go to see the actual exhibits at the scene of the atrocity. In 1944, the editorial staff of *The Camp* appeared to be taking the view that the British were merely misguided. In December an article was published on the Royal Navy, in January 1945 a description of how a mayor in Britain shook hands with a German prisoner, and in February 1945 a statement by repatriated German POWs—to the effect that the attitude of officers and guards in British POW camps was above reproach—was reproduced. All this was too clumsy to deceive anybody, while an attempt in May 1944 and afterwards to form a 'Free British Corps' to fight the Russians was little short of puerile. The circular* sent to POW

* The circular read as follows:
As a result of repeated applications from British subjects from all parts of the world wishing to take part in the common European struggle against Bolshevism, authorisation has recently been given for the creation of a British Volunteer unit. The British Free Corps publishes herewith the following short statement of the aims and principles of the unit.
1. The British Free Corps is a thoroughly British volunteer unit conceived and created by British subjects from all parts of the Empire who have taken up arms and pledged their lives in the common European struggle against Soviet Russia.
2. The British Free Corps condemns the war with Germany and the sacrifice of British blood in the interests of Jewry and International Finance, and regards this conflict as a fundamental betrayal of the British people and British Imperial interests.
3. The British Free Corps desires the establishment of peace in Europe, the development of close friendly relations between England and Germany, and the encouragement of mutual understanding and collaboration between the two great Germanic peoples.
4. The British Free Corps will neither make war against Britain or the British Crown, nor support any action or policy detrimental to the interests of the British.
                        Published by the British Free Corps

camps was couched in appealing terms and good English, but the time of launching the appeal could scarcely have been worse judged. In the event the response to it was negligible.

A more subtle idea was the setting up of 'holiday camps'. The one at Genshagen, near Berlin, for other ranks, was opened in June 1943 'to promote a better feeling between the opposing nations when the war is over'. Not only was it to give men 'a better outlook' and 'relaxation from the tragedies of war' by 'educational, physical and social activities', but it was to be 'a spiritual centre where the men could be brought closer to Him who alone can bring peace to this suffering world'!* In effect those who ran the camp did not attempt any direct propaganda with the quotas of men who were sent to it. Two hundred prisoners were sent at a time, and they were kept in the camp for 4 weeks. Apart from the entertainment provided by the prisoners themselves, they had music by German instrumentalists and opera-singers, films, lectures, outings to Potsdam, sports facilities and indoor games. Many of the men selected for a 'holiday' were those who had been working in mines or on other unpleasant jobs, so it is not surprising that some at least found it an enjoyable break.

A similar camp for officers was set up in Berlin about the same time, and officers were detailed by the Germans to go to it. In 1944 the camp was moved to a Schloss at Steinburg in Bavaria, near Straubing on the Danube, and although the Germans still insisted that a certain quota from each camp should attend, its selection was left to the senior British officer in consultation with the camp medical officer. In some Oflags the choice was made from among those whose health would benefit from the change or those whose long hours of work at some camp administrative task had earned them a long rest. Almost every camp quota included one officer primed with information, for Steinburg became of great value to British POW camps throughout Germany as a clearing house for news, intelligence and ideas.

The camp at Steinburg was on the fringe of the Bavarian forest, a region of pine-clad hills and rich valleys dotted with neat half-timbered villages clustered round onion-shaped church steeples. Ideal walks were easily accessible in this area and inmates could stroll at any time in the forest meadows adjacent to the Schloss. There was accommodation for about 40, ten to a large bedroom together with a large dining room and a comfortable reading room. According to a New Zealand officer the atmosphere could be summed up: '. . . no wire, pleasant rooms, spring beds, soft mattresses, no

---

* Quoted from an article in *The Camp* of 20 February 1944.

petty restrictions, all the walks you want with small parties led by
guides rather than surrounded by guards. . . .'* The camp was amply
supplied with Red Cross food; the cooks were efficient; the interpreters were men of university education; and the library was well
stocked—although the Germans had included a few propaganda
volumes for the gullible. First-class photographers among the staff,
from whom photographs were readily available to send home, and
the plying of prisoners with a liberal supply of letter forms, were
among the more subtle moves to create goodwill towards Germany.
But this elementary and gentle 'indoctrination' had little success.
The activities of the Abwehr and the experiences of escapers who fell
into the hands of the Gestapo was bound to make it an uphill task.

The Japanese made no attempt to indoctrinate or brainwash their
prisoners. No doubt they could see no need for subtlety when a
simple or more easily implemented policy of frightfulness could
achieve what they wanted. But the Russians had no such illusions
and their campaign to indoctrinate thousands of German POWs with
Communist ideologies emerges as one of the strangest episodes of
World War II. In October 1941 the Red Army sent a directive to all
its interrogators which stated in part: 'From the very moment of
capture by the Red Army and during the entire period of captivity,
officers and men of the enemy forces must be under continuous
indoctrination by our political workers and interrogators.'† Captured Germans were herded into political camps, and put through
the Red indoctrination mills. Week in, week out, each day from
dawn to dusk the prisoners were subjected to lessons in Marxist
practice. As a result, many of them came to believe that their crime
was not invading Russia, but that they had been anti-Communists.
Where efforts to propagandize German *Kultur* in both World Wars
had a minimal effect, the Red programme gained hundreds of German converts. Of these not least in stature and propaganda worth was
General von Paulus, captured at Stalingrad.

After the war token of the indoctrinated Germans, Japanese and
Italians were profitably employed by the Soviet Union to sow
propaganda for the 'kind' Communists at times when elections were
in the offing or the national Communist parties needed a boost.

Meantime the Chinese Communist forces who had learned the
technique of manipulating of POWs from the Russians were also
using indoctrinated prisoners as a psychological warfare weapon. As
Mao's force overran areas of China, prisoners from Chiang Kai-

---

* *Official History of New Zealand in the Second World War: Prisoners of War*, by
W. Wynne Mason, p. 394.
    † Eugene Kinkead, *In Every War But One* (W. W. Norton Inc., New York 1959),
p. 98.

Shek's Nationalist forces were treated solicitously and well fed. Those who responded 'righteously' to such treatment and showed a desire to change sides were permitted to go back to their own lines to tell other Nationalists how well they had been treated. The remainder were given a choice: change sides or be shot. Thus, by the time the Korean War broke out the Communist nations were thoroughly experienced in the exploitation of POWs as a psychological warfare weapon, and the Chinese appear to have worked out a definite policy for a 'war within a war' behind the barbed wire. The result was that the American and British troops who were taken prisoner—some 8000 in all—were soon to discover that their struggles against Communism were by no means at an end. The Communist policy regarding the UN prisoners had two main purposes: a short-term aim of using them in the propaganda war against Western 'imperialists'; and the longer object of returning men to the West as avowed Communists. Indoctrination courses served both purposes. Officers were usually segregated soon after capture and as soon as a natural leader stepped forward he would be removed. The object was to destroy the soldier's sense of discipline and loyalty based on rank and place authority in the hands of 'Progressives'. (These individuals were graduates of the 'Peaceful Valley' camp, and others who accepted Communist schooling. Prisoners who refused to show the 'proper spirit' were considered 'Reactionaries'.) When the prisoners were reckoned to have been reduced to a uniform level, the Chinese and North Koreans set about their 're-education' programme. The first step in this process was a specialized interrogation. 'Pak's Palace', near Pyongjang, was one of the worst camps endured by American POWs undergoing such interrogation. This North Korean establishment, which was outside the jurisdiction of the Chinese, had an exceptionally high mortality rate, and a reputation for the tortures inflicted on prisoners. The chief interrogator was a sadist, Colonel Pak, and his assistant was known to the POWs as 'Dirty Pictures' Wong.

The camp was under the administration of a Colonel Lee, and there were several other interrogators on the team. But Pak and Wong were symbolic of the institution. 'The Palace' wanted military information and men were required to answer a questionnaire. Coercion began as soon as a prisoner refused to talk. Verbal abuse would be followed by threats, kicks, cigarette burns and promises of further torture. American airmen were singled out for exceptionally brutal treatment. The purpose was to get the airmen to confess that they had been involved in germ warfare. And of 59 American airmen subjected to pressure, 38 eventually made admissions of guilt which were used later as Communist propaganda.

Following the interrogations prisoners were classified according to their political convictions. A POW might start the hard way—and be punished by restricted rations and other privations. But if he began to show the 'proper spirit' and cooperate with his captors, he was lectured and issued with Communist literature. A docile prisoner, who read the literature and listened politely to the lectures, was graduated to a better class. Finally he might be sent to 'Peaceful Valley'. In this lenient camp the food was relatively good and prisoners were given tobacco. Here they graduated as 'Progressives'. According to the official British Government Report on the Korean prisoner camps* a man who became a progressive was expected to do more than passively accept Communism. He had to become a propagandist and help the Chinese, not only by assisting them with military information but also by informing on his fellow prisoners— revealing their plans and thoughts and helping to spread Communism among them. He was also expected to write and explain to his friends and relatives at home the justice of the North Korean cause. One American officer who was to be used as an informer after interrogation was kept in solitary confinement for three weeks, handcuffed in a small thatched hole in the ground, from which he was taken only to be beaten. When he returned to his fellow POWs in the prison camp he was morally and physically broken. But he retained sufficient presence of mind to tell the other officers never to discuss anything in his presence, as he had been sent back to act as an informer. Thus, because he was unable to give his captors the information they wanted, he was subjected to further torture and although he survived the war he died within two weeks of his release from prison.

The so-called 'lenient policy' adopted towards 'liberated' UN soldiers in Chinese POW camps was not extended to 'reactionaries'— those who refused to go along with their programme. For such men who refused to be re-educated or forsake the capitalist cause, and 'learn the truth', the Chinese considered physical violence was justifiable. Solitary confinement, Chinese style, was among the worst of the tortures. According to one victim the 'normal' method was to make the prisoner stand or sit to attention with legs outstretched in complete silence from 4.30 am to 11 pm daily. For the remainder of the time the man was allowed to sleep but was aroused continually by the guards 'to make sure he was still there'. There were no beds and no bedding. Shoes and all clothing, other than underclothes, were often taken away even in the middle of winter; washing facilities were often denied, sometimes for months on end. The British Government's report describes how a private of the Glou-

* *Treatment of British Prisoners-of-War in Korea* (HMSO, London 1955).

cestershire Regiment spent 6 months confined in a box 5 ft by 3 ft by 2 ft.

Apart from the beatings, kicks and slaps administered by guards, depriving prisoners of food and water—inadequate and unsatisfactory as it usually was—was another method of helping 'self-reflection'. Stringing up uncooperative prisoners was another means of inducing men to talk. Bound hand and foot, a hangman's noose would be slipped round the man's neck and the other end of the rope passed over a beam. He would then be hoisted up on his toes and the noose rope tied to his ankles. At this point the prisoner was told that if he slipped or bent his knees he would be committing suicide, for which his captors could not be held responsible. Alternatively a prisoner's wrists and ankles would be bound and a rope tied to his wrists pulled over a beam so that the prisoner was left standing on his toes. In that position he would be left for hours.

Reactionaries and *active* reactionaries in particular* were often subjected to particularly brutal treatment. In winter such men are reported to have had water poured over their feet. In temperatures of well below 20 degrees of frost, the water froze, and with their feet embedded in solid blocks of ice the prisoners were left to reflect on their crimes. If a man stood up to such treatment, it was possible that the Chinese would eventually give up and send him to a camp as mild as any—if any POW camp in North Korea could be described as mild. In this respect the Chinese were unpredictable: indeed on occasions they showed contempt for a man who submitted readily to bullying. All in all a docile prisoner did not gain much by his docility, and sometimes he gained nothing.

But once a man broke down and admitted guilt, he was expected to write a confession of crimes which he—and the Chinese—knew he had never committed. On the basis of this confession he could be tried and sentenced, although it was more usual for him merely to be told that the trial had been held and that the sentence had been such and such a punishment. The sentence invariably consisted of solitary confinement, and, according to the circumstances, the prisoner served all or some or none of it. If he was released at once he was liable to be warned at frequent intervals that his sentence had merely been suspended and that he could be made to serve it if he did not show that his 'repentance' was 'sincere'. Sometimes, having served the sentence, the prisoner was sentenced to another term or was kept in solitary confinement long after his sentence had actually expired. One British officer sentenced to 6 months actually served fifteen; another British officer, similarly sentenced to six months, served

---

* 'Active' reactionaries were those individuals who opposed the Progressives in the groups to which the latter had been assigned.

eighteen. Many such prisoners never returned to their compounds but were sent to a penal camp.

When a man steadfastly refused to cooperate, the Chinese usually moved him to another camp so that he would not hinder the conversion of his fellows. At the very beginning of the war attempts were made to re-educate all ranks together (with officers and other ranks taking orders from Chinese-appointed squad leaders). But this soon proved to be a failure and officers were segregated; this segregation was subsequently carried a stage further with the removal of senior NCOs from the other ranks' camps. Yet this segregation of officers, NCOs and other ranks by no means removed all the 'reactionaries', and 'uncooperative' other ranks continued to be weeded out, and sent to OR penal camps where discipline was 'stricter' and rations kept at the minimum required for survival. The equivalent officer penal camp contained prisoners sentenced for participating in various 'plots' or 'reactionary activities', or for having a 'hostile attitude'; officers and air-crews captured after January 1952; and those who because of their former duties were considered by the Chinese as 'spies'. All were regarded as rather 'special criminals', and until the armistice was signed, food and treatment in this camp were consistently bad.

But the worst effect of segregation stemmed from the withdrawal of leadership. In some camps this resulted in a breakdown of discipline, and decay of morale, the consequences of which were filthy conditions, disease and mistrust.

The revelations of a Japanese officer, who spent four years from 1945 to 1949 as a POW of the Russians, showed that the indoctrination programme in North Korea was based on Soviet techniques.* The Progressives were expected to lecture the reactionary groups, to write speeches condemning capitalism and 'American aggression in Korea', and to make propaganda broadcasts. Some did, and the most progressive of the Progressives even formed a group known as the 'Peace Fighters'. Such individuals were few and far between.† Nevertheless, the blizzards of propaganda and hurricanes of violent oratory to which they were subjected did have an effect on quite a number of prisoners. The 229 captured Turks, who were singled out in the beginning as a special target for indoctrination, were completely unaffected. Their rock-like discipline stood them in good stead and when things got difficult they retreated behind their language barrier. Haranguing men through an interpreter is not the easiest

---

* 'Yamomoto', *Four Years in Hell* (Tokyo 1952).
† When the Korean War ended only one British soldier and 21 Americans chose life under the Communists; 11 other Americans were retained by the Communists against their will but subsequently released.

way of putting across an indoctrination problem. Some 978 British soldiers were captured in Korea, nearly all of whom went through the indoctrination mill without absorbing its message. Of the 7190 captured Americans, 4428 survived to return to the US (2730 died and 470 others have been recorded 'missing'). It was against this group of 7000 that the Communists concentrated their efforts, and it was then that the indoctrination programme had most success. Fundamentally this was because the American GIs were utterly unprepared for what was to happen after their capture. Hardly had they recovered from the shock of capture when they had their first interrogation. It was usually conducted by an officer—often educated in the United States and nearly always a fluent English conversationalist—in the presence of a 'progressive'. Military information was sought, but the prisoner was also quizzed on his home life and educational background. Only a handful of POWs were able to maintain silence and nearly all of them went beyond the 'name, rank, number' formula. Interrogation sessions often concluded with a demand that the prisoner should write up his own personal history for the benefit of his interrogators. But whatever he produced in the way of a biographical sketch was rarely sufficient, and he was usually compelled to write more and in greater detail. What he did write was often used against him—the slightest discrepancy and he was accused of lying; he might even learn that he had written a confession of some kind.

When Colonel Frank H. Schwable, an American marine, was repatriated from Korea, he was required to appear before a military court of enquiry to answer charges that he had confessed to knowledge of the UN Forces using germ warfare. (On his return home, Schwable had repudiated his confession, saying it had been made under duress.) In fact the pressures applied to Schwable to get him to make his 'confession' were typical of those brought to bear by the Chinese on many men in Korea. Humiliated, cold, starved and isolated in solitary confinement, the answers he gave to a succession of interrogators were probed and twisted until his memory and ability to think coherently were affected. In the end his resistance broke, and the Chinese began to imprint their own version of the 'truth' on his mind. The outcome was inevitable. His tormentors were able to get him to admit his crime of being concerned with bacteriological warfare.

A British officer, Major (now Major-General) Anthony Farrar-Hockley, has also described how a man can eventually come to believe what his interrogators have implanted in his mind, given the right physical and mental approach.*

* BBC Broadcast: *The Spirit in Jeopardy*, 2 January 1955.

... The Chinese are past masters at this technique. They wouldn't tell me what they wanted. Whenever we got near to something substantial they would immediately come back to it from another angle. We'd all go round it, but I'd never find out what it was. And then they would go away and leave me thinking. . . . 'Now was that it? No, it couldn't have been that. I wonder if it was so-and-so. And that's what they were trying to do. They were trying to get me to a state when the idea would suddenly come: bingo, and I would begin to wonder whether I'd thought of it or they had. . . .'

The Chinese were quick to realize that the longings for peace among men desperate to get home would, if properly handled, provide excellent propaganda material. So 'peace' soon became the major theme of the indoctrination campaign. From lectures on 'peace' it was only a short step to POW 'peace' committees to persuade other prisoners to sign 'peace petitions'. As such appeals came from supposedly spontaneously formed groups of captives they were expected to have more effect in the free world than Chinese-prepared appeals. There was also the hope that members of camp 'peace committees' might on their return home found similar organizations and so extend Communist influence in their own country. Another advantage was that prisoners who joined peace committees would find it more difficult to refuse to cooperate with the Chinese on other matters. The British Government Report quotes one British officer's account of the preparation of a peace appeal in Camp 5:

The Chinese were anxious to get the officers to sign a 'peace appeal'. Their timing, as usual, was excellent. Several officers had been returned to the compound who had undergone severe punishment for alleged and actual offences. The moral effect on their comrades was at its peak when a 'petition for the cessation of hostilities' was produced for signature.

Using the battered condition of those who had just returned to the compound as an example of what could happen to anyone who showed himself to be 'an enemy of the people', and having encouraged some of these men to relate the horrors of 'the treatment', they were able to get the signature of all the officers. . . .

From a British other rank came another account of the peace petition signing: 'Prisoners were taken out on parade and ordered to sign the Stockholm Peace Appeal—there was no question of the signing being voluntary. Threats of cutting down food supplies were used to persuade prisoners to sign other petitions. . . .'

Most of the inmates of the Korean-run 'Peace Fighter Camp'

(Camp 12) were recruited in small groups either from the 'Bean Camp' near Suan—a POW transit camp—or from the notorious 'Caves' (Camp 9) run by Colonel Kim, the commandant of Camp 12. At 'The Caves', which was run by the North Korean police primarily for South Korean prisoners, treatment was brutal, medical care non-existent, food inadequate, and the death-rate high. Men were literally confined in caverns; there were no latrines, they were forced to sleep without blankets, and food was thrown at the captives. In contrast with these degrading conditions, the food at Camp 12 was good; medical attention was available, and prisoners were issued with bedding, clothing, cigarettes and soap. Thus the temptation to succumb to Colonel Kim's appeal to join his Peace Fighters' Camp was great, and many prisoners who consented to a move did so in the belief that by doing so they would stay alive, whereas if they stayed in the 'Caves' they would probably die.

Once in Camp 12 prisoners were expected to produce any type of propaganda material asked for. The Koreans wasted little time on explanations, although they did make some attempt to indoctrinate prisoners, realizing that the more indoctrinated they were the better the propaganda. So long as the prisoners did what was required of them they were well treated; if they became uncooperative they were usually softened by threats of a return to the 'Caves'. Yet not all succumbed. One British sergeant consistently refused to sign any petition even when he was told that he could be shot for refusing to obey an order. He was eventually returned to the 'Caves', and although he survived his punishment probably discouraged others from following his lead.

Every available propaganda tool was employed in the Chinese indoctrination programme. Via pamphlets and a weekly newspaper, the *Peace Fighters' Chronicle*, propaganda supporting the work of the peace committees was fed to the captives. In the *Chronicle* articles on the preparation of surrender appeals, atrocity stories, and broadcasts for the Peking or Pyongyang radio were published. Foreign journalists were also harnessed to the effort. Until the last few weeks of the war, independent visitors and organizations such as the International Red Cross were barred by the Chinese from the POW camps; on the other hand facilities for visits by Communists and Communist sympathizers were readily arranged. British visitors included Mr Alan Winnington of the *Daily Worker*, Mr Wilfred Burchett, an Australian correspondent of the left-wing French magazine *L'Humanité*, Mr Michel Shapiro of the *Daily Worker*, Mr Jack Gaster, a London solicitor and member of the British Communist Party, and Mrs Monica Felton, chairman of the British National Assembly of Women—a society affiliated to the Women's

International Democratic Federation, an international Communist 'front' organization.

Winnington, whose lurid reporting of the Korean War—including a description of a germ warfare raid which he claimed to have witnessed—invariably followed the Communist line, visited Camps 1 and 5 on a number of occasions. (The fact that he once referred to captured officers as 'a lot of bloody Fascists' may have accounted for his not visiting the officers' and sergeants' camp.) At these camps he had personal talks with selected prisoners and lectured on such subjects as the Korean peace talks, the progress of the world 'peace' conferences, and the 'appalling conditions' in the US and Britain. At Camp 5 (the Progressives' Camp) he appeared to be fairly welcome, but at Camp 1 his lectures were often greeted with shouts of 'You'll hang' and so on.

The other *Daily Worker* correspondent, Shapiro, received similar treatment. One sergeant of the Royal Ulster Rifles, who was suffering from dysentery and the early symptoms of beri-beri from which he died later, told Shapiro that he was the 'poorest example of an Englishman I've ever seen, and if I could get my hands round your scrawny neck I'd wring it'. Shapiro had him marched out with the comment: 'I'll have you shot!' At about the same time Shapiro lectured a number of American prisoners, telling them that they were 'warmongering dogs' who deserved to die like dogs. Gaster, who visited China and North Korea in March 1952 as a member of the 'International Association of Democratic Lawyers' to investigate charges of germ warfare and atrocities committed by United Nations troops, went to Camps 1 and 5. On his return to Britain he contributed to the *Daily Worker* a glowing account of camp conditions. 'Prisoners,' he wrote, 'get more meat, more fats and more sugar to eat than anyone in Britain receives from a ration book.'

The indoctrination of UN prisoners in Korea so far described was all part of the Communist battle for the minds of UN prisoners. While this struggle was going on, another battle was raging in the POW camps in South Korea, where Communist prisoners were continuing the war for military and political advantage. Their actions were not governed by any indoctrination programme—unless it was one which had affected the prisoners' leaders before they became captives. As it is pertinent to the whole question of whether captors should automatically initiate and pursue an indoctrination programme, this use of prisoners as a psychological weapon in war is deserving of mention.

In the late spring of 1951, when armistice negotiations opened in Korea, the Chinese and North Koreans had taken about 60,000 prisoners, of whom about 50,000 were Koreans. On the other side, the UN Forces had captured about 160,000 communist prisoners. As the Koreans were rapidly absorbed into the North Korean War effort—being given the option of enlisting in the Communist army or paying the ultimate penalty for their bourgeois sins—the proportion of POWs behind barbed wire was about 15 to 1 in favour of the UN. In any other conflict up to World War II this would have represented a powerful weapon in the hands of the UN truce negotiators. Unfortunately there was one complicating factor. A large number of the POWs in UN hands did not wish to return to Communist control. Many of them had been unwilling Communists anyway, press-ganged into soldiering for North Korea. Others had sampled a little of the 'imperial warmongers'' gravy—albeit behind barbed wire—and found it to their taste. So they had no wish to be repatriated. For the UN their attitude represented something of an ideological victory. For the North Koreans, however, it was a totally unacceptable loss of face. The fact that they had been unable to attain a military success was bad enough; that a large number of their people should be unwilling to return to the Communist fold was even more unpalatable. So they set about reducing the percentage of those whose views had changed by their glimpses of the non-Communist way of life.

In effect this was not such a difficult task as might be imagined. Most of the Communist POWs were confined in huge camps on Koje-do Island to the south of the Korean peninsula. Their food, clothing and housing were adequate—indeed lavish by Korean standards; guarding arrangements were lax; and within their compounds the prisoners were permitted to organize and run their own show more or less as they liked. In workshops equipped by the Americans as rehabilitation training centres, the POWs were not prevented from turning out Communist placards, flags and news-sheets; and unbeknown to the camp authorities they were also making weapons. Virtually no supervision was exercised by guards inside the wire, and inspections were few and far between, so the Communist hierarchy in the compound was allowed to tighten its grip unchallenged.* Hard core Communists had quickly taken over the reins of leadership inside the compounds, and orders were passed to them from the north. In any civil war an agent from one side can

---

* Unfortunately the attitude of protective agencies exacerbated the situation. Some members of the UN were hypersensitive over the treatment of POWs. These, the International Red Cross and the Neutral Nations Inspection Teams (called NITS by all Americans!), harassed the Koje-do camp authorities regularly regarding POW rights and privileges. None of these agencies could enter North Korea because of the blunt refusal of the Communists, and they tended to compensate by being twice as officious at Koje-do.

usually pass himself off as a civilian only a few yards from the barbed wire of a military installation—and vice versa. So it was comparatively simple for the North Koreans to get messages to their men behind the wire. But they went further than this. Control of their prisoners was strengthened by infiltrating more high-grade Communists into the compounds. Jeon Moon Il, alias Pak Sang Hyong, for instance, had risen to be the vice-chairman of the North Korean Labour Party. But in 1952, Jeon Moon Il, officially listed as Private Pak, was the head of a political committee in the Koje-do POW camp. Responsible to him there was a complete network of North Korean officers, who had simply walked into the UN lines with their hands up, brandishing UN surrender leaflets.

When the situation eventually boiled over, it was found that the prisoners' 'cell organization committees' had organized kangaroo courts, strong-arm squads and executioners. In March 1952 there was a riot in Koje-do, and two months later the prisoners seized the American camp commandant, Brigadier General Francis T. Dodd, and a US regimental combat-team had to be sent in to restore order. To obtain Dodd's release the Americans had virtually to promise that the UN would 'stop persecuting and terrorizing' prisoners into opting *not* to return to their homelands when hostilities ceased. As such a promise implied that the UN had been actually persuading prisoners to forsake their Communist beliefs, this was a propaganda victory for the Chinese and North Korean delegates at the truce talks. This was a situation that had never happened before. In World War II German and Italian POWs moved tractably to the rear under the command of their own officers, and captured Japanese—who considered themselves dead in the eyes of their Emperor—needed to be protected only from their Korean fellow-prisoners. But in the UN POW camps the Communist Chinese and North Koreans had organized themselves into a military force almost as formidable as the regiments they had left in the north.

Communist plans intercepted in mid-1952 revealed that the prisoners were ordered deliberately to misunderstand orders, to ignore the instructions of POW camp authorities and to stage demonstrations and riots. Mutinies at Koje-do and Cheju-do during September showed that these orders had got through and were being carried out. Finally on 14 December 1952—the same day the Chinese rejected a United Nations resolution calling for peace in Korea— 9000 civilian internees at Pongan attempted a mass break-out. In the course of the fighting which followed, 85 prisoners lost their lives and 113 were wounded. A Communist summary of the results of this operation recognized that heavy casualties had been expected, but went on to say that '... our fighting comrades ... were determined to die a glorious death . . . and although the task imposed on us by the party and the fatherland could not be fulfilled . . . the main purpose was to develop "a class fight to give the enemy a crushing defeat. . . .""*

Ominously UN Command HQ noted that the measures permitted under the Geneva Convention would not destroy the Communist organization inside the UN POW camps. A Communist POW, therefore, had to be regarded 'not as a passive human being in need of care and protection until he could be returned to his home but as still an active soldier determined to fight on in whatever way his leader dictated'.†

Thus, in Korea, war was extended in a very positive sense into the prisoner of war camp. On the one side there was a fight for the minds of the prisoners; on the other side prisoners were used by their own people to earn political and military advantage. Of the two battles the more dramatic, but probably less significant in the strategic sense, was the battle for the prisoners' minds. Before the evidence of the indoctrination campaign used by the Communists in Korea had been properly sifted, it was popularly supposed that 'brainwashing' techniques had been employed to 'wash' a man's mind and then fill it with Communist doctrine. However, a US Government Committee set up to investigate what happened to American POWs in Korea concluded that any 'brainwashing' that had been done was limited to the extraction of confessions having a special propaganda value, such as those concerned with germ warfare. Nevertheless, even if brainwashing was not used, there is little doubt that the Communists were able to use rudimentary psychology on their prisoners—and not too scientifically at that—to further their aims. If they hoped to convert large numbers of American and British troops to Communism, their indoctrination programme was a miserable failure.‡ But they did undoubtedly achieve considerable propaganda advantages. And propaganda is of great value, especially in war, and most especially in Asia and that part of the world adjacent to or behind the Iron Curtain. Peoples from India to the Philippines and from Poland to Siberia could hear stories and see pictures of men ostensibly accepting the Communist line and condemning that of the West. To the great mass of uncertain people or those whose knowledge of

* Press release from the UN Command of 28 January 1953, and George S. Prugh, 'Prisoners of War', *Dickinson Law Review* (1956), p. 123.

† 57th Report of the UN Command for the period 1–15 November 1952; 28 US Dept. State Bulletin 690 (1953).

‡ The voluntary educational programmes for German POWs run by the British and Americans between 1943 and 1945 are credited with a much higher degree of success than the compulsory Chinese programme. See Dean Tollefson, 'Enemy Prisoners of War', *Iowa Law Review* (1946), pp. 51–77.

the West was restricted only to the information which was allowed to trickle under the Iron Curtain, such propaganda probably had a considerable impact. Modern war is in part a war of ideologies—a struggle for the mind of man. And the side which appeals to the reason and captures the mind of an enemy soldier may often capture his body without any further struggle. Like the interrogation battle, the war for the mind of a man comes down to a battle of wits. And it is one which a soldier who has not been educated to understand what he may be up against will surely lose.

13
Freedom

Between the extreme alternatives of escape and repatriation at the end of the war there are several other ways in which a prisoner of war may regain his freedom while the fighting is still going on. In the majority of cases only one of these is really feasible and its implications for the prisoners concerned are not pleasant.

Practical as well as humanitarian considerations often prompt a captor nation to repatriate sick and wounded prisoners. The prime reason for holding men as POWs is to stop them taking any further part in a war, and as sick and wounded men are no longer able to do so there is little point in keeping them. Indeed, the fact that they need extra care is an added incentive for getting rid of them. In April 1942 about 129 British sick and wounded were exchanged for 919 Italians in Smyrna harbour. Hospital ships from Bari and Alexandria took the repatriates to Smyrna and the actual exchange was effected in mid-harbour under the supervision of the International Red Cross and the Turkish military authorities. A year later two other parties totalling about 1600 British were exchanged for about 5700 Italians, many of whom were civilians. This is an example of what can happen.

Unfortunately the arranging of an exchange of sick and wounded is not as easy as one would imagine. Past experience has shown that even disabled persons have taken an active part in hostilities after being exchanged, and a captor state is reluctant to let prisoners go free unless it is absolutely sure that they are out of the war for good and all. Political motives also intervene. Repatriated sick and wounded POWs will talk about the deprivations they and other prisoners have undergone. And this information can be exploited as propaganda prejudicial to the captors. For the amputees, the blind, and the cot cases this is a heart-breaking reason for refusing to send them home. But that will not necessarily trouble the captors. A totalitarian regime may well prefer prisoners to die rather than be repatriated.

Even if the repatriation or exchange of sick and disabled POWs is agreed, the question of eligibility often provides another hurdle. According to the Geneva Convention (Articles 109–110) the 'beneficiaries' of such an exchange are those whose mental or physical capacity has been gravely diminished because they are suffering from an incurable disease or wound, or because of an illness from which they are not likely to recover within one year. The task of deciding which prisoners fall into these categories is that of a mixed medical commission, comprising two neutral representatives of the International Red Cross and a doctor appointed by the captor state. Men recommended by POW camp doctors or the delegates of humanitarian agencies visiting the camps are examined by the commission and if they are found to fulfill the conditions their names are put on the list for repatriation. Those who are familiar with bureaucratic arguments will appreciate that this process takes time—time during which a man who may be considered as eligible in the unlikely-to-recover-in-a-year may well be downgraded into a get-well-in-four-or-five-months category. In the long run everything depends on the good will of the belligerents, combined perhaps with a fear that retribution will follow if there is a violation of the Geneva rules.

Apart from the repatriation of sick and wounded, Article 109 of the 1949 Geneva Convention provides for prisoners who have had a long spell in captivity to be repatriated or interned in a neutral country. This provision is motivated by a desire to save prisoners from mental disorders and degenerations which accrue from 'barbed-wire disease'. The same difficulties as those applying to the sick and disabled are likely to hamper the working of any repatriation of long-term POWs. The captors' determination to exploit their POW labour force or their efforts to indoctrinate the prisoners may be additional hardships. Only if a reciprocal arrangement is sufficiently tempting is an exchange of prisoners likely to materialize during hostilities. If it does, then the POW who is likely to benefit will probably have spent two or three years behind the wire, be over 45 years of age, married and have children. Fit young men, as most soldiers are, have little hope in this field.

It is possible, of course, for prisoners to be released on parole. In the past men have been given their freedom on promising not to take any further part in current hostilities. However, as parole is a form of agreement, it requires the consent of both parties, i.e. captor and prisoner, neither of whom is under an obligation to give or accept parole. A general parole is never granted without ascertaining the individual's attitude. But once he has accepted parole, a prisoner is under an obligation which neither he nor his government should violate. An understanding of this sort carries obvious disadvantages. Yet there are some corresponding benefits which may attract a captor state to the parole system. Releasing POWs on parole frees guards for other duties, and the captors no longer face the onerous burden of providing food and accommodation for the men behind the wire. When the captors themselves are short of food this may be a major consideration.

The principal obstacle of the granting of parole in modern war is likely to be the large number of prisoners involved. Releasing them on their mere word without a promise by the prisoners' own government would be a risk, and there would always be some doubt about the supervision necessary to ensure the parole was scrupulously observed. For more than a hundred years these considerations have discouraged both captors from granting parole and the prisoners from accepting it, and in this century the practice has become almost extinct.* From a humanitarian point of view release on parole has much to offer by way of mitigating the deprivations of prisoners of war. Regrettably, however, it is a custom and system which is unlikely to be revived.

Like parole, the ransoming of prisoners of war is almost a relic of the past, and there is little hope of the custom being resuscitated on any appreciable scale. Ransom implies release of prisoners in exchange for money, but anything may be given as a price and this kind of ransom is not absolutely ruled out. In recent years Cuban rebels were released by Castro on receipt of millions of dollars worth of medical supplies provided by American sympathizers.

But if ransom, parole and exchange are unlikely prospects, the prisoner of war can always hope that a change in the course of the war will bring his liberation. In World War II the Italian capitulation brought an early release for thousands of prisoners. G. S. Stavert, who had had more than enough of POW life after six months' captivity, describes his liberation as 'the best moment of his life'— although his eventual return to the UK in a succession of dreary transit-camps was 'a bit of a let down'. In this context the realization that freedom is close at hand is the greatest morale raiser.

At Fontanellato in 1943 [Stavert writes], we had plenty of hope with the invasion of Sicily in progress, led by Monty and the Eighth Army who of course could not possibly fail, the end of our sentence was in sight. Exactly what form it would take nobody

* During World War I, the French Government released some German officers on parole in France, but as Germany did not reciprocate the French withdrew the privilege.

could say, but it was bound to be only weeks away. All we had to do was pass the time in patience till the day arrived. At Capua, we baited the guards, fouled up the counts, and took little notice of the Capitano; how could you, when he regularly came on parade with several days' growth on his chin? At Fontanellato (after a bit of sharpening up by the SBO) we behaved. The Commandante, a Colonello of the old school, responded by handing over control to the SBO after the armistice. As a consequence we got a few hours' warning, and when the German convoy arrived we had already gone. They arrested him instead.

In this instance the Germans took charge of the Allied prisoners when the Italians surrendered, and subsequently took the prisoners with them when they retreated. On other occasions retreating armies have been known to kill their prisoners. Napoleon killed Turkish prisoners at Jaffa rather than have them return to reinforce the army opposing him, or weaken his own army by providing escorts to send the prisoners to Egypt. When the invasion of Japan was contemplated in 1945 the Allied planning staffs feared that the Japanese would massacre their captives. This fear lingered right up to the time of the Japanese surrender.

14

Repatriation
and After-effects

For the vast majority of prisoners of war freedom comes only after the shooting has stopped. The Geneva Convention of 1949 stipulates that POWs should be released and repatriated when 'active' hostilities end, and in the normal course of events this is what happens.* But this is not always the case. Victor nations sometimes retain prisoners of war as hostages until the peace terms they impose are accepted by the vanquished. In 1918 the German Armistice dictated the 'immediate repatriation without reciprocity . . . of all Allied and United States prisoners of war, including those under trial and condemned'. The Allies, on the other hand, were free to dispose of their prisoners as they thought fit. Twenty-seven years later the Allied Powers did not repatriate all the prisoners of war for a long time, and in some cases the prisoners were absorbed into their local economy. It was 1949, four years after the ending of 'active' hostilities before the Russians announced that they had returned all the Germans they were holding in captivity. More recently still, India has been holding 90,000 Pakistani prisoners captured during the fighting over Bangladesh, which ended in 1971.

Most prisoners of war are only too anxious to go home at the earliest opportunity. But one feature of the ideological wars in recent years has been the number of prisoners who have exchanged their loyalty and refused to go home. In the Korean War there was intense political ferment inside the UN POW camps, and the prisoners divided into Communists and non-Communists. Many Koreans and Chinese had been forcibly pressed into the Communist armies, and they had no political belief; indeed in thousands of cases they had a

---

* The 1929 Convention was less accommodating. It provided that prisoners should be repatriated 'in accordance with the terms to that effect in the Armistice agreement, and in the absence of such provision in the Armistice immediately after the conclusion of a peace treaty' (Article 75).

general hatred of their rulers. These men, and others whose glimpse —albeit from behind the wire—into non-Communist life had altered their outlook, petitioned the UN not to allow them to be repatriated. The Chinese and North Koreans suggested that such prisoners should be offered a choice in a properly organized screening operation. When the screening was completed, however, and it became known that only about 50 per cent of the total POWs held by the UN would voluntarily return to Red China or North Korea, the Communist representatives at the peace talks in Panmunjon demanded that all captured personnel must be repatriated regardless of their politics.

President Truman, responding to this demand, declared that 'forced repatriation was repugnant to the free world' and that America would not force anyone to return to Communist slavery. American public opinion was behind the President although fears were expressed that this development would prolong the war and delay the return of the American troops in Korea. In the event, the tortuous story of the captives of Korea came to an end when the non-repatriates were released in the demilitarized zone created under the terms of the Korean Armistice. The Chinese sailed to Formosa, and the Koreans reported to the South Korean authorities; their problems had been resolved humanely.

On this occasion the number of prisoners who did not wish to be repatriated was extraordinarily high. The conflict in Korea, like that in Indo-China, was essentially a civil war, exacerbated by ideological differences. Wherever these conditions prevail a similar situation is likely to arise. What then is the position of the POWs who do not wish to be repatriated? For the captors this could well be a serious problem. On humanitarian grounds no man should be compelled to return to his own country against his wishes. On the other hand it can be argued that no state should be compelled to keep prisoners merely because they express a wish not to be repatriated. The number of POWs involved may ultimately decide the issue; but the prisoners' financial position, their standard of living, local labour jealousies, and social and religious prejudices may also impair their chance of being granted asylum in a foreign country. (If a POW says that he wishes to be given asylum in one country and refuses it in another, the situation becomes even more complicated.)

From what has been said the question of non-repatriation is not likely ever to become a burning issue among prisoners of war reared in a Western culture. Those who are not clamouring to return home as soon as the war ends are likely to remain an insignificant minority. Once hostilities cease, the transition from prisoner to free man is likely to occur very quickly.

The end came suddenly, thank God [Colonel Thomas recalls]. Any longer and our time was fast running out. We felt that as individuals physically the end was very near and those who could make any logical mental conclusions by this time were certain that that dirty, nasty, little Commandant would have brought into full play his complete sadistic repertoire to gradually (yes! it would have been gradually) dispose of the superior scum he had had in his charge during his so-called 'war'.

This, in fact, is the beginning of a traumatic period comparable only with that which follows the shock of capture. At the time of his capture, the sudden realization that he had been cut off from all that he has ever known, the POW's psychological spring is wound up. When he is freed, the spring is suddenly released. In captivity he has spent most of his day and much of the night thinking out ways of killing time, and absorbing himself in things that do not conjure up too much of the past. Because the future is uncertain, he has tried not to think too much about it; because it is too depressing he puts thoughts of home out of his mind. Behind the wire a man's horizon narrows, his work becomes sullen. Sooner or later—unless he is an individual of exceptional willpower—the prisoner adjusts to it. At the same time his responsibilities diminish; everything is found, the routine worries of earning a living are removed, and the POW moves slower and slower with the stream.

With freedom, everything changes; and the ex-prisoner has to start growing up all over again. The world will have moved on in his absence. As Stavert found, even after 6 months, 'people'—meaning people who had not been in captivity—seemed to have changed. Some prisoners may even experience a feeling of reluctance when it comes to leaving their camp and returning to the world. Flight-Lieutenant W. B. Towler, whose liberation was assured as Russian tanks burst through the gates of his camp, hesitated when he was offered a lift back to a British unit by the driver of a US scout car. He had left six bars of soap, 300 cigarettes and a greatcoat behind and he wondered whether the proffered lift was worth the sacrifice of these precious objects. Sidney Sheldrick was overcome with a feeling of sadness when he learned that the war was over and he would be going home. Up to the very last minute he was employed

on the most terrible of all working parties—that of the burial squad, and I had the task of taking my comrades on their last journey. Every morning we took up five, and most afternoons the same number. We only had wood for five coffins, so the coffins had a hinged bottom so that a few feet from the bottom we unhooked the coffin bottom with long bamboo poles and, as the body fell the few extra feet, we lifted the coffin out so it could be used again. . . .

An enormous gap exists between the misery which Sheldrick describes and life in surroundings where the crucial issue of the moment might be whether or not the wife's mother should come to stay. The gap can be bridged, but time, patience and understanding are needed. A. C. Goodger considers that many POWS found the return home to be the worst aspect of imprisonment. . . .

Having dreamed of returning to an England we had known in 1939, we were shocked to discover the differences which the war had made, not only to the country itself, but to the people, who had perhaps quite naturally become very hard, while we presumably had become soft. For example, we discovered early on that even genial chaff was intolerable in our confined quarters, and became unusually tolerant and amiable. Even a friend of mine, who had been in Jap hands for three and a half years, most of the time in hospital, expressed a preference for POW life after being home for a few months. On the other hand, the few dreams I have had since, of being captured again, have filled me with horror.

Assessing the effects of captivity on individuals is not easy. At the end of World War II officialdom did not regard the fact that an ex-serviceman had been a POW as of any significance for his rehabilitation and no special records were maintained. A comparison of the post-war history of ex-prisoners of war with those of a similar sample of other ex-servicemen would necessitate considerable research. Nevertheless it is possible to draw some conclusions from the limited number of ex-captives of World War II from Europe and the Far East who have contributed to the making of this book.

Any wide generalization about the physical condition of POWs is difficult because of the enormous variety of camp conditions and individual experiences. Conditions varied in different countries, and inside these countries, in different camps and different periods of the war. Quite often the camp commandant was a major influence in this respect. Clearly a man's physical condition on release depended on the length of his captivity and his own personal experiences. If he had worked in the Silesian coal mines or on the Burma-Siam railway at its worst; if he had been in one of the less fortunate columns that marched across Europe in the closing stages of the war; if he had been subjected to severe exposure and privation while in attempts to escape; if he had fallen into the hands of the Gestapo or been beaten and tortured by the Kempetai or the OGPU, he would probably be in a worse state than if he had not had one or more such experiences. Food, medicine, accommodation and local climatic conditions all had an influence. In general it may be said that POW conditions in the Far East were more damaging to health than those in Europe. If the latter turned out to be better than most prisoners expected the former turned out generally worse. Yet some men released from captivity in Europe were in a worse physical condition than some from the Far East. Many repatriates from Europe were below their normal weight when they were liberated; many found that they tired easily and lacked their former vitality and endurance; a considerable number—especially among the older men—had digestive troubles and rheumatism. Some found that these effects wore off after a few months of good food and comfortable living. Others complain that they have persisted, or—if they did seem to wear off—they have returned to plague middle age.

Generally speaking, repatriates from the Far East and the Soviet Union were suffering from the effects of malnutrition. Those from the Far East were also still suffering from tropical diseases such as malaria; their condition varied from merely being somewhat underweight to extreme emaciation; some still had dysentry or beri-beri; many found their eyesight had suffered; a number had contracted hernias; and others had a variety of aches in muscles and joints. Some found it took a year of care and good feeding to get back to their normal condition; the worst cases needed two years medical treatment; a few attribute a relapse and their present condition to the hardships of POW camp life. Some were prevented by their physical handicaps from taking up their pre-war occupations, or returning to their jobs in tropical climates.

But it is the mental effects of captivity which are probably the most difficult to assess. Here again the individual's reaction to captivity depends on the length of time he spent as a POW, the strain of the work he had to do, the facilities of recreation or education, and any drastic experiences he might have undergone during interrogation or disciplinary punishment. Those who occupied their minds in captivity seem to have come off best. Some, like Owen Greenwood, believe that they benefited from their experiences.

Here again I must keep almost entirely to my personal feelings and reactions. Naturally it took some months to get back to anything approaching normal, as I was in an extremely nervous state and still suffering from various tropical illnesses, etc., so that I was physically in pretty poor shape when I got back to the UK. Over the years, however, I would say that my general characteristics have returned very nearly to what they were before capture. I mention this point because many people are considered to have changed a good deal as the result of their POW experiences. I am probably more tolerant of my fellow men although impatient of the moaners and those who indulge in self-pity and there is quite a fair sprinkling of those among ex-prisoners. If I am more mellow now, it must be remembered that it is over a quarter of a century since I was released and this may be merely the result of Anno Domini. *On balance, however, I think it would be fair to say that, from the point of view of character, I have benefited from my sojourn behind bamboo.* I value life and I enjoy life and I certainly do not under-estimate my good fortune at having survived three and a half years of extremely uncomfortable imprisonment.

Some men felt deeply what they imagined to be the disgrace of capture, and regular soldiers sometimes felt their careers had been ruined by it. Cyril Whitcombe was a major in the Royal Artillery when he was captured:

Financial losses due to loss of promotion and career can never be assessed, but when one thinks of the compensation that is given now in the form of lump sums for early compulsory retirement, it is rather hard to think about what we should have had. . . . I think my chief disappointment when I returned home was the lack of consideration and understanding of those in authority at the time. I find it a little difficult to express my feelings in words. All most of us asked was to be allowed to be able to take up life as far as possible where we left it. As a gunner I expected to be allowed to be posted to an Artillery unit. But no! Would I like to go to the Pioneer Corps or maybe the Ordnance Corps? I was rising 48 and overdue for promotion to Lt-Colonel. I had qualified for the Staff College, passed my promotion exams and always got good confidential reports, so apart from being a bit rusty I was perfectly capable of running a Regiment. When I resisted those in the War Office Selection Board and went to see the War Office myself I was told to get any job I could as Lt-Colonel and after three months in the rank I would be promoted if I got a good report. This I did, but I never got back to the regiment though they did promote me. Every time I tried to get some sort of reasonable treatment I was told, 'We've promoted you, what else do you want.' So in due course I was retired in 1948—a dissatisfied customer. Then came a year of struggling to get a job. I'd got my Lt-Colonel's pension—then £650 p.a.—and I was 51. At last in September 1949 I was offered the task of starting a Home for ex-Officers under the auspices of the Officers' Association. It was not a princely salary but I did get a home for myself and wife, eventually all found, though not at first. This job I did for nearly eleven years and I did feel I was doing something useful. . . .

To many of the younger men in captivity the lack of freedom of movement was a greater trial than it was to those whose mental resources had had more time to develop before capture. (One elderly officer in a German POW camp who had been a businessman considered his time in the POW camp as the most tranquil holiday he had known for years.) Young healthy men often break down before the older and weaker ones; and they complain about their aches and pains more than the others. Some of them worried during their captivity as to whether physical deprivations would leave some permanent impairment of their bodily functions: respiratory, digestive or sexual. The older men were less concerned. A man who has suffered from various disabilities and learned to live with them is often better off than the young robust individual. Subject to several qualifications, therefore, it appears that the best age to become a POW is the early forties when body and mind have become mature.

Restlessness and an inability to settle, a deterioration in their powers of concentration and memory, and a tendency to be easily affected emotionally—especially by a pathetic film or music—a feeling of awkwardness in meeting strangers, a strong dislike of crowds and queues and an overpowering desire to be quiet and alone are common complaints of POWs in the early years after their repatriation. Many ex-POWs of World War II were inclined to resent and oppose restrictions on their freedom of action. 'If anyone tried to order me around I take strong exception,' one of them has said. While such an attitude could easily derive from situations other than captivity, no doubt the latter tended to accentuate it. For most of these men such after-effects tended to disappear after some months of normal living. 'I was probably fairly useless, nervous and difficult to begin with,' wrote Owen Greenwood,

but everyone was extremely tolerant and my rehabilitation was no doubt speeded up by their indulgence. Among my 'colleagues' in the Far East, one has become a partner in a world-renowned firm of architects, another has risen to the top in RAF Intelligence and a third has recently retired from a leading position in a Merchant Bank, so it would seem that our experiences have not interfered much with our careers. You say 'Oddly enough a good many ex-POWs have also done well.' I think perhaps this is not so odd, because to have survived at all shows a degree of resilience, of determination and of intolerance to red tape and various forms of petty bureaucracy that one ought to get on. Of course, there is the other side of the coin. Those less fortunate, with worse physical handicaps, such as blindness, severe neuroses and chronic illness have had a much harder time, but they seem to be fewer than one would expect, and they in their way show, as they always did, remarkable fortitude.

J. V. Webb thought that he might always have been

moody and irritable, and given to outbursts of rage. Perhaps it was the effect of the war as a whole. When the war started I was a 15-year-old schoolboy, and when it finished I was a 21-year-old POW. But at least I survived. The physical effects of captivity were more easily noticeable, as we all suffered from what was probably dysentry, although we blamed it on the cabbage soup. I only know it was a long time before my bladder worked properly, and nearly 5 years before I could sleep a whole night without having to get up and relieve myself.

Many ex-POWs—especially those from the Far East—found it hard to understand what civilians had to grumble about even in austerity England. They might be excused for listening unsympathetically to the occasional civilians who told them of the long hours they had worked during the war and the difficulties they had had with clothing coupons or the rationing system. And it is not surprising that these men should also comment on what seems to them to be an inordinate waste of food in the outside world, as well as that complacency, self-satisfaction and even intolerance of those who had not shared their experiences. No doubt much of this was reaction to the contrast between reality as the ex-prisoners found it, and the enchanted picture which they had built up in their minds and which had sustained them during the blackest days in their distant camps.

While some men have discounted their period of captivity as a 'dead loss' the vast majority regard it as an experience which taught them much. It is natural that those who spent years slaving as manual labourers and struggling to keep alive in appalling conditions, only to return broken down physically if not mentally, should feel that not only were their years in POW camps wasted years, but years whose effects would dog them throughout the rest of their lives. For these men it was 'a waste of time', a period in which they lost everything. But the majority—especially those who were imprisoned in Europe—experienced long periods during which conditions were bearable, and during which they had the strength and urge to make good use of their time. These men, who returned to normal health soon after repatriation, were as definite that they gained from captivity knowledge which might never otherwise have come their way. Nearly every ex-POW will claim that he learned more of human nature in a couple of years of captivity that he could have done in two decades of normal life. There are few who do not speak nostalgically of the comradeship of their days of captivity, and the ex-prisoners of war associations which have been formed almost everywhere are no doubt born of a natural understanding which grew up from the common experience of captivity and the desire to continue the mutual help which so many men found to be its main redeeming feature.

Later [wrote Captain Johnson], with a fuller knowledge of all that had been happening outside the barbed wire, we realized how much we—who have endured and were not overcome—must all strive to banish forever the guilty madness of war.

15

A Code for Survival

In World War II the death-toll of prisoners reached an unprecedented level, estimated at between six and ten million.* Never in any war have so many POWS perished. Of all British and American prisoners approximately 11 per cent died in captivity—most of them from malnutrition or deliberate neglect; some 45 per cent of the Germans imprisoned in Soviet camps and 60 per cent of the Russians captured by the Germans did not live to return home either. Staggered by these statistics the representatives of 57 nations met in Geneva in 1949 to hammer out higher standards for POWS and revise the Geneva Convention. The outcome of their deliberations was the 1949 Convention, details of which are discussed in Appendix A.

The 1949 Convention, like its predecessors, provides a set of rules protecting prisoners of war. Like other international agreements it is one of the fruits of the civilized world. And if there are wars in which some of the participants have refused to acknowledge this civilization, or seceded from it, prisoners may not derive much benefit from the rules followed by their own side. In the past they may have profited from the reluctance of nations to behave badly towards prisoners in their hands because they are concerned about what happens to their fighting men in the enemy's hands. Allied POWS in Germany in World War II clearly benefited from this reciprocity, and it remains a very real bulwark against abuses. But the benefits of reciprocal respect depend on the value attached to individuals, which has been one of the main features of established creeds and of Western civilization. In Asia many people have always had different

---

*It is difficult to arrive at a more accurate total, because the statistics do not exist. No one knows, for instance, exactly how many men died in the Japanese camps, how many Russians in German camps (believed to be about three million out of a total of five million), or how many Germans died in the USSR. (The official German estimate puts the number at 1·5 million out of a total of 3,460,000.)

instincts, which rise rapidly to the surface in war. During World War I, it was apparent that Turkey was not interested in Turks who were captured, and in World War II Japan and Russia were not interested in their nationals who became prisoners of war. In Korea and Vietnam Communist interest appears to be not in the individual as such, but only his worth as a political weapon. The Japanese, the Russians, the North Koreans and the Viet Cong have not been interested in reprisals because they did not care what happened to their captured troops. Such attitudes present a serious threat to future POWs.

Another threat stems from a historical change in conditions. Until recently most wars have been fought by nations of comparatively equal economic potential. The exception were colonial-type wars in which only limited forces were engaged and in which the numbers of European or American prisoners were never high. Their captors—whether they were dervishes or American Indians—were not even expected to comply with civilized rules. In World War II Japan had advanced in many ways, but the living standards of the Japanese were well below those of the West even in peace time. Korea, Vietnam, the Arab nations of the Middle East, China and even the Soviet Union still have a long way to go before they attain the standards of the West. In this respect one conclusion of the German investigators into the fate of German POWs in Russia is especially significant. No evidence was uncovered to suggest that the Russians deliberately tried to starve their prisoners to death. Malnutrition followed in the wake of inefficiency, indifference and corruption. But the Russians had a vested interest in the Germans as manpower to replace that which they had lost. This was reason enough to keep them alive. The point, however, is that prisoners of war cannot expect standards of food and shelter higher than those of their captors, even if their health suffers because of their conditions.

Historical changes have also undermined the established system of protective agencies. One of the main pillars of the Geneva Convention is the reliance on neutrals as protecting powers. By the end of World War I no great nation of power and influence remained uninvolved, and there was a shortage of minor neutral states. The same situation occurred in World War II, when the protection role again devolved on a few neutrals whose strength and influence was woefully inadequate. Under the United Nations Charter a nation is not even considered to be peace-loving if it fails to join in with the right side. So only minor powers are likely to be uncommitted and available to carry out the functions of the protective agencies. Because minor power means minor influence their ability to oversee the working of the Convention will be weak.

For POWs the United Nations Charter has introduced a further complication. In the old days, a belligerent nation could earn the respect of the neutral world by the way it behaved during hostilities. In modern times the United Nations declares one side to be the aggressor and its actions are outlawed in advance. Pressure of world opinion reduces the size of the neutral world, and so there is little to be gained by treating prisoners decently. Nor is decent behaviour encouraged by the knowledge that defeat in total war will be followed anyway by total retaliation. Also, in the event of victory, there will be no great power remaining after the war whose criticism would make much difference to a cynical victor. All in all, therefore, the outlook for future POWs is as grim as before—if not more so. And as war seems unlikely to be abolished and efforts to control what happens when it breaks out seem to promise even more complications, the problems of POWs must be considered pragmatically.

Whether anything more can be done on an international level seems doubtful. The existing Geneva Convention, which was the outcome of prolonged and difficult negotiations, defines limits to which most countries were prepared to go in 1949 towards establishing a set of rules for controlling what happens in war. Marginal improvements might be effected, but as some states were unwilling to adopt the 1949 Convention, even more states can be expected to oppose improvement. If so it leads nowhere to give the rules a false bill of health. In any case there can be no assurance that any new convention will be observed more faithfully than previous regulations have been. Nor is it certain that all countries will adhere to the old convention. And even if both adherence and future observance were assured, it could not be assumed that the content of a new convention would be adequate. In fact, it is almost mathematically certain to be inadequate. Whatever is globally adopted must come down to the lowest common denominator, and this lowest common denominator usually comes nowhere near what is essential. Consequently, while international efforts to devise rules to regulate war can be appreciated as steps in the right direction they rarely reach the point where exclusive reliance can be placed on them.

What then can be done on a national level to protect POWs? Here again the field is limited. A powerful country can, to some extent, rely on reprisals to protect its nationals who become prisoners of war. Competing with a barbaric enemy may, however, make competition impossible without coming down to the enemy's level and lowering the country's own honour and reputation. This does not, of course, mean that some reprisals which are less reprehensible may not be successful. Whoever wins the war can punish the other side's war criminals, and what is expected from other nations in the way of treatment of prisoners of war can be spelled out in peace time, and what will happen by way of reprisals and war criminals can be specified even before a shot is fired.

A policy of fairness and kindness towards enemy prisoners is an alternative to reprisals, and incompatible with them. Such a policy has the advantage of avoiding cruelty towards helpless human beings and of being morally superior to the policies of many other nations. Poor countries may be forced into bad treatment of prisoners through their very poverty; economic warfare may aggravate the situation. In past wars Britain and the United States have been fortunate in this respect; economic pressures have never been so severe as to reflect in their treatment of POWs. Moreover, in World War II, adequate food and humane treatment showed a profit. Starved and bullied prisoners will not do the best work, and prisoners fed and treated well in Britain and America contributed to the Allied war effort by doing work for which civilians would have been needed. Without necessarily doing work of a military nature they released civilians.

Good treatment of prisoners of war also makes a profound impression in enemy countries. Even if it is not advertised the true facts soon reach the families of enemy prisoners; through these families they will reach other nationals. Good treatment can also be mentioned in radio broadcasts to enemy countries, and as the facts are true, this kind of propaganda cannot be reversed later. On the other hand reprisals against enemy prisoners may easily be ineffective; the enemy may be a country which does not care much for individual lives, and still less for the lives of those who have been captured.

In retrospect it appears that most of the atrocities committed and threatened in recent wars have been military blunders. Atrocities embitter, and threats frighten an enemy population into prolonged resistance, while the decent treatment of prisoners encourages surrender. Even among people who have been indoctrinated with fanaticism, decent treatment will break the wall of fanaticism and encourage surrender. On the other hand there is no real danger of troops reared and nurtured in the Western world being attracted by offers made by some totalitarian state; they are too firmly convinced of the superiority of conditions at home to be lured by the promises of a better world behind an iron or bamboo curtain. But if this is not true, there must surely be benefit if both sides compete to attract the greater number of surrenders. If either side starts such a competition, the other will be forced to follow suit. And such a competition could do as much for prisoners of war as either international regulations or harsh treatment.

On the personal level, the way a man comes through the ordeal of being a prisoner of war depends on a number of factors. Sir John Burns, a prisoner of the Japanese who worked on the notorious Burma railway in World War II, has expressed his views as follows.*

I speak only of the Railway as that is where my experience was. . . . Let me attempt to list the factors which influence survival and then to elaborate as to why I have chosen them: Age; Mental and Physical Balance and Fitness; Luck.

I have restricted the list to just these three main factors and I have ignored those factors which affected a small minority only. Perhaps to some extent this is conditioned by the fact that in some cases at least I tended to despise the ways and means adopted: Hanging round the Japanese cook-house in the hope of food surplus to requirements, trading with the Thais when it meant in stolen goods, cashing IOUs at £1 to one tical—say fourteen to one —although I did in fact do this and honoured the IOU after the war, and a variety of other more or less dishonest practices.

So: *Age:* This in my view was the greatest single factor and the best survival age to be old enough to be mature mentally but still young enough to stand up to the physical effort needed to work on the railway. This age varied with the individual but I would place thirty as near the ideal: The very young could reach a point where life no longer seemed worth living and the will to survive disappeared: A factor in this was, of course, the constant tension and the underlying fear of falling foul of the Japanese and being ill-treated: Punishment varied from a simple slap on the face to a beating to the point of near death and included standing in front of the guardroom for 24 hours and having a limb broken with a blow from a male bamboo: One never knew when one might unwittingly offend nor what the punishment might be: The more nervous or apprehensive one might be the greater the chance of committing an offence.

The too old simply exhausted their physical resources. The Japanese did not accept age as a reason for not working on the railway; they simple said, 'Not too old to fight, not too old to work.' With physical exhaustion often came mental exhaustion, and again the underlying tension and fear of the consequences of error, real or imagined, played its part.

Mental and physical balance and fitness: This is so obvious as hardly to need elaboration. Some are just unfitted mentally but this does not apply only to prisoners; it applies to war in all its aspects and perhaps in this age of strain to life itself. Physically

* Letter to the author.

the overweight at the time of the capitulation were more susceptible to beri-beri and other deficiency disease. The lean seemed to
survive better on the meagre diet—the lowest I experienced was
8 ozs of rice per day and very little else.

Luck: Undoubtedly an important factor. There was the luck of
what particular work one had to do. Clearing the track was
probably the hardest work. A working party was given a section
of jungle to clear and this had to be finished before returning to
camp. Again the section, in fact the luck of the section, one drew
lots for them, was a factor. Trees had to be felled and cleared and
bamboo clumps destroyed and removed as well as clearing the
undergrowth. The luck of the Japanese engineer private in charge
—some were better than others. There was the luck of the
particular sickness from which one suffered. A large enough jungle
ulcer—something which was extremely visible—usually meant
being sent to the base hospital camp. Malaria and dysentry are not
visible sicknesses and unless one had an actual fever at a time
when sick parades were held for the Japanese to decide who went
to the hospital camp one simply continued to work.

There were other forms of luck: For example, the Japanese
soldiers at one point were putting their Thai money—printed in
great quantity by the Japanese—into goods. Watches and particularly Rolex watches were readily purchased. I had a Rolex wrist-
watch—admittedly it did not go—but it was snapped up for
50 ticals. I could buy bananas, peanuts and sometimes eggs which
supplemented the rations. So also I was considered good for an
IOU and this too helped. My battalion officers, we were separated
from our Indian troops, adopted a policy of mutual help. When
we went into our first POW camp in Singapore some had money
some had not. So we each subscribed half of what we had to a
battalion fund. With that money we bought eggs, peanuts and
anything else as and when available in the black market and when
we started to move to Thailand we bought marmite with the
balance of the fund and we each had a jar to take with us. Easily
carried and a source of vitamin B.

In sum therefore: Age first, mental and physical balance second
and luck third. There is not much to choose between age and luck
in importance and influence, and perhaps after all it was luck
what age one happened to be.

Lieutenant-Colonel I. G. Thomas, who was also a prisoner of the
Japanese, was sent to a camp in Korea: 'Only the fittest survived,'
he wrote,* 'but each man I am sure—as I was—was continually

* Letter to the author.

asking himself how much longer I can go on being so lucky. Yet there
was still a pact with oneself to survive but what the hell for God only
knows.' A German view of life in a Russian POW camp is similar:
'What with the cold, hunger and exhaustion, those of us who survived
often found ourselves envying those who died.'*

In the relatively humane conditions of a German, Italian, British
or American prison camp the question of actual survival was less
important. Most prisoners in the Western camps had little doubt
that they would live through the ordeal; their concern was more with
the duration rather than the hardships of imprisonment.

'A lot has been written since the war on the great feeling of
comradeship and mutual help which flourished in Stalags,' writes
Mr J. V. Webb, who was captured in Normandy in August 1944.†

> If this is true, I must have been very unfortunate in my sur-
> roundings, for in my experience it was a case of every man for
> himself, or at least every small group working for its own survival.
> Possibly officers behaved differently, and really did act as they do
> in all the escape films, but the other ranks had too much work to
> indulge in all the elaborate escape plots. . . .

From these illustrations it is clear that the captive's personal
philosophy is the critical factor behind the wire. In an alien society
physical torture, psychiatric pressures and modern high-powered
indoctrination techniques can be expected to put this philosophy to
the test. Modern wars are fought for the minds of men, and they are
won or lost by the men who are best equipped and trained in all their
aspects. Proficiency with weapons is no longer sufficient, fighting
skills must be reinforced by will—by moral character and basic
beliefs instilled long before a man becomes a soldier. Natural pride,
a sense of honour and a sense of responsibility need to be established
long before 'basic training'. War has been defined as a 'contest of
wills'. A trained hand holds the weapon. But the will, the spirit of the
individual—these control the hand. In a war for the minds of men
moral character, will and spirit are more important than ever before.

Finally, there is the vexed question of how a man should conduct
himself under interrogation. Under the Geneva Convention he is
required to give 'number, rank, name and date of birth'—nothing
more. By the end of World War II this formula was already becoming
unrealistic; the prisoner himself often wore badges which revealed
extra information, and if the captors wanted more they generally got
it. Mr J. V. Webb had been with his unit for only three weeks, and
he hardly knew his company commander's name.

* Godfrey Lias, *I Survived* (Evans Bros. Ltd, London 1954), p. 24.
† Letter to the author.

But the German interrogator took one look at my shoulder flashes and said: 'I see that you are in the 5th Wilts, 129 Brigade, 43rd Division. What is your brigadier's name?' In the best POW tradition Webb refused to answer . . . mainly because I did not know.

In this instance the Germans were not especially interested, or they might have pressed the point at the Dulag where Webb and his fellow prisoners were subjected to a more sophisticated interrogation. '. . . The RA observer who was captured with us was questioned for several days, as the Germans were convinced that our 25-pounders were belt-fed and wanted to discover the mechanism employed.'

After the Korean War, authorities on the subject of interrogation concluded that the 'Number, rank, name—and nothing more' code was impossible. If Communist interrogators could bend tough characters like Cardinal Mindszenty, it was wholly unrealistic to expect men with a lower 'breaking point' not to go beyond the traditional formula. Nearly every prisoner had divulged something, so the question was: why should a man endure purgatory when his breaking was inevitable? This view was published in an article in the US magazine *The Saturday Evening Post*.* The most logical and effective answer to interrogation and indoctrination, the author declared, would be a campaign of mass lying. Fighting men should be permitted to say anything the interrogators wanted them to say— or sign anything, or appear on TV—drawing on their imaginations to elaborate their statements in order to make them seem absurd to the outside world. The theory was that this sort of compliant mendacity would not expose the prisoner to the risk of punishment; and such widespread and exaggerated falsehood would make it worthless anyway. Various in-between alternatives to the 'Number, rank, name' code and the 'Talk, sign or confess anything' solution were also advocated. All were rejected on the grounds that one of the most powerful assets of the Western World is its love of truth. Moreover, the man who signed some sort of confession might well be charged as a war criminal. Once he confessed, an unscrupulous enemy would label him a war criminal and he would no longer be entitled to the protection of the Geneva Convention.

In the US, where 192 of the 7190 Americans captured in Korea were thought to have committed 'serious offences'† in captivity, a

---

* D. V. Galley, 'We Can Baffle the Brainwashers', 22 January 1955.

† 'Serious offences' included collaboration with the enemy, making germ warfare confessions, or 'ratting' on fellow prisoners. Of the 192 accused Americans 21 elected not to return to the US but to live in China. Expediency, opportunism and fear of reprisal, rather than a sincere conversion to Communism are believed to be the root causes underlying their decision.

special committee was set up to formulate a new code of conduct for members of the US Armed Forces. The Americans were concerned not so much about the 192 minority, but that 2730 of their men had died or were killed in captivity. This amounted to 38 per cent of those captured, as compared with the 11 per cent death rate among American prisoners in World War II. Evidence of men who had been prisoners in both wars was heard, and experts in international law were consulted. The latter pointed out that there was nothing in the Geneva Convention which precluded a man from talking during an interrogation. Indeed, there are clauses indicating he might discuss his employment, his finances, his health, or even the conditions of his captivity, if necessity demanded. The 'Number, rank, name' formula was merely a method of making sure he gave his captors no *military* information. After condemning the feasibility of teaching men to out-talk and outwit Communist interrogators, the US committee decided that any new code of conduct for POWs must be on the basis of no information beyond 'Number, rank and name'. If, however, prisoners were coerced beyond their ability to resist—as happened in Korea—they must reveal as little information as possible. And on no account must they disclose any vital military information '. . . and above all [there must be] no disloyalty in word or deed to their country, their service, or their comrades'.*

The Code of Conduct recommended by the US committee, and subsequently adopted by the US Armed Forces, has six clauses:

  I I am an American fighting man. I serve in the forces which guard my country and our way of life. I am prepared to give my life in their defense.

 II I will never surrender of my own free will. If in command I will never surrender my men while they still have the means to resist.

III If I am captured I will continue to resist by all means available. I will make every effort to escape and aid others to escape. I will accept neither parole nor special favors from the enemy.

IV If I become a prisoner of war, I will keep faith with my fellow prisoners. I will give no information or take part in any action which might be harmful to my comrades. If I am senior, I will take command. If not I will obey the lawful orders of those appointed over me and will back them up in every way.

 V When questioned, should I become a prisoner of war, I am bound to give only name, rank, service number and date of birth. I will evade answering further questions to the utmost of my ability. I will make no oral or written statements disloyal to my country and its allies or harmful to their cause.

* Report of the US Secretary of Defense's Advisory Committee on Prisoners of War, August 1955, p. 18.

VI I will never forget that I am an American fighting man, responsible for my actions, and dedicated to the principles which made my country free. I will trust in my God and the United States of America.

In simple terms these reduce to: no surrender; no parole; no information; discipline and loyalty. As guides to both collective and individual survival these are principles which could be adopted by anybody who faces the possibility of becoming a POW.

1

Conclusion

The lot of the prisoner of war has never been a happy one. In almost every war since the beginning of time criminal individuals and cruel governments have added to the misery of helpless people who are at their mercy. Moreover the profound historical changes which have taken place since the turn of the century have brought little benefit. Since August 1914 the magnitude of the problems associated with prisoners of war has been growing. Total war has meant the total mobilization of manpower; the concomitant of vast armies has been vast numbers of prisoners of war. Belligerent nations with limited resources have lowered the standards of treatment of prisoners of war, employed them as slave labour, and allowed the weaker ones, who could not be usefully employed, to die. Guerillas and Freedom Fighters have added a new dimension to the old problems. Under the rules which were established before World War I a population living under the heel of an occupying power was expected to behave as a group of civilians. Today, as likely as not, a part of this population will fight on as guerillas. And when guerillas join the fray, it becomes difficult to tell a civilian from a soldier who is evading capture, or a prisoner of war who has escaped from his camp. Because this development affects the very status of prisoners of war, it is probably the most significant change which has come about since World War II.

Wars are now no longer fought merely in order to defeat an army and enforce terms of armistice and peace but for what one side or the other will term survival. In such circumstances the effectiveness of international prescriptions like the Geneva Convention is in doubt. Both sides aim at the complete annihilation of the other, and wars are fought without any regard for the traditional concepts of humanity and chivalry. No amount of barbarism or destruction is too great when one ideology is determined to subjugate another. Thus, say the pessimists, it is a futile waste of time to attempt to regulate such wars: they will be beyond the pale of law, and any laws relating to prisoners of war are doomed to failure. The trend in this direction is exemplified in the wanton violations which occurred in World War II and subsequently in the Korean and Vietnam wars.

Nor unfortunately does the trend towards barbarism end with the termination of actual fighting. Novel types of armistices and unconditional surrender have become increasingly fashionable. The purpose of armistice agreements is no longer merely to secure suitable peace terms. There is now the desire to punish, to exterminate, to enslave and to degrade. Prisoners held by a defeated country are liberated; but those held by the victor are kept as hostages until a harsh peace is accepted by the vanquished. Where an ally is forced to surrender there is often a tendency nowadays to convert the defeated into a co-belligerent army. A prisoner of war may suddenly have to fight against the friends of his own country.

A harsh armistice is then followed either by the defeat of the erstwhile victor—as happened to Germany in the two World Wars—or else by a novel kind of peace which hardly deserves the name. The measures taken against the enemy do not end with the end of the war; on the contrary, helplessness of the vanquished now supplies new and increased opportunities. Sometimes no peace treaties come about for years; in the meantime an ugly twilight prevails in which horrors do not fall much short of the worst period of the actual war. The defeated country is helpless, cannot insist on what should be done and is forced to sign away what rights it may have. This kind of situation—the continuation of 'cold' war into the post-'hot' war period—has many consequences. One of them is to delay the repatriation of prisoners of war and to use them as slave labour or as a bargaining counter to obtain concessions in the original peace treaty. Other than reversion to a shooting war or some form of economic bribe there appears to be no remedy.

The historical changes which have occurred and affect, among others, the plight of prisoners of war, go deeper and have a more general scope than modifications in the conduct of war. The fact is there has been a serious downward trend in the level of civilization and a perturbing upward trend in brutalization. Until the turn of the century there was a constant improvement, although the increase in materialism should have been recognized as a danger signal. There was until then more and more of a rule of law, and less and less of cruel barbarism. Ultimately this trend extended to the more backward and more barbaric countries. No region in the world remained entirely uninfluenced. This was as true in Russia and Asia as it was in darkest Africa. Then, somehow, the tide turned—first slowly and

then with increasing rapidity. The situation now is that we are confronted not with primitive barbarism which might mitigate in time, but with one of the gravest symptoms of decline—a return to more cruelty and a morbid refinement of measures designed to pain, degrade and destroy human beings. There are not many regimes left today where arrest and detention without trial do not occur. The concentration camp is becoming an almost global institution from Siberia to Eire; from Argentina to India. Callousness is increasing; extraordinary tribunals are multiplying. Political court decisions and arbitrary judgement in criminal prosecutions are more frequent. Purges are institutional, if only to the extent of depriving multitudes of their accustomed livelihood. Compulsory migrations, rare since the days of Assyria, are not uncommon. Torture shows a tendency to come back, despite all the surface tendencies towards the coddling of ordinary criminals. At first the reports came from some police states and from the more backward regions; then they became more frequent. In concentration camps torture seems to be institutional. If these tendencies are strong in times of 'peace', they cannot help being even stronger in times of war and to have their effects on the treatment of POWs. Technological changes may have contributed to the deteriorating position of prisoners of war. But the root cause lies in the transition taking place in the character of civilization itself. We may well be at a transitional stage comparable with the fall of the Roman Empire, or the termination of mediaeval civilization. If so the treatment of POWs may be no worse than it was in either of these two periods. Corrective action is no longer merely a question of individual remedies. There is a profound and general problem, going to the very root of things, and that is to stop the trend towards brutalization. This was one of the worst signs of decay in a mature civilization when torturing of Roman citizens became customary some little time before the Fall of Rome.

It is perhaps merely a natural result of the weakening of the moral fibre of a whole civilization that more barbaric and more backward countries reverted to earlier habits of barbarism. A rising civilization would have continued to lift up countries like Russia and Japan. As it was, a Western World, shaken in its own moral roots, had to witness unparalleled outbreaks of arbitrary rule and of increased brutality. Not only that, but countries which had been civilized long ago—countries like Germany and Italy—adopted, temporarily at least, the outlooks and attitudes of savages. At present it is not clear whether the moral disease is healing or whether the infection is spreading. Countries which are savage in peace time can hardly be expected to be anything but savage in their treatment of helpless POWs. Perhaps that is one of the simplest and most tragic explanations of what happened in Japan, in Nazi Germany, in Korea, in Algeria and in Vietnam.

It is sometimes forgotten that achievements like the Hague Convention were, incomplete as they may be, mature fruits of a definite civilization. In wars involving belligerents which have refused to join this civilization or have seceded from it, neither the traditional rules nor the established methods of enforcing them are likely to be adequate. Despite many abuses the law protecting prisoners of war worked fairly well up to 1941. It profited from the facts of reciprocity. Because a country was concerned about those of its own fighting men who were captured, its government was usually reluctant to go too far in abuses of the international prescriptions. And although this advantage has been eroded, it has not yet disappeared. Allied POWs of the Axis powers clearly benefited from it in World War II. But while the value attached to individuals has been one of the main features of established creeds and of Western civilization, many peoples of Asia have always had different instincts. After brutalization began to run its course in the West and Western influence diminished, old instincts were revived and even strengthened. During World War II it became apparent that countries like Japan and the Soviet Union were not interested in Japanese or Russians who became prisoners of war. The result was another breach in the established rules. The Japanese Government was not interested in Allied threats of reprisals because it was totally unconcerned about the fate of captured members of the Imperial Japanese Forces. The Soviet Union's attitude, although perhaps not quite so harsh as that of the Japanese, was also one of general lack of interest in captured Russians, and reprisals against Russia were not effective when Germany resorted to them. It seems therefore that the world is confronted with attitudes and historical changes of grave implications against which the proper remedies have not yet been worked out.

What of the future? War is as old as the world, and the likelihood of it becoming extinct seems very remote. And so long as there are wars, there will continue to be problems over the treatment of prisoners.

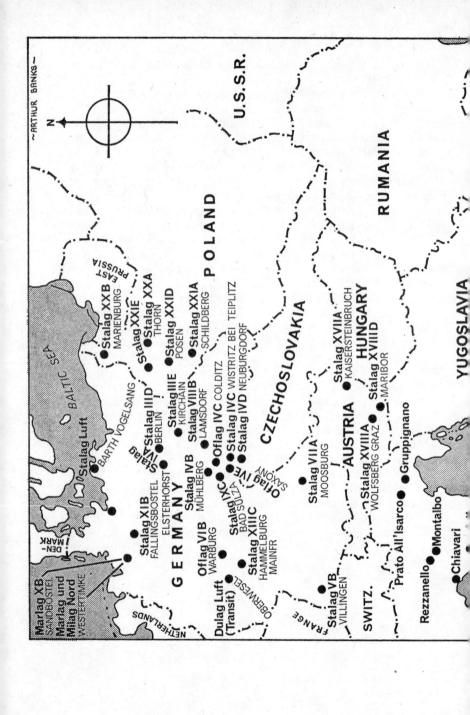

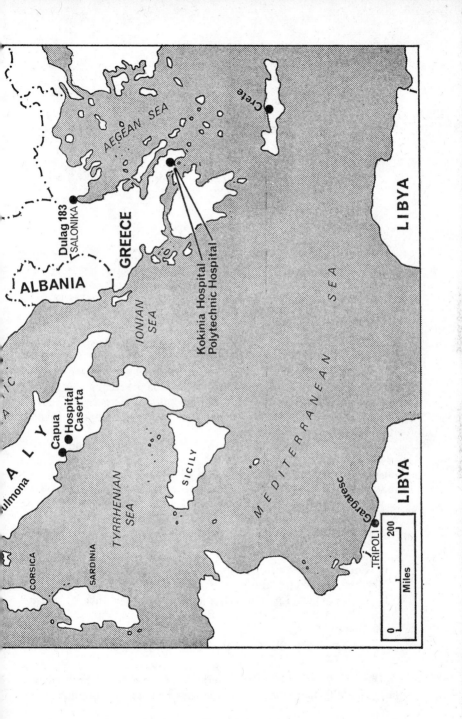

APPENDIX A

The 1949 Geneva Convention relative to the Treatment of Prisoners of War

In July 1945 the United States suggested to the President of the International Committee of the Red Cross that experts on prisoner of war affairs should meet to record their experiences of the working of the Geneva Convention of 1929 during World War II. The ICRC approved, and sixteen nations sent their experts to Geneva in April 1947; the Soviet Union was not represented but some of her satellite nations were. At the meeting the experts tabulated their recommendations for a revised Convention, and in August 1948 the ICRC called a conference in Stockholm to re-draft the 1929 Convention. Some 60 nations attended and a draft text embodying the recommendations of the experts was prepared for the Diplomatic Conference in Geneva during 1949. Subsequently the new Convention was approved, and formally ratified by 61 nations.

The 1929 Convention had been based on the principles enunciated in the Hague Regulations of 1899 and 1907, and it did much to ameliorate the horrors of war. But experience in World War II indicated clauses where it might be improved. One of its fundamental faults was its adoption of national standards rather than absolutes. Illustrative of this fault was Article 11, which provided:

> The food rations of prisoners of war shall be equal in quantity and quality to that of troops at base camps.
>
> Furthermore, prisoners shall receive facilities for preparing, themselves, additional food which they might have.
>
> A sufficiency of potable water shall be furnished them. The use of tobacco shall be permitted. Prisoners may be employed in the kitchens.
>
> All collective disciplinary measures affecting the food are prohibited.

The rations of a British or American soldier may not be particularly palatable to an Oriental, but at least he could live on them. On the other hand the British or American troops cannot remain healthy on a diet of dried fish and rice. Article 26 of the 1949 Convention (which replaced Article 11 of the 1929 Convention) was thus redrafted as follows:

> The basic daily food ration shall be sufficient in quantity, quality and variety to keep prisoners of war in good health and to prevent loss of weight or the development of nutritional deficiencies. Account shall also be taken of the habitual diet of the prisoners.
>
> The Detaining Power shall supply prisoners of war who work with such additional rations as are necessary for the labour on which they are employed.
>
> Sufficient drinking water shall be supplied to prisoners of war. The use of tobacco shall be permitted.
>
> Prisoners of war shall, as far as possible, be associated with the preparation of their meals; they may be employed for that purpose in the kitchens. Furthermore, they shall be given the means of preparing, themselves, the additional food in their possession.
>
> Adequate premises shall be provided for messing.
>
> Collective disciplinary measures affecting food are prohibited.

The amended article is a distinct improvement on the 1929 standard, which was regarded as having caused a good deal of suffering and many deaths in Japanese POW camps. But even the new version is not entirely satisfactory. If the captor nation is short of food—as might well be the case if it is being effectively blockaded—it might be very difficult to abide by the terms of Article 26. A plea that it is impossible to carry out an order is of course the usual excuse for non-compliance. In effect the only solution to the captors' problem would seem to be to transfer the prisoners to some other country (which is a party to the Convention) or even repatriate them.

Despite such faults the 1949 Convention is, nevertheless, an improvement on its 1929 predecessor. Many of the earlier ambiguities are eliminated, and matters which were left to the humane discretion of the signatories in 1929 have been spelled out more fully. Moreover Article 127 of the 1949 text prescribes wide dissemination of the provisions of the revised Convention. One of the causes for the 1929 Convention being abused derived from ignorance on the part of POWs as well as those of the captor nation who were concerned with its administration. If the 1949 Convention is widely publicized, as its Article 127 requires, much of this abuse should disappear.

It is not proposed to reproduce the 1949 Convention in detail but to present what are perhaps the important changes in concept and philosophy regarding treatment to be accorded prisoners of war now and in the future.

Major Points in the 1949 Text

Article 4 defines prisoners of war in detail. It included all those in the 1929 text and introduces several new categories of persons who, when captured, are entitled to be treated as prisoners of war. Among these new categories are those

> who accompany the armed forces without actually being members thereof, such as civilian military aircraft crews, war correspondents, supply contractors, members of labour units or of services responsible for the welfare of the armed forces, provided that they have received authorization from the armed forces which they accompany, who shall provide them for that purpose with an identity card . . .

and also members of crews of the merchant marine and of civil aircraft.

Article 5 of the Convention prescribes the duration of the obligation of the Detaining Power:

> The present Convention shall apply to the persons referred to in Article 4 from the time they fall into the power of the enemy and until their final release and repatriation.

The 1929 Convention had no specific article comparable to that just quoted, and in its absence, commanders in World War II occasionally believed that they could decide when captivity began. (In one instance a party of enemy troops were told that they would not be treated as prisoners of war until they removed the mines which had been planted by their forces. In terms of Article 5 this is illegal: captivity commences as soon as an enemy has been overpowered or is weaponless, when he has voluntarily and individually ceased to fight, or when his commander has surrendered on his behalf.)

Article 7 is important because it stresses that a POW retains his rights. It provides:

> Prisoners of war may in no circumstances renounce in part or in entirety the rights secured to them by the present Convention, and by the special agreements referred to in the foregoing Article, if such there be.

This consolidates the principle that the obligations of the Convention are national in character, and cannot be altered by the action of an individual prisoner.

Article 12 reiterates the doctrine of national responsibility, and recognizes individual responsibility for the treatment accorded prisoners of war. A more important provision of Article 12, however, is the establishment of a right in the Detaining Power to transfer prisoners of war to another Power under certain prescribed safeguards:

> Prisoners of war may only be transferred by the Detaining Power to a Power which is a party to the Convention and after the Detaining Power has satisfied itself of the willingness and ability of such transferee Power to apply the Convention. When prisoners of war are transferred under such circumstances, responsibility for the application of the Convention rests on the Power accepting them while they are in its custody.
>
> Nevertheless, if that Power fails to carry out the provisions of the Convention in any important respect, the Power by whom the prisoners of war were transferred shall, upon being notified by the Protecting Power, take effective measures to correct the situation or shall request the return of the prisoners of war. Such requests must be complied with.

At the Geneva Conference this article gave rise to a long debate. Some of the nations were unwilling to free a Detaining Power, which transferred prisoners of war to another Power, from responsibility for the application of the Convention to these prisoners of war while they were in the custody of the Power accepting them. Others wished to place full and sole responsibility on the transferee Power. The present article represents a practical compromise. When the Convention was signed the Soviet Union and her satellites recorded a reservation on this article in the following terms:

> The Union of Soviet Socialist Republics does not consider as valid the freeing of a Detaining Power, which has transferred prisoners of war to another Power, from responsibility for the application of the Convention to such prisoners of war while the latter are in the custody of the Power accepting them.

The 1929 Convention said nothing about the subject of transfers. Nevertheless, it was the practice of belligerents to transfer prisoners from one ally to another. And it was generally accepted as allowable under international law. But there was considerable difference of opinion as to whether the captor had the Conventional responsibilities. This was an involved question because of the national standards contained in the 1929 Convention. A prisoner taken by the British is entitled to the same ration as British garrison troops. Similarly a man captured by troops of the US Army is entitled to the ration of an American 'base' soldier. In both cases these rations were substantially different from the rations of French troops. The question arose as to whether a prisoner transferred by the United States to France was entitled to the ration of the United States base troops or that of France. Many similar questions arose, and none was answered satisfactorily.

Article 13 of the 1929 text enumerated the principle of humane treatment:

> Prisoners of war have the right to have their person and their honour respected. Women shall be treated with all the regard due to their sex.
>
> Prisoners retain their full civil status.

This was substantially broadened by Article 13 of the 1949 text:

> Prisoners of war must at all times be humanely treated. Any unlawful act or omission by the Detaining Power causing death or seriously endangering the health of a prisoner of war in its custody is prohibited, and will be regarded as a serious breach of the present Convention. In particular, no prisoner of war may be subjected to physical mutilation or to medical or scientific experiments of any kind which are not justified by the medical, dental or hospital treatment of the prisoner concerned and carried out in his interest.
>
> Likewise, prisoners of war must at all times be protected, particularly against acts of violence or intimidation and against insults and public curiosity.
>
> Measures of reprisal against prisoners of war are prohibited.

Article 17 is concerned with the early identification of prisoners. In World War II prisoners of war were often evacuated from beach-heads before nominal rolls had been taken. If any of the ships in which the prisoners were evacuated had been sunk and the prisoners gone down with them, there would have been no record to identify those who had been lost. So Article 17 was designed to cover such a contingency.

> Each Party to a conflict is required to furnish the persons under its jurisdiction who are liable to become prisoners of war with an identity card showing the owner's surname, first names, rank, army, regimental, personal or serial number or equivalent information, and date of birth. The identity card may, furthermore, bear the signature or the fingerprints, or both, of the owner, and may bear, as well, any other information the Party to the conflict may wish to add concerning persons belonging to its armed forces. As far as possible the card shall measure 6·5 × 10 cm. and shall be issued in duplicate. The identity card shall be shown by the

prisoner of war upon demand, but may in no case be taken away from him. . . .

This provision offers an easy solution to the problem of hasty evacuation. The duplicates of each identity card may be collected prior to evacuation and they constitute a basis for a nominal roll. The provision that the identity card 'may in no case be taken away from him' does not preclude the taking of the duplicate. The intention is that the prisoner of war shall at no time be without means of identification.

Article 23 provides for national or local standards of protection to be used as a basis of protection for prisoners:

> . . . prisoners of war shall have shelters against air bombardment and other hazards of war, to the same extent as the local civilian population. With the exception of those engaged in the protection of their quarters against the aforesaid hazards, they may enter such shelters as soon as possible after the giving of the alarm. Any other protective measure taken in favour of the population shall also apply in them. . . .

Article 26 concerning food rations, which have been discussed already, contains another important stipulation to the effect that 'adequate premises shall be provided for messing'. This same principle was carried through in other articles dealing with religious worship and medical attention.

Articles 29–32, the provisions concerning hygiene and medical attention, represent an amplification of the 1929 text. Monthly medical inspections of prisoners of war are now required to be made and these must include the checking and recording of the weight of each prisoner of war as well as 'periodic mass miniature radiography for the early detection of tuberculosis'.

Articles 34–37 stress the right of prisoners of war to 'enjoy complete latitude in the exercise of their religious duties', including attendance at the service of their faith and the right of

> Chaplains who fall into the hands of the enemy Power and who remain or are retained with a view to assisting Prisoners of War, shall be allowed to minister to them and to exercise freely their ministry amongst prisoners of war of the same religion, in accordance with their religious conscience.

Article 39 which emphasizes Article 127 (to which reference has already been made), requires every camp commandant of a POW camp to make sure that the provisions of the Convention are known by his camp staff and guards. Under the direction of his government he is held responsible for their application.

Articles 46–48 deal with the transfer and evacuation of prisoners. When these articles were drafted the memory of the Burma railway and the Bataan Death March were still green in the minds of the delegates to the Geneva Conference, and the aim was to outlaw future catastrophes of this nature. Thus Article 46 prescribes:

> The Detaining Power, when deciding upon the transfer of prisoners of war, shall take into account the interests of the prisoners themselves, more especially so as not to increase the difficulty of their repatriation.
>
> The transfer of prisoners of war shall always be effected humanely and in conditions not less favourable than those under which the forces of the Detaining Power are transferred. Account shall always be taken of the climatic conditions to which the prisoners of war are accustomed and the conditions of transfer shall in no case be prejudicial to their health.
>
> The Detaining Power shall supply prisoners of war during transfer with sufficient food and drinking water to keep them in good health, likewise with the necessary clothing, shelter and medical attention. The Detaining Power shall take adequate precautions especially in case of transport by sea or by air, to ensure their safety during transfer, and shall draw up a complete list of all transferred prisoners before their departure.

The Employment of Prisoners of War

At the Geneva Conference the question of how—and to what extent —prisoners of war could be employed by a Detaining Power gave rise to considerable debate and the expression of many differences of view. At the outset the only thing the delegates could agree upon was that the provisions set out in the 1929 Convention were inadequate and ambiguous. According to its Article 31, 'Labour furnished by prisoners of war shall have no direct relation with war operations. . . .' But what constituted a direct relation with war operations was a matter of personal opinion or guess. Clearly Article 31 needed revision. So too did its related article which prohibited use of prisoners of war at unhealthful or dangerous work. Many nations felt that work which might otherwise be dangerous (such as mine removal) was not prohibited, if the prisoner of war was thoroughly trained and properly equipped for the work.

In the event, it was decided to enumerate the classes of work on which prisoners might be compelled to work, and **Article 50** establishes these:

> Besides work connected with camp administration, installation or maintenance, prisoners of war may be compelled to do only such work as is included in the following classes:
> (a) agriculture;
> (b) industries connected with the production or the extraction of raw materials, and manufacturing industries, with the exception of metallurgical, machinery and chemical industries; public works and building operations which have no military character or purpose;
> (c) transport and handling of stores which are not military in character or purpose;
> (d) commercial business, and arts and crafts;
> (e) domestic service;
> (f) public utility services having no military character or purpose.

Should the above provisions be infringed, prisoners of war shall be allowed to exercise their right of complaint, in conformity with Article 78.

In **Article 52** the removal of mines or similar devices has been defined as dangerous work, and it states that

> unless he be a volunteer, no prisoner of war may be employed on labour which is of an unhealthy or dangerous nature.

The conditions of labour for prisoners of war have been elaborately improved (**Articles 51–57**) and of special interest is the provision contained in **Article 55**:

> The fitness of prisoners of war for work shall be periodically verified by medical examination at least once a month. The examinations shall have particular regard to the nature of the work which prisoners of war are required to do.
>
> If any prisoner of war considers himself incapable of working, he shall be permitted to appear before the medical authorities of his camp. Physicians or surgeons may recommend that the prisoners who are, in their opinion, unfit for work, be exempted therefrom.

Financial Problems of POWs

In the 1929 text there were only two Articles dealing with the prisoners' financial problems. This left too much to the discretion of the Detaining Power, and the 1949 Convention devoted eleven articles (Articles 58–68) to more comprehensive instructions on the subject.

Article 23 of the 1929 Convention provided:

> Subject to private arrangements between belligerent Powers, and particularly those provided in Article 24, officers and persons of equivalent status who are prisoners of war, shall receive from the Detaining Power the same pay as officers of corresponding rank in the armies of that Power, on the condition, however, that this pay does not exceed that to which they are entitled in the armies of the country which they have served. This pay shall be granted them in full, once a month if possible, and without being liable to any deduction for expenses incumbent on the Detaining Power, even when they are in favour of the prisoner.
>
> An agreement between the belligerents shall fix the rate of exchange applicable to this payment; in the absence of such an agreement, the rate adopted shall be that in force at the opening of hostilities.
>
> All payments made to prisoners of war must be reimbursed, at the end of hostilities, by the Power which they have served.

In World War II the changing value of currencies and the difficulty of negotiating an arrangement with the enemy made the implementation of this Article utterly impracticable. Every belligerent used its own discretion in the interpretation of the Article—some more generously than others. At the end of the war the suffering of hundreds of thousands of ex-prisoners was exacerbated by the collapse of their countries' monetary systems. Illustration of the detail resorted to in the 1949 Convention is gleaned from **Article 60** which fixes a monthly advance of pay as follows:

> The Detaining Power shall grant all prisoners of war a monthly advance of pay, the amount of which shall be fixed by conversion, into the currency of the said Power, of the following amounts:
>
> Category I: Prisoners ranking below sergeant, eight Swiss francs.
>
> Category II: Sergeants and other non-commissioned officers, or prisoners of equivalent rank, 12 Swiss francs.
>
> Category III: Warrant officers and commissioned officers below the rank of major, or prisoners of equivalent rank, 50 Swiss francs.
>
> Category IV: Major, lieutenant-colonels, colonels, or prisoners of equivalent rank, 60 Swiss francs.

Category V: General officers, or prisoners of war of equivalent rank, 75 Swiss francs.

However, the Parties to the conflict concerned may by special agreement modify the amount of advances of pay due to prisoners of the preceding categories.

Furthermore, if the amounts indicated in the first paragraph above would be unduly high compared with the pay of the Detaining Power's armed forces or would, for any reason, seriously embarrass the Detaining Power, then, pending the conclusion of a special agreement with the Power on which the prisoners depend to vary the amounts indicated above, the Detaining Power:

(a) shall continue to credit the accounts of the prisoners with the amounts indicated in the first paragraph above;

(b) may temporarily limit the amount made available from these advances of pay to prisoners of war for their own use, to sums which are reasonable, but which, for Category I, shall never be inferior to the amount that the Detaining Power gives to the members of its own armed forces.

The reasons for any limitations will be given without delay to the Protecting Power.

And **Article 66** dealing with termination of captivity:

On the termination of captivity, through the release of a prisoner of war or his repatriation, the Detaining Power shall give him a statement signed by an authorized officer of that Power, showing the credit balance then due to him. The Detaining Power shall also send through the Protecting Power to the government upon which the prisoner of war depends, lists giving all appropriate particulars of all prisoners of war whose captivity has been terminated by repatriation, release, escape, death or any other means, and showing the amount of their credit balances. Such lists shall be certified on each sheet by an authorized representative of the Detaining Power.

Any of the above provisions of this Article may be varied by mutual agreement between any two Parties to the conflict.

The power on which the prisoner of war depends shall be responsible for settling with him any credit balance due to him from the Detaining Power on the termination of his captivity.

Article 68 establishes a right of claim for injury or losses—an important matter not included in the 1929 Convention:

Any claim by a prisoner of war for compensation in respect of any injury or other disability arising out of work shall be referred to the Power on which he depends, through the Protecting Power. In accordance with Article 54, the Detaining Power will, in all cases, provide the prisoner of war concerned with a statement showing the nature of the injury or disability, the circumstances in which it arose and particulars of medical or hospital treatment given for it. This statement will be signed by a responsible officer of the Detaining Power and the medical particulars certified by a medical officer.

Any claim by a prisoner of war for compensation in respect of personal effects, monies or valuables impounded by the Detaining Power under Article 18 and not forthcoming on his repatriation, or in respect of loss alleged to be due to the fault of the Detaining Power or any of its servants, shall likewise be referred to the Power on which he depends. Nevertheless, any such personal effects required for use by the prisoners of war whilst in captivity shall be replaced at the expense of the Detaining Power. The Detaining Power will, in all cases, provide the prisoner of war with a statement, signed by a responsible officer, showing all available information regarding the reasons why such effects, monies or valuables have not been restored to him. A copy of this statement will be forwarded to the Power on which he depends through the Central Prisoners of War Agency provided for in Article 123.

Mail

One of the most bitter features of captivity experienced by prisoners is the lack of news from home. Even in the best circumstances long delays in the transit of mail to and from POWs are unavoidable. One need only consider censorship requirements and the routes that the prisoners' mail must take to realize the truth of this.

Article 71 attempts to alleviate the problem.

Prisoners of war shall be allowed to send and receive letters and cards. If the Detaining Power deems it necessary to limit the number of letters and cards sent by each prisoner of war, the said number shall not be less than two letters and four cards monthly, exclusive of the capture cards provided for in Article 70, and conforming as closely as possible to the models annexed to the present Convention. Further limitations may be imposed only if the Protecting Power is satisfied that it would be in the interests of the prisoners of war concerned to do so owing to difficulties of translation caused by the Detaining Power's inability to find sufficient qualified linguists to carry out the necessary censorship.

If limitations must be placed on the correspondence addressed to prisoners of war, they may be ordered only by the Power on which the prisoners depend, possibly at the request of the Detaining Power. Such letters and cards must be conveyed by the most rapid method at the disposal of the Detaining Power; they may not be delayed or retained for disciplinary reasons.

Prisoners of war who have been without news for a long period, or who are unable to receive news from their next of kin or to give them news by the ordinary postal route, as well as those who are at a great distance from their homes, shall be permitted to send telegrams, the fees being charged against the prisoner of war's accounts with the Detaining Power or paid in the currency at their disposal. They shall likewise benefit by this measure in cases of urgency.

As a general rule, the correspondence of prisoners of war shall be written in their native language. The Parties of the conflict may allow correspondence in other languages.

Sacks containing prisoner of war mail must be sealed and labeled so as clearly to indicate their contents, and must be addressed to offices of destination.

All parties to the Convention (belligerent or neutral) through whose country prisoner of war mail or relief shipments pass must provide free transport and should

military operations prevent the Powers concerned from fulfilling their obligations to assure the transport of shipments referred to in Articles 70, 71, 72 and 77, the Protecting Powers concerned, the International Committee of the Red Cross or any other organization duly approved by the Parties to the conflict may undertake to ensure the conveyance of such shipments by suitable means (railway wagons, motor vehicles, vessels, or aircraft, etc.). For this purpose the High Contracting Parties shall endeavour to supply them with such transport and to allow its circulation, especially by granting the necessary safe conducts.

Penal and Disciplinary Sanctions

In the 1949 text the entire chapter on penal and disciplinary sanctions is divided into three parts:

(a) General provisions covering matters of general application to both the other parts.
(b) Disciplinary sanctions.
(c) Judicial proceedings.

The fundamental principles laid down in the Hague Regulations of 1907, reasserted in the 1929 text, were re-adopted whereby

> a prisoner of war shall be subject to the laws, regulations and orders in force in the armed forces of the Detaining Power; the Detaining Power shall be justified in taking judicial or disciplinary measures in respect of any offense committed by a prisoner of war against such laws, regulations or orders. However, no proceedings or punishments contrary to the provisions of this chapter shall be allowed.

But some new and important principles were introduced, and old ones were broadened and clarified.

Article 83 provides that

> the Detaining Power shall ensure that the competent authorities exercise the greatest leniency and adopt, wherever possible, disciplinary rather than judicial measures.

Article 87 provides that:

> When fixing the penalty, the courts or authorities of the Detaining Power shall take into consideration, to the widest extent possible, the fact that the accused, not being a national of the Detaining Power, is not bound to it by any duty of allegiance, and that he is in its power as the result of circumstances independent of his own will. The said courts or authorities shall be at liberty to reduce the penalty provided for the violation of which the prisoner of war is accused, and shall therefore not be bound to apply the minimum penalty prescribed.

Treatment of War Criminals

Article 85 provides that 'prisoners of war prosecuted under the laws of the Detaining Power for actions committed prior to capture shall retain, even if convicted, the benefits of the present Convention'. This particular clause led to an irreparable cleavage between the Soviet Union and her satellites on the one hand and the remainder of the nations represented at the 1949 Conference on the other. The trouble stemmed from the war crimes trials which followed World War II. The United States sponsored the article containing a principle which most of those administering the affairs of POWs during World War II believed was contained in the 1929 Convention. But the US Supreme Court, ruling on the trial of the Japanese General Yamashita, held that the provisions of the Convention were not applicable to trials for offences committed by a soldier *before* he became a prisoner of war. As war crimes would almost certainly be committed prior to capture, this decision implied that men who were suspected war criminals would not be entitled to the rights of a prisoner of war until they were cleared of suspicion. At the Geneva Conference the United States delegate held that the essential guarantees of a fair trial should be provided to all POWs. The US would punish all war crimes, he said, but a simple judicial system was preferable for all POWs—whether they were charged with committing offences before capture or after. Regardless of the nature of the crime and when it was committed the conditions for executing the sentence should conform to **Article 108**:

> Sentences pronounced on prisoners of war after a conviction has become duly enforceable, shall be served in the same establishments and under the same conditions as on the case of members of the armed forces of the Detaining Power. These conditions shall in all cases conform to the requirements of health and humanity.
>
> A woman prisoner of war on whom such a sentence has been pronounced shall be confined in separate quarters and shall be under the supervision of women.
>
> In any case, prisoners of war sentenced to a penalty depriving them of their liberty shall retain the benefit of the provisions of Articles 78 and 126 of the present Convention. Furthermore, they shall be entitled to receive and dispatch correspondence, to receive at least one relief parcel monthly, to take regular exercise in the open air, to have the medical care required by their state of health, and the spiritual assistance they may desire. Penalties to which they may be subjected shall be in accordance with the provisions of Article 87, third paragraph.

This article adopts the standard accorded to troops of the Detaining Power, but this standard must also meet the requirements of health and humanity.

Without **Article 85** the treatment of a war crimes suspect would be left to the discretion of individual nations. The entire conference, with the exception of the Soviet Union and her satellites, agreed and adopted Article 85, but the Soviet Union recorded a reservation:

> The Union of Soviet Republics does not consider itself bound by the obligation, which follows from Article 85, to extend the application of the Convention to prisoners of war who have been convicted under the law of the Detaining Power, in accordance with the principles of the Nuremberg trial, for war crimes and crimes against humanity, it being understood that persons convicted of such crimes must be subject to the conditions obtaining

in the country in question for those who undergo their punishment.

On the face of it this reservation appears innocuous enough but a studied analysis shows that men convicted of war crimes can be given unlimited sentences, and the conditions under which they serve these sentences are not defined.

Escape

In the 1929 Convention it was laid down that POWs who escape and are recaptured shall not be punished in respect of their escape. But the text did not make it clear what constituted a completed or successful escape. So **Article 91** in the new Convention was phrased to cover this:

> The escape of a prisoner of war shall be deemed to have succeeded when:
> (1) he has joined the armed forces of the Power on which he depends, or those of an allied Power;
> (2) he has left the territory under the control of the Detaining Power, or of an ally of the said Power;
> (3) he has joined a ship flying the flag of the Power on which he depends, or of an allied Power, in the territorial waters of the Detaining Power, the said ship not being under the control of the last named Power.
>
> Prisoners of war who have made good their escape in the sense of this Article and who are recaptured, shall not be liable to any punishment in respect of their previous escape.

It is generally accepted that it is the POW's duty to try to escape, and acts committed solely in furtherance of escape are to be dealt with lightly. For example, the maximum punishment for the theft of a motor-car, stolen in the course of an escape to make a get-away, would be confinement for thirty days—the maximum disciplinary punishment. And **Article 93** provides:

> Escape or attempt to escape, even if it is a repeated offense, shall not be deemed an aggravating circumstance if the prisoner of war is subjected to trial by judicial proceedings in respect of an offense committed during his escape or attempt to escape.
>
> In conformity with the principle stated in Article 83, offenses committed by prisoners of war with the sole intention of facilitating their escape and which do not entail any violence against life or limb, such as offenses against public property, theft without

intention of self-enrichment, the drawing up or use of false papers, or the wearing of civilian clothing, shall occasion disciplinary punishment only.

Prisoners of war who aid or abet an escape or an attempt to escape shall be liable on this count to disciplinary punishment only.

Punishments

Some disciplinary punishments for minor offences are laid down in **Article 89,** and the procedure for dealing with these offences is defined in **Article 96:**

Acts which constitute offenses against discipline shall be investigated immediately.

Without prejudice to the competence of courts and superior military authorities, disciplinary punishment may be ordered only by an officer having disciplinary powers in his capacity as camp commander, or by a responsible officer who replaces him or to whom he has delegated his disciplinary powers.

In no case may such powers be delegated to a prisoner of war or be exercised by a prisoner of war.

Before any disciplinary award is pronounced, the accused shall be given precise information regarding the offense of which he is accused, and given an opportunity of explaining his conduct and of defending himself. He shall be permitted, in particular, to call witnesses and to have recourse, if necessary, to the services of a qualified interpreter. The decision shall be announced to the accused prisoner of war and to the prisoner's representative.

A record of disciplinary punishments shall be maintained by the camp commander and shall be open to inspection by representatives of the Protecting Power.

Termination of Captivity

(A) DURING HOSTILITIES

Article 110 prescribes the conditions under which sick and wounded prisoners of war may be repatriated direct or accommodated in a neutral country. It also sets out the conditions which prisoners of war accommodated in a neutral country must fulfill in order to permit their repatriation:

If no special agreements are concluded between the Parties to the conflict concerned, to determine the cases of disablement or sickness entailing direct repatriation or accommodation in a neutral country, such cases shall be settled in accordance with the principles laid down in the Model Agreement concerning direct repatriation and accommodation in neutral countries of wounded and sick prisoners of war and in the Regulations concerning Mixed Medical Commissions annexed to the present Convention.

Upon the outbreak of hostilities, Mixed Medical Commissions shall be appointed to examine sick and wounded prisoners of war and to make all appropriate decisions regarding them. The appointment, duties and functioning of these Commissions shall be in conformity with the provisions of the Regulations annexed to the present Convention.

The wounds or sickness need not be the result of battle to make a POW eligible for repatriation. Unless the injury is self-inflicted, prisoners of war who meet with accidents also enjoy the benefit of the provisions of the 1949 Convention as regards repatriation or accommodation in neutral country. It is also prescribed that no repatriated person may be employed on active military service.

(B) AT THE CLOSE OF HOSTILITIES

The principle of release and repatriation without delay after the cessation of active hostilities is re-asserted in **Article 118**. At the time of signing of the present Convention some of the signatories to the Convention still held German and Japanese prisoners. Under the terms of the new article they would be in violation of the Convention for retaining them for so long.

Enforcing the Convention

Article 126 says:

Representatives or delegates of the Protecting Power shall have permission to go to all places where prisoners of war may be, particularly to places of internment, imprisonment and labour, and shall have access to all premises occupied by prisoners of war; they shall be allowed to go to the places of departure, passage and arrival of prisoners who are being transferred. They shall be able to interview the prisoners, and in particular, the prisoners' representatives, without witnesses, either personally or through an interpreter.

But the real teeth for enforcement of the Convention—supplementing the usual sanctions of International Law (i.e. world-wide condemnation and fear of reprisal)—is found in **Articles 129–130**, which require signatories to undertake to enact any legislation necessary to provide effective penal sanctions against people who commit—or order others to commit—'any grave breaches against persons or property protected by this Convention'. These breaches are defined as: 'Wilful killing, torture or inhumane treatment, including biological experiments, wilfully causing great suffering or serious injury to body or health, compelling a prisoner of war to serve in the forces of a hostile Power, or wilfully depriving a prisoner of war of the rights of fair and regular trial.'

APPENDIX B

The Protecting Power and Humanitarian Agencies

The Protecting Power

The *Protecting Power** is a neutral state which has accepted the responsibility of protecting the interests of another state in the territory of a third—with which, for some reason such as war, the second state has broken off diplomatic relations. (For obvious reasons this third state is known as the *Detaining Power* in the case of prisoners of war.)

In a war, therefore, the Protecting Power functions as an intermediary between two belligerents for the overall welfare of prisoners of the state from whom it has received its mandate as Protecting Power.

The earliest recorded indication of the concept of Protecting Power came in the thirteenth century when the Venetian Resident in Constantinople was charged with the protection of Armenians and Jews. But the modern genesis of Protecting Power is attributed to developments which occurred during the Franco-Prussian War in 1870–1871, when both sides imposed stringent restrictions on enemy aliens and expelled enemy consuls. This led to an expansion of the functions of Protecting Powers, and probably for the first time in history the belligerents were represented by Protecting Powers—with Britain looking after French interests in Germany, and the United States, Switzerland and Russia doing the same for the various German states.

In subsequent wars the precedents established in the Franco-Prussian War were followed, albeit with some variations. In the Sino-Japanese War the United States acted as Protecting Power for both sides, and Germany did the same for both belligerents in the Italo-Turkish War and the Sino-Soviet War of 1929. At the other extreme, Germany acted as the Protecting Power for Turkey in

---

* In this context the Protecting Power must not be confused with the protecting state exercising powers over a protectorate.

Greece during the Greco-Turkish War of 1897, while three other nations—Britain, France and Russia—acted jointly for Greece in Turkey. During the Spanish-American War Britain acted as Protecting Power for the United States, while France and Austro-Hungary acted jointly for Spain. (It was in this war that a belligerent, the United States, specifically requested medical inspection of the camps in which POWs were held.) This practice of using more than one friendly state as Protecting Power has virtually disappeared, although at one time in World War II Spain was acting as the Protecting Power for Japan on the American continent, while Sweden acted for her in Hawaii and Switzerland in American Samoa.

By the time World War I burst upon Europe the role of the Protecting Power was firmly established, as an international custom. And in the course of that conflict public opinion in all the countries at war came to recognize the benefits of having a channel through which the belligerents could communicate on matters such as those affecting the welfare of POWs. Finally, in 1929, the institution of Protecting Power was officially recognized when the Prisoners of War Convention was adopted by the Diplomatic Conference in Geneva. In 1949 the existing Geneva Convention confirmed the Protecting Power and expanded the definitions of its functions in greater detail.

By the 1949 Convention the duty of a Protecting Power is 'to safeguard the interest of the Parties to the conflict' (Article 8).

The specific functions of a Protecting Power are not spelled out in detail; most of them are expressed either in the form of duties of the Detaining Power or as the rights of prisoners of war. In the British Army's Manual of Military Law the Protecting Power is termed 'the principal organ . . . for ensuring the observance of the Convention'. Whether and to what extent the captor state observes the international regulations relating to POWs largely depends on the Protecting Power. In practical terms this means visits to POW camps to inspect general camp arrangements, accommodation, food, clothing, canteen and recreation facilities, the conditions under which POW labour is employed, and to observe judicial proceedings against the prisoners. In addition to this the Protecting Power often has to reconcile the views of the two belligerents regarding the interpretation of the Geneva Convention. Under Article 127 the Protecting Power's representatives may talk to POWs and ask them about their conditions; under Article 8, the captor nation is required to give the Protecting Power all the help it needs to carry out its tasks.

As might be expected, those who do the actual work of the Protecting Power generally face a difficult, thankless task. Initially, if not later, a captor nation tends to see the Protecting Power's inspectors as investigators into its activities. And if inspection reports are adverse, the captors are prone to accuse the Protecting Power of prejudice in favour of their enemy. At the POW camps themselves the camp staff are usually older men, veterans of another war or seasoned campaigners. And they resent the interference of the young neutrals. So visits are barred on the grounds of military exigency or some other excuse. (On one occasion, for example, the Germans would not permit visits to certain camps on the grounds that there should be no inspections of camps on 'the line of communications'. Visits to factories where prisoners were working have also been prohibited because such visits might divulge 'trade secrets'.) Suggestions and offers of assistance in cases involving delinquencies and disciplinary infractions committed by POWS have also been resented.

These are only a few of the handicaps which representatives of the Protecting Power have to face. Some of the handicaps are based on fears by the captors which are unfounded; with patience and tact these can often be overcome. But this has not always been the case, and instances have arisen when violations have been overlooked to avoid friction at the time, with the hope of better relations in the future.

In World War II there was a good deal of controversy over the status of a Protecting Power whose mandate came from a country which had been overrun. If a state ceases to exist because it is occupied, the Protecting Power's mandate is presumed to be extinct; on this account Protecting Power facilities were denied to Belgian, Danish, Dutch, French, Norwegian, Polish and Yugoslav prisoners whose countries had been occupied by the Germans. By this interpretation of international law a Protecting Power must have a sponsor for whom he is to work. And if a sponsoring belligerent state is not recognized by the other belligerents the implication is that it cannot appoint a Protecting Power to look after his interests in the latter's territory. North Korea, Communist China and Israel have all faced this situation in recent years.

Another dilemma arises when two governments exist—one puppet and one in exile. Both may claim the right to appoint a Protecting Power, and it is obvious that the occupying power would favour the choice of the puppet regime. A similar situation arises when a nation is utterly defeated and occupied, as happened with Germany and Japan in 1945. At this particular time POWS are in most need of an intermediary to regulate the victor's behaviour.

Finding a neutral nation of sufficient strength and influence to act as Protective Power who can be of any real help to POWS is another problem. In a global war it is likely to be impossible, and even in local wars it may be difficult if the war involves the great powers of East and West. In the Korean War the UN could not find five real neutrals. One novel solution to the problem which has been suggested depends on what is termed 'direct representation'. This represents a breach with traditional procedure, by which enemy diplomats packed their bags and returned home when a war broke out. 'Direct representation' would require diplomats to stay at their posts to look after the welfare of their own country's captured and detained personnel. Among other things they would be responsible for notifying prisoners' next of kin and for seeing that prisoners were treated in a manner compatible with the economic condition of their enemies. They would hear the prisoners' complaints and try to get some corrective action from the enemy government. As diplomats they might be expected to work objectively; in any case the information they transmitted back to their governments would be censored.

Whether any government would be willing to allow enemy diplomats to remain in the country to look after POWs is another matter. Diplomats, with their personal connections and intelligence machinery, are more dangerous than enemy civilians. So their freedom of action would probably be restricted, and this would limit their capacity to help POWs. As any such arrangements would be mutual, however, the arrangement might be viable. Reciprocity would guarantee the diplomats safety—as far as anybody's safety can be guaranteed in modern wars. And although they would not be as comfortable or popular in time of war as in peace, they would be performing a vital function.

Humanitarian Agencies

Apart from the Protective Power which looks after the interests of prisoners, there are other private organizations which work to the same end. In 1814 a group of French women formed a society to solicit, collect and distribute aid to French POWs in Germany. During the Crimean War another group of voluntary workers organized assistance for Russian prisoners in Britain and France and for British, French and Italian POWs in Russia. In the American Civil War an organization known as the 'Sisters of Charity' threw food over the wire to Union prisoners in the Southern POW camp at Charleston in South Carolina, and provided bandages and food for prisoners in the notorious camp at Andersonville. But it is the Red Cross which is the best known of the humanitarian agencies. National Red Cross Committees and the International Committee of the Red Cross (the ICRC) have done sterling work during the wars of this century.

Under the terms of the Geneva Convention POWs are allowed to receive food in addition to that supplied by their captors; and without it their health in two world wars would undoubtedly have suffered. 'The Red Cross parcels saved our lives' is a phrase which occurs repeatedly in letters from prisoners. The task of organizing the food and other relief parcels containing clothes, comforts, games, musical instruments and a myriad other items was carried out by National Red Cross Societies. Through the ICRC in Geneva they also put prisoners in touch with their families and vice versa. The Geneva Code provides for correspondence between prisoners, their relatives and their friends. Such correspondence usually starts with a prisoner sending two cards—a 'capture' card and the 'special' card—to the Central Agency of the ICRC and their next of kin shortly after capture. Apart from these two cards the POW is entitled to write two letters and four post-cards per month, and if he has not heard from his relatives for a long time—and can pay the charges—he may even be allowed to send telegrams. This is what is permitted. Unfortunately the rules are not always followed. The Japanese disregarded the rules in World War II, and since then they have been ignored in the Korean, French Indo-China and Vietnam Wars. Prisoners taken by the Communists in these wars were not allowed to send the 'capture' or 'special' cards, and sometimes not permitted any other form of correspondence. In many cases this has resulted in the prisoners' next of kin coming to believe that the prisoner was dead.* Apart from the mental anguish caused by such a situation, complications have arisen when wives have re-married or insurance policies have been collected.

Letters and parcels to and from POWs are supposed to be carried free and exempted from customs levies. Getting them to their destinations, however, is not always free from difficulties. At the beginning of World War II parcels were sent to British POWs in Germany via Belgium, and after the German occupation through France and Switzerland; with the fall of France they were sent through Portugal, Spain and—for a time—unoccupied France until a route was eventually found via Lisbon and Marseilles. But the ships which carried them were exposed to all the normal war risks of vessels on the high seas and often bombed and torpedoed. From time to time the packages were pilfered on their journeys and the climax was reached when some thousands of parcels were lost between Britain and Geneva.

To resolve the problem, Dr Junod of the ICRC suggested that the Red Cross must charter its own ships. The German naval authorities gave their consent to the plan, provided the British Admiralty also

---

* At the time of writing the North Vietnamese are known to hold many more American prisoners than the 589 which they admit. Some of the 1216 Americans listed as missing are believed to be among those they have not declared.

agreed. The initial British reaction was unfavourable, but the Admiralty eventually gave way and for the rest of the war ships with 'C-International' painted on their sides sailed openly across the Atlantic flying the Red Cross emblem and through the Mediterranean with cargoes destined for POWs in Europe. These were neutral ships, manned by neutral crews, and a representative of the ICRC travelled on every voyage.

Whether a similar arrangement could be put into operation in another world war is a matter for conjecture. The use of nuclear weapons may close some of the shipping avenues, and devastate the ports. An increased volume of mail consequent on the involvement of millions of participants in the hostilities and their subsequent capture or detention will be one more complication; censorship problems will probably be another.

Food parcels present a unique problem which deserves mention at this point. In the two world wars they have occasionally been used for purposes other than that intended by the Geneva Convention. Instances have occurred where escape instructions have been pressed into gramophone records; propaganda material has been sent on other occasions. Furthermore, if the captors are themselves short of food the prisoners' parcels give rise to jealousy. Even among the prisoners themselves differences between parcels arising from the greater economic prosperity of one prisoner's nation compared with another, or the financial means of their next of kin, can create intense feeling behind the wire.

None of these problems should be confused with the overall service of the Red Cross to which great credit should be given. The ICRC has done magnificent work in the past and continues to do so. Its function as an intermediary and inspector in wartime is not an easy task for any neutral.

Apart from the ICRC other international organizations have also contributed to the alleviation of the sufferings of POWs. Of these the YMCA, the World Students' Congress and the Vatican deserve special mention.

ACKNOWLEDGEMENTS

The author would like to express his thanks to the many institutions and individuals who have helped him, and without whose assistance this book could never have been written in its present form.

I am especially grateful to Brigadier John Stephenson OBE, of the Royal United Service Institution—with whom the idea for a book about Prisoners of War originated, and whose interest in it has continued through to publication.

Many ex-POWs of different nationalities have responded from all over the world to my appeal for information about their experiences. I should like to thank those who prefer to remain anonymous as well as those whose names are recorded here: G. P. Adams Esq, Mrs J. W. Allgrove, H. W. Ashton Esq, J. S. Atkinson Esq, Rev. Louis A. Bralant, Sir John Burns, A. T. Casdagli Esq, P. Cheeseman Esq and the staff of the Victoria Theatre, Stoke on Trent, Captain C. T. Collett, L. J. Crickmar Esq, Rev. S. J. Davies MBE, QHC, CF, E. Dyson Esq, Mrs A. Ellis, H. Faulk Esq, Sir John Fletcher-Cooke CMG, N. L. Flower Esq, R. W. Giddings-Green Esq, Lieut.-Col. C. Gilbert, D. Glover Esq, A. C. Goodger Esq, Owen Greenwood Esq, A. Greenshields Esq, L. St. Clare Grondona Esq, Professor G. W. Imberger, Captain K. C. Jacob, F. R. Jelley Esq, Lieut-.Col. G. Johnstone RADC, A. Karabus Esq, V. G. R. Kenward Esq, Rev. W. V. C. Lake, Rev. W. V. S. Leatherdale, C. H. Lee Esq, B. Long Esq, G. E. Lyons Esq, R. Merryweather Shaw Esq, J. R. Milford Esq, Lieut.-Col. H. Moyse-Bartlett MBE, Commodore L. N. Mungavin Military and Naval Attache to H. E. The Ambassador of Pakistan in London, Rev. J. S. Naylor, Colonel W. B. Purnell, Wing Commander J. R. Preedy, L. H. Renton Esq, J. L. Rice Esq, H. Romney Esq, H. A. Savill Esq, General Sir Reginald Savory KCIE, CB, DSO, MC, S. L. Sheldrick Esq, Commander C. S. Sheppard, Lieut.-Col. A. W. Shirley MBE, TD, R. R. Snalham Esq, W. R. Spikeman Esq, Commander A. S. Stavert MBE, Lieut.-Col. I. G. Thomas, W. B. Towler Esq, F. Waddington Esq, T. S. Waiting Esq, C. G. Webber

Esq, Lieut.-Col. C. C. Whitcombe MBE, H. O. Whiting Esq, Captain K.Williamson RN, J. H. Witte Esq.

For the assessment of, and comments on, their diverse experiences I alone am responsible; if any of these interpretations appear to be out of keeping with the facts or views of the individuals concerned the fault is patently mine.

The help and advice of M. Jean Pictet, Vice-Chairman of the Comité International de la Croix Rouge, and of M. Jacques Moreillon and M. Paul Vibert of the same organisation were invaluable during my research. So too was the assistance afforded by Professor Erich Maschke and Doctor Helmut Wolff of the Wissenschaftliche Kommission für Deutsche Kriegsgefangenengeschichte, and M. H. Michel, Directeur de Recherche au Centre National de la Recherche Scientifique of the French Comité d'Histoire de la 2e Guerre Mondiale and M. S. Champion of the French Ministère des Anciens Combattants in Paris. I am grateful also for the cooperation of the Proprietors and Editor of the German magazine *Quick*, and the Editors of the *Sunday Times, The Daily Telegraph*, The *Yorkshire Post*, and *Soldier;* and to the librarians of the Royal United Service Institution and the Harrogate Public Library. I must also express a special obligation for permission to include the copyright material quoted and acknowledged in the text.

Finally I must acknowledge the contribution made by my wife Alexandra, whose translating, interpreting and typing abilities have been invaluable.

Thanks are due to the following Authors and Publishers for permission to quote from the books mentioned: Henri Alleg, *The Question*, John Calder (Calder & Boyars); A. T. Farrar-Hockley, *The Edge of the Sword*, Frederick Müller; H. C. Fooks, *Prisoners of War*, Stowell Printing Co; *The Spirit in Jeopardy*, an extract from a broadcast by the BBC; J. Hargest, *Farewell Campo 12*, Michael Joseph Ltd; Ronald Hastain, *White Coolie*, Hodder & Stoughton Ltd; Jean Hélion, *Ils ne m'auront pas*, E. P. Dutton (New York); Betty Jeffrey, *White Coolies*, Panther Books Ltd.

The author and publishers wish to thank the Imperial War Museum for providing the illustrations for this book, with the exception of figs 9–11, 13, 18 and cover, Keystone Press Agency Ltd, 12 Mr Albert Grant, and 21 Heinrich Bauer Verlag.

BIBLIOGRAPHY

1 Published Books

Abell, F. *Prisoners of War in Britain, 1756 to 1815: A Record of Their Lives; Their Romance; and Their Sufferings*, Oxford University Press, London 1914

Adams, G. P. *No Time for Geishas*, Leo Cooper, London 1973

Allan, J. *No Citation*, Angus & Robertson, London 1955

Allbury, A. G. *Bamboo and Bushido*, Robert Hale, London 1960

Alleg, H. *The Question*, Braziller, New York 1958

Attiwell, K. *The Rising Sunset*, Robert Hale, London 1957

Baber, D. *The Guarded Years*, Heinemann, London 1956

Barber, N. *Sinister Twilight*, Fontana, London 1960

Beck, F. and Godwin, W. *Russian Purge and Extraction of Confessions*, Hurst & Blackett, London 1951

Beckwith, Capt. E. G. C. *The Quill*, Country Life Ltd., London 1947

Belmonte, C. *Ervaringen mit gefangenkampen op Java en in Japan*

Böhme, K. W. *Gesucht wird. . . .*, Süddeutscher Verlag, München 1968

Bohn, H. *Die Letzten*, Markus Verlag GMBH, Köln 1954

Boissier, P. *Histoire du Comité de la Croix-Rouge: De Solferino à Tsoushima*, Plon, Paris 1963

Brandt, W. *Das Recht der Kriegsgefangenen im Landkriege*, Julius Abel, Greifswald 1919

Brougher, Brig.-Gen. W. E. *South to Bataan, North to Mukden*, University of Georgia Press, Athens, Ga. 1972

Burney, C. *Solitary Confinement*, Clerke and Cockeran, London 1952

Cahen-Salvador, G. *Les Prisonniers de Guerre 1914–1919*, Payot & Cie, Paris 1929

Cooper, A. R. *The Adventures of a Secret Agent*, Muller, London 1957

Cooper, A. R. *Born to Fight*, Blackwood, London 1969

D'Anthouand, Baron A. and Hecht, E. *Les Prisonniers de Guerre*, A. Colin, Paris 1915

Davie, M. R. *The Evolution of War: A Study of its Role in Early Societies*, Yale University Press, New Haven, Conn. 1929

Davies, Rev. S. J. *In Spite of Dungeons*, Hodder & Stoughton, London 1954

Davis, N. H. *Prisoners of War: A Study in the Development of International Law,* American Council on Public Affairs, Washington, DC 1942

Deeley, P. *Beyond Breaking Point,* Arthur Barker, London 1971

Evans, A. J. *Escape and Liberation,* Hodder & Stoughton, London 1945

Farrar-Hockley, Capt. A. *The Edge of the Sword,* Frederick Muller, London 1954

Fletcher-Cooke, Sir John. *The Emperor's Guest,* Leo Cooper, London 1972

Fooks, H. C. *Prisoners of War,* Stowell Printing Co., Federalsburg 1924

Forster, J. *Heldentum nach Ladenschluss,* Gerhard Stalling Verlag, Hamburg

Gerard, J. *My Four Years in Germany,* Doran, New York 1917

Gerlach, H. *Odyssee in Rot,* Nymphenburger Verlagshandlung, München 1958

Graham, J. and Thomas, J. *Joe in Germany,* privately printed by: The Surrey Fine Arts Press, 1946

Hansen, K. K. *Heroes Behind Barbed Wire,* Van Nostrand, Princeton, NJ 1957

Hargest, Brig. J. *Farewell Campo 12,* Michael Joseph, London 1945

Harvey, F. W. *Comrades in Captivity: A Record of Life in Seven Prison Camps,* Sidgwick & Jackson, London 1920

Hastan, Ronald. *White Coolie,* Hodder & Stoughton, London 1947

Heinemann, F. W. *Das Kriegsgefangenenrecht im Landkriege nach moderner volkerrechtlichen Auffassung unter besonderer Berucksichtigung des Genfer Kriegsgefangenen-Abkommens von 27,* Tekok, Krefeld 1929

Hélion, J. *They Shall Not Have Me,* Dutton, New York 1943

Hingorani, R. C. *Prisoners of War,* N. M. Tripathi Private Ltd., Bombay 1963

Jeffrey, Betty. *White Coolies,* Angus & Robertson, London 1954

Junod, Dr M. *Le Troisième Combattant,* Payot, Paris 1950 (published also as *Warrior Without Weapons,* by Jonathan Cape, London 1951)

Kern, E. *Dance of Death,* Collins, London 1951

Kinkhead, E. *In Every War But One,* W. W. Norton, New York 1959

Krist, G. *Prisoner in the Forbidden the Forbidden Land,* Faber & Faber, London 1938

Lewis, Lt.-Col. G. and Mewka, Capt. John. *History of Prisoner of War Utilization by the United States Army, 1776–1945,* US Dept. of Army, Washington 1955

Lewis, M. *Napoleon and His British Captives*, Allen & Unwin, London 1962

Lias, Godfrey. *I Survived*, Evans Bros., London 1954

Maschke, Dr E. (Editor).* *Zur Geschichte der deutschen Kriegsgefangenen des Zweiten Weltkrieges*, E. & W. Gieseking, Bethel/ Bielefeld 1972 (Official History of the German POWs in the Second World War, compiled by the Scientific Commission for the History of the German Prisoners of War, Munich)

Vol. I, K. W. Bohme: Die deutschen Kriegsgefangenen in Yugoslawien 1941–1949

Vol. II, D. Cartellieri: Die deutschen Kriegsgefangenen in der Sowjetunion—Die Lagergesellschaft

Vol. III: Die deutschen Kriegsgefangenen in der Sowjetunion— Der Faktor Hunger

Vol. IV: Die deutschen Kriegsgefangenen in der Sowjetunion— Der Faktor Arbeit

Vol. V: Deutsche in Straflagern und Gefangnissen der Sowjetunion

Vol. VI: Die deutschen Kriegsgefangenen in der Sowjetunion— Aus dem kulturellen Leben

Vol. VII: Die deutschen Kriegsgefangenen in sowjetischer Hand— Eine Bilanz

Vol. VIII: Die deutschen Kriegsgefangenen in der Sowjetunion— Antifa

Vol. IX: Die deutschen Kriegsgefangenen in Polen und der CSR

Vol. X/1: Die deutschen Kriegsgefangenen in amerikanischer Hand—USA

Vol. X/2: Die deutschen Kriegsgefangenen in amerikanischer Hand—Europa

Vol. XI/1: Die deutschen Kriegsgefangenen in britischer Hand

Vol. XI/2: Die deutschen Kriegsgefangenen in britischer Hand— Re-education

Vol. XII: Die deutschen Kriegsgefangenen im Gewahrsam Belgiens, der Niederlande und Luxemburgs

Vol. XIII: Die deutschen Kriegsgefangenen in französischer Hand

Vol. XIV: Geist und Kultur der deutschen Kriegsgefangenen im Westen

Vol. XV: Die Deutsche Kriegsgefangenenschaft des Zweiten Weltkrieges

Meerloo, J. A. M. *The Rape of the Mind. The Psychology of Thought Control: Menticide and Brainwashing*, World Publishing Co., New York 1956

* These publications are not available to the general public but copies are held in the leading American libraries.

Muller-Bringmann, W. *Das Buch von Friedland*, Musterschmidt-Verlag, Gottingen 1966

Myers, Bessie. *Captured*, Harrap, London 1941

Norman, D. *Road from Singapore*, Hodder & Stoughton, London 1970

Oliver, Dame Beryl. *The British Red Cross in Action*, Faber, London 1966

Pape, R. *Boldness Be My Friend*, Elek, London 1953

Peacey, Belinda. *The Red Cross*, Muller, London 1958

Peacock, B. *Prisoner on the Kwai*, Blackwood, London 1966

Potter, A. *Verses by British Internees*, privately published at the British Internees Camp La Grande Caserne, St Denis (Seine) 1944

Pyke, Geoffrey. *To Ruhleben and Back*, Constable & Co., London 1916

Reel, A. F. *The Case of General Yamashita*, University of Chicago Press, Chicago 1949

Risner, R. *The Passing of the Night,* Random House, New York, 1974

Roberts, D. R. *Spotlight on Singapore*, Gibbs & Phillips, London 1965

Robertson, T. *The Golden Horseshoe*, Evans Bros., London 1960

Rowan, S. *They Wouldn't Let Us Die,* Jonathan David, Middle Village, NY 1973

Scotland, Lt.-Col. A. P. *The London Cage*, Evans Bros., London 1957

Short, J. T. *Prisoners of War in France from 1804 to 1814*, Duckworth, London 1914

Silkin, J. *Out of Battle: The Poetry of The Great War*, Oxford University Press, London 1972

Slater, F. *As You Were*, Hutchinson, London 1946

Simons, J. E. *While History Passed*, Heinemann, London 1954

Spoight, J. M. *War Rights on Land*, 1911

Strong, Tracy (Editor). *We Prisoners of War*, Association Press, New York 1942

Strupp, K. (Editor). '*Kriegsgefangene*' (Worterbuch des Volkerrechts u. der Diplomatie, Vol. I, pp. 743–749), de Gruyter, Berlin 1924

Taft, W. H. (Editor). *Service With Fighting Men*, Association Press, New York 1924

Van der Post, L. *The Prisoner and the Bomb,* William Morrow,

Vattel, E. *Le Droit des Gens,* Carnegie Institution of Washington, 1916

Vidal-Naquet, P. *Torture—Cancer of Democracy: France and Algeria 1954–62*, Penguin Special, London 1963

Wentzel, F. *Single or Return*, W. Kimber, London 1958

Williams, E. *The Book of Famous Escapes*, W. W. Norton & Co. Inc., New York 1954

Yamamoto, Y. *Four Years in Hell*, Tokyo 1952
Yehezkel, Hameiri. *Prisoners of Hate*, Keter Books, Jerusalem 1970

2 Pamphlets and Documents

(A) COMITÉ INTERNATIONAL DE LA CROIX-ROUGE

The Activities of the International Committee of the Red Cross in the Arab Countries from 1955 to 1970 (D 1206b), Geneva 1971

Proceedings of the Meeting for the Study of Treaty Stipulations Relative to the Spiritual and Intellectual Needs of Prisoners of War and Civilian Internees, Geneva 1947

Conflit de Corée—Recueil de Documents, Vol. I and II (to 30 June 1952), Geneva 1952

Report of the ICRC on its Activities during the Second World War (1 September 1939 to 30 June 1947) . . . , Geneva 1948

Report of the Efforts made by the International Committee on behalf of 'Partisans' taken by the Enemy . . . , Geneva 1946

Report on the Work of the Conference of Government Experts for the Study of the Convention for the Protection of War Victims . . . , Geneva 1947

The ICRC and the International Convention relative to Prisoners of War and Civilians, Geneva 1945

The Central Tracing Agency, Pamphlet D 714b, Geneva 1952

ICRC Annual Report 1971, Geneva 1971

Can the Status of Prisoners of War be Altered? (Rene-Jean Wilhelm), Geneva 1953

Retention of Members of the Army Medical Services fallen into Enemy Hands (Jean S. Pictet), Geneva 1950

(B) UNITED NATIONS

Standard Minimum Rules for the Treatment of Prisoners: Recommendations, UN Dept. of Economics & Social Affairs, New York 1958

(C) US GOVERNMENT

Communist Interrogation, Indoctrination and Exploitation of Prisoners of War, US Dept. of the Army Pamphlet, No. 30–101, 1956

Development of Law Relative to Treatment of Prisoners of War (Brig.-Gen. J. V. Dillon, US Dept. of the Air Force, Washington 1957. Report from the *Miami Law Quarterly* of December 1950)

(D) MISCELLANEOUS

3rd Conference Internationale de Pathologie de La Captivité, Confederation Internationale des Anciens Prisonniers de Guerre, Paris 1967

Prisoner of War, Horace Marshall & Sons on behalf of the British Red Cross Society, London 1943

POW, Report of the US Secretary of Defense Advisory Committee on Prisoners of War, Washington DC 1955

Shall Brothers Be: An account written by American and British prisoners of war of their treatment at the hands of the Chinese People's Volunteers and Korean People's Army in POW camps in Korea, The Chinese People's Committee for World Peace, Peking 1952

Das Schicksal der Deutschen Kriegsgefangenen des Zweiten Weltkrieges, Erich Maschke, Verlag E. & W. Gieseking, Bielefeld, München 1962

Taschenbuch des öffentlichen Lebens 1971, Dr Albert Oeckl, Festland Verlag GMBH, Bonn 1972

Penal Sanctions for Maltreatment of Prisoners of War, Colonel Howard S. Levie (reprinted from the *American Journal of International Law*, Vol. 56, No. 2, April 1962)

The Employment of Prisoners of War, Colonel Howard S. Levie (reprinted from the *American Journal of International Law*, Vol. 57, No. 2, April 1963)

Prisoners of War and the Protecting Power, Colonel Howard S. Levie (reprinted from the *American Journal of International Law*, Vol. 55, No. 2, April 1961)

Asylum to Prisoners of War, Major R. R. Baxter (reprinted from the *British Year Book of International Law*, 1953)

Prisoners of War: The POW Battleground, George S. Prugh (*The Dickinson Law Review*, Vol. 60, 1956)

Treatment of British Prisoners of War in Korea, Report by the British Ministry of Defence, HMSO, London 1955

Wir Mahnen Die Welt (Verband der Heimkehrer, Kriegsgefangenen und Vermissten-Angehorigen Deutschlands e.V.), 1952

Freiheit Ohne Furcht—Zehn Jahre Heimkehrerverband

3 Articles

America: 'Conflict Over POWs', 17 October 1953, 90:63
'Atrocities in Korea', 12 December 1953, 90:283

Commentary: 'Prisoners of War: Treatment of Prisoners in Vietnam, Korea, and Communist Countries', January 1974, 57:30–37

Commonwealth: 'Exchange of Prisoners', 21 August 1953, 58:479
'Indian Village; Prisoner Exchange', 30 October 1953

Fortune: 'Germ Warfare: The Lie That Won', November 1953, 493:6

Life: 'Back After Eight Years', 6 April 1953, 34:30–31

Heiden, K. 'Why They Confess', 20 June 1949, 92–94

'Prisoners of Pardon', 5 October 1953, 35:26

'Big Lie; How Reds Got Germ Confessions', 9 November 1953

Look: Wilson, Richard. 'How US Prisoners Broke Under Red "Brainwashing"', 2 June 1953, 80–83

Newsweek: 'Without Honour', 13 July 1953, 42:30

'Sick POWs', 17 August 1953, 42:58

'Riots and Repatriation Rules', 12 October 1953, 42:36

'Secret Agony of the POW's', 9 April 1973, 81:30 ff.

'POW's: The Price of Survival', 16 April 1973, 81:26 ff.

Quick: 'Keiner Sollte Wissen Wie Sie Starben', Nr 11–32, 1972

Readers Digest: Swift, S. K. 'How They Broke Cardinal Mindszenty', November 1949, 55:1–10

Saturday Evening Post: Gallery, D. V. 'We Can Baffle the Brainwashers', 22 January 1955

Time: 'Brainwashing', 8 October 1951, 58:39–40

'Cowardice in Korea', 2 November 1953, 62:31

'Germ Warfare: Forged Evidence', 9 November 1953, 62:22

'Beyond the Worst Suspicions', 9 April 1973, 101:20 ff.

US News and World Report: 'Real Story of Returned Prisoners', 29 May 1953 (tape recordings of GIs back from Korea)

'Truth vs Promises in Korea', 14 August 1953, 35:35

US News and World Report: Peterson, C. B.

'Prisoners Swayed; Didn't Fall, Interview', 28 August 1953, 35:28

'Back to the Germ Warfare Hoax, Tortures; US Officer's Own Story', 18 September 1953

'Where are 944 Missing GIs?', 18 December 1953, 35:77–78

Lawrence, D. 'To the Unreturned Prisoners'

George Washington Law Review: 'Coerced Confessions of Prisoners of War', Vol. 24, No. 5, April 1956

4 Unpublished Works

Hands Up for You the War is Ended, a musical documentary produced by Peter Cheeseman at the Victoria Theatre, Stoke in 1971

A Gunner Goes to War by James Hendrick Witte

History of Changi by Group Captain H. A. Probert, MBE, MA, RAF

White Coolie by J. R. Milford

POW Days in Siam by C. H. Lee

Index